ONE MINUTE TO MIDNIGHT

A collection of essays

By

Dr. Irving Moskowitz

ISBN: 978-0-578-23442-7 (Paperback)

Library of Congress Control Number: 00000000000

Front cover image by Yechezkel Moskowitz.
Book design by Yechezkel Moskowitz.

Printed in the United States of America.

First printing edition May 2020.

Chovevei Tzion Publishing
471 Sheridan Blvd. Suite 60
Inwood, New York, 11096

https://choveveizion.org/

"If I forget thee, O Jerusalem, let my right hand forget its skill. Let my tongue cleave to the roof of my mouth, if I remember thee not; if I set not Jerusalem above my utmost joy"

Psalms 137:5-6

PREFACE

It was June 17th, 2016; I was on a flight to Israel, escorting my grandfather to his final resting place when the concept of this publication came into being. I was sitting in my cabin seat, eyes drenched and overwhelmed with the significant loss that had just struck my family. True, the illness that had taken his conscience away from us, had done so many years ago, but in the end, that hope by all of us that perhaps Zaidy would come back to us, show us the way, as he did all those years ago, lingered in our minds. As I reflected on all of this and more, it occurred to me that my grandfather had written articles for over a decade, circulated widely - most prominently in the Jewish Press, known as "One Minute to Midnight." Using the pen as his sword, my grandfather waged war against the entire establishment. Those who attempted to stand in the path of his mission to secure a Jewish future in the land of Israel were not left unscathed. Sure, he offended, but he also inspired, and in the scope of history, that is all that mattered. With that notion, I made the promise, mainly to myself, that I would make sure the world heard the messages that my saintly grandfather propagated throughout his life. Perhaps, a new generation would be inspired as well.

It took approximately a year to get to this project and start my journey into the depths of my grandfather's mindset. The first step was to track down the coveted articles. I discovered, with the help of my good friend and executive director of Chovevi Tzion - Nachman Mostofsky, that the Jewish Press had access to all the articles, right here in New York City. There was a catch; however, the archives were all in hard copy form, so it would be a long and tedious process to find all of them - and that predictably it would be costly. With that, I reached out to my grandmother and proposed the idea, to which she responded very warmly and generously. The prospect of having the writings of her husband readily available in her mind was a good idea. With the help of the Jewish Press editorial staff, all the papers from that period were manually reviewed, locating the "One Minute to Midnight" op-eds within. The articles were then scanned, dated, and sent over for review. Once my grandmother started seeing the fruit of our labor, she recalled that she had written a series of letters and articles published between 1975 to 1980 in a column entitled HaMatzav, a collection of her thoughts on current events and trips to Israel at the time. Once we had everything together, we outsourced the copywriting, typesetting, and cover design to Fiverr – a story in itself (tech these days) ...

With the review of the articles, I discovered that they were timeless. The recurring theme, the Jewish quest for survival and sovereignty, was vital throughout. To my grandfather, the concept of a Jewish state for the Jewish people was to be accepted as the core principle of the Jewish consciousness. To my grandfather, the notion of Jews not subscribing to the idea of a sovereign Jewish nation in their historical homeland was the ultimate betrayal to their faith and the Jewish nation. In my mind, this stemmed from my grandfather being a beautiful illustration of what it meant to be a proud Jew, forever faithful to the Jewish people in their quest for freedom of persecution and full rights to self-determination in their eternal homeland. With that said, my grandfather did not shy away from being critical of any US or Israeli officials he thought posed a threat to Jewish interests, even when others were afraid to do so. My grandfather would scoff at the idea of dual loyalty, and I recall he once told me, "I have no issue of having dual loyalty; I am loyal to one people; the Jewish people." Indeed, and as these articles reflect most sensibly, my grandfather was loyal to the Jewish people and their needs first after foremost. And as is illustrated in these pages time and time again, he had every reason not to. As he saw in real-time, so-called friends of Israel throughout history, have betrayed the Jewish people, and thus it was his mission to say what he believed was the truth, no matter what the time or the place might be.

Those that my grandfather was most critical of were none other than the American Jewish Community, whom he felt were the worst threat to the future existence of the Jewish state and the Jewish people. In my grandfather's mind, a lack of Jewish pride creates a void within the Jewish people's soul. Such a void results in a Jewish people who are unwilling to stand firm in defense of the Jewish state due to embarrassment, shame, or even self-hatred. In my grandfather's eyes, "the failure of American Jews to come to Israel's defense is simply unforgivable". Sadly, not much has changed since he expressed such sentiment as some sects within the Jewish community, in my mind, have weaponized Judaism against a sitting President of the United States. A president who, ironically, is arguably the greatest friend of the Jewish people in modern history.

Interestingly, there were times when my grandfather's writing transcended the needs of the Jewish people, albeit rarely, and addressed the core issues of globalization and the threat it poses to the American economy. A classic example of such sentiment can be found in the article titled "How the Arabs Wrecked America's Economy (1.10.92). My grandfather, within these pages, espoused ideas that were way ahead of their time and ended up being implemented by the current sitting president over thirty years later. Although critical at times, my grandfather was a man who genuinely respected and admired the United States, the place of his birth. Still, as a Jew, he knew it was not his home; instead, it was a temporary place, and our final destination was nothing other than our birthright as Jews - Israel. Indeed, my grandfather made it his first and foremost goal to protect the interests of the Jewish people - specifically Israel. Nonetheless, as a good citizen who wished for the best in the American safe heaven, he viewed his criticism as constructive. Calling for reformations in the way Americans did business on an international scale, he wanted to see a powerful and stable America that acts as the vanguard for liberty and justice for all.

Our grandfather, Grandpa or Zaidy, as we called him, was never the one to shy away from his opinions. He was strong, pure, and without a doubt, a visionary. He had no fear of being critical of anyone he felt would God forbid steer the Jewish people away from the path of sovereignty and self-determination. US Presidents, Israeli Prime Ministers, Congressmen, Senators, Members of the Israeli Parliament and Major Jewish Organizations, even his closest friends; no one was spared of his sharp and pointed criticism when he felt they deserved it. My grandfather was fearless. A severe critic of George Bush Sr. and then Bill Clinton, my grandfather, was the manifestation of the verse (Deuteronomy 1:17) "Fear no man, for judgment, is God's." He was the living embodiment of the verse (Psalm 118:6) "The LORD is with me; I will not be afraid; for what can mere mortals do to me?" To see such intensity was awe-inspiring. Imagine growing up in the shadow of such a person; it was inspirational, it was a source of pride, it grounded all of us, and as my siblings and cousins can attest, it without a doubt made us who we are today.

My grandfather always relished the opportunity to discuss history, current events, and the impact that they have on the Jewish community presently and throughout its past. He had a strong sense of foresight, ahead of his time in a significant way, and knew the world for what it was when many others hadn't the courage to acknowledge it. So many of his comments were relevant to the present times. So many predictions or calls to action for various core issues came to be. One perfect example was his investment in the city of David and supporting its growth over the years, in which my grandmother continues the tradition to this very day. I was recently sitting in the Shiva house with Ambassador David Friedman, with the passing of his mother. I pointed out to him that while it might be the case that by the opening of pilgrimage road, he upset middle eastern and European Union government officials, but there was one man who was grinning from ear to ear; our Zaidy.

My grandfather was a patriot and an ardent Zionist, a living manifestation of Herzel, Jabotinsky, and Rabbi Tzvi Hirsch Kalisher. He was a fusion of the love for our historic homeland combined with an intense passion for our rich Jewish culture based in the scripture and ethics that gave credence to our claims for the land in the first place. This notion motivated him to invest night and day building a business empire, amassing a fortune, all for the sake of his love - the Jewish people and Jerusalem. This passion did not stop him from spending time with us whenever he could. When we would walk into his office, he would take a few moments to stop what he was doing and talk to us about anything we wanted as long as it was about Israel. When he had time, he would take a day off from his tireless work (there were no cell phones then) to take us to the Zoo or the merry go round and buy us ice cream. All of us still look back on those days; we were kids with not a clue within whose presence we were.

Shabbat was a special day for my grandfather because it was an opportunity for him to slow down and enjoy his family. He enjoyed the day as it provided him with a much-needed respite from his hectic week. The Friday night meal at my grandparents' home was a joyous occasion with the family gathered around the table enjoying the splendor, Shabbat. Divrei Torah and Shabbat songs were bountiful as well, with my grandmother's fantastic cooking truly making his Shabbat table a place that gave him such joy and Yiddish nachas (Jewish pride from offspring). One Friday night, I remember saying the blessing after meals with extra trepidation and zeal, he was so impressed, and he gave me 50 dollars to spend on myself. My parents took me to Toys R Us, and I bought a remote-control car that I had seen on a TV commercial.

There were many more memories from the time he was with us, he walked among us and inspired us to continue his work for days and years to come. The way I see it, this book presents the readers, as it did to me, a little glimpse of the giant that he was, I am so grateful I had the opportunity to partake, just this little bit, in his work. We pray that through its dissemination, it should be a merit for myself and the greater family as we continue to forge ahead in the mission that he has set for our family, and for generations to come.

Yehi Zichro Baruch, may his memory be blessed and may the inspiration within these pages be a source of comfort for his lofty soul until the final redemption. Amen.

EDITOR'S NOTE

In regard to the editing of the essays in this book, I attempted, conceptually, to leave the articles with all the style and punctuation as they appeared in the newspaper at the time. I would like to believe that the articles didn't receive any major edits by the editors as the articles made their way to the press, as my grandfather was a masterful writer. With that said, there were some places where I made a small adjustment, specifically, where I felt the error in punctuation or grammar was due to a typo missed by the editor in the newspaper clip and not due to an error of the actual author.

I did the same for the articles that came to my possession after the idea was conceptualized. The articles of my grandmother titled "HaMatzav," which were published in a local Federation newspaper between 1975 to 1980. As with my grandfather's essays, I did all I can to maintain the style of those as well.

All in all, these articles are, for the most part, the same as they appeared in print all those years ago; I hope the reader will find these essays as insightful and as instructive as I found them. I hope that the reader will comprehend their timeless message to the Jewish people and the inspiration within for generations to come.

November 3, 1989
Israel's Ten Points' of Advice for Bush

Now that the Bush Administration has embraced Egypt's "Ten Point Plan" for turning Judea and Samaria into a Palestinian Liberation Organization (PLO) state. Israel should turn to Bush and offer him its own "Ten Points" of advice. The list should include:

1. Stop undermining your ally. Israel is America's only trustworthy friend in the Middle East. By encouraging the creation of a Palestinian state, you are endangering the security of your most important strategically.

2. Stop wasting American taxpayers' dollars on aid to the Arab countries. The billions that the U.S. gives Egypt and other Arab states every year would be better spent on countries that help further American interests. Egypt today is as unreliable as Iran was in 1979; at any moment, the Mubarak regime could be overthrown and replaced by a pro-Soviet or fanatical Moslem leadership.

3. Honor your commitments. The U.S. has a poor record of standing by its pledges: South Vietnam and Taiwan are examples of that. When you promise to support Israel, stick to it.

4. Use Israel as the cornerstone of the Western alliance. With the West Europeans cozying up to Moscow, you need a reliable, militarily capable ally to keep the Soviets in check. Israel can be an important partner in defense of the West if you allow her.

5. Recognize Jerusalem as Israel's capital. The Israeli public will never agree to surrender Jerusalem to the Arabs, any more than the American public would agree to surrender Washington to Gorbachev. It's time you faced reality.

6. Do something about the Arab refugees. The 600,000 Arabs living in refugee camps in Judea and Samaria are the source of the rioting of the last

20 months. American aid could help resettle them in Arab countries where they could live peacefully among their co-regionists.

7. Speak out against human rights violations in Arab countries. The State Department always has plenty to say whenever Arab rioters claim to be mistreated by Israel; why is there not similar outrage when striking demonstrators who are not threatening with rocks and petrol bombs, but are shot to death in Jordan or Algeria?

8. Call for more democracy in the Arab world. The Arab masses deserve the right to elect their leaders, just as Americans do.

9. Stop criticizing the Jewish settlers. Jews have a right to live in their country wherever they choose, be it Hebron, Washington, Toronto, London, respectively, just as do Americans, Canadians or British. Anyone who seeks to deny that right is a racist.

10. Break off your talks with the PLO. America has no business consorting with Arafat's bloodthirsty henchmen. Rescue American honor before it's too late.

November 10, 1989

Israel's "Ten Points" For Egypt

Egypt's "ten-points plan" for Judea, Samaria, and Gaza have been delivered to the Israeli government for its study and consideration. Since Cairo is freely dispensing unsolicited advice to Jerusalem, it would not be unreasonable for Jerusalem to turn around and present Cairo with "ten points" of advice. The list could look something like this:

1. Stop spending billions of dollars on weapons, and start spending it on your poverty-stricken masses. The Egyptian people need butter, not guns.

2. If you really intend to remain at peace with Israel, withdraw your troops from the Sinai and let those soldiers go home to families; Why should they languish in the hot desert sun when they could be back in Egypt helping the country as part of its workforce?

3. Stop publishing anti-Semitic propaganda. Your government-controlled press overflows with anti-Semitic rhetoric, and that is a clear violation of your peace treaty with Israel.

4. Permit trade and tourism with Israel. The peace treaty required it; why won't you honor it?

5. Stop sheltering Nazi war criminals. As of the 1970s, more than 6,000 ex-Nazis were living in Egypt. Nasser granted them haven in the 1950s, and Sadat continued that vile tradition. If you are really at peace with the Jews, then why are you sheltering their murderers?

6. Expel the PLO from Egypt. Right now, there are PLO terrorist buses and offices in all of Egypt's major cities, as well as El-Arish, near the border with Israel. The peace treaty clearly prohibits you from allowing such hostile forces to operate on your territory.

7.   Absorb some of the Arab refugees from Gaza. Why should they be languishing in refugee camps under an Israeli administration which they despise, when they could be living in Egypt with their fellow Arabs?

8.   Urge the wealthy Arab oil states to absorb the Arab refugees from Judea and Samaria. Saudi Arabia and its neighbors could easily take in the 600,000 or so refugees. You should prod them to make the humanitarian gesture.

9.   Try democracy. Your dictatorship isn't a fair means of governing. The Egyptian people have a right to elect the leaders of their choice. It's time for "one man, one vote" in the Land of the Pharaohs.

10. Get off Israel's back. Israel doesn't demand that you attend an international conference to solve your border dispute with Libya: you have no right to demand that Israel attend such a conference to discuss its border disputes with Jordan and Syria.

December 1, 1989

Those German Train Transports Are Rolling Again

German trains are transporting humans again, only this time the crowds of bystanders are clamoring to join the transports, instead of pushing Jews onto the trains. How times have changed! Forty-five years ago, German trains carried their passengers to death camps. Today, they carry their East German passengers to a life of freedom.

The international community has extended its wholehearted sympathy to the transports. Statesmen have issued declarations of encouragement. Journalists have excitedly chronicled each new development. How odd that the Jews were being transported, the statesmen were silent, and the journalists were busy covering other stories. The Jews, it seems, were expendable.

The dramatic difference between the world's reaction to the German transports of 1944 and its reaction to those of 1989 underlines several important points for Jews to remember.

First: this is a cold world, a world of realpolitik in which diplomatic expediency, not morality, is the decisive factor in the shaping of a nation's foreign policy. The same international community that turned its back on the Six Million could easily turn its back on Israel. The same United States that broke its promises to South Vietnam and Taiwan could easily break its promises to Israel.

Second: today's American Jewish leaders dare not repeat the sin of silence committed by American Jewish leaders during the Nazi era. Beleaguered Israel desperately needs vigorous American Jewish support to stave off U.S. pressure. Jewish leaders should be initiating protests, marches, instead of meekly accepting the pro-Arab line that President George Bush and Secretary James Baker are promoting.

Third: grassroots Jews have an enormous responsibility in the present crisis. Every televised transport of Germans to the West should stir in the heart of every American Jew to pledge that he or she will never again stand idly by while Jews are transported to the west, whether from East Europe to the Nazi death camps, or from Israel westward into the Mediterranean, as the Arabs intend.

December 29, 1989

Will A Unified-Germany Bring World Jewry To Its Senses?

Suddenly, the specter of a unified, rising Germany haunts Europe afresh. The dismantling of the Berlin Wall, the freedom of movement across the border dividing East Germany from West Germany, the talk of a massive West German aid package for the East Germans, all point to the possible emergence of a powerful reunified Germany seeking a dominant role in European and world affairs.

Jews should sit up and take notice. The last time Germany was powerful and unified, six million Jews became its victims. Today, the four million Jews of Israel are threatened by the massive, deadly arms shipments that both East and West Germany have provided to the Arabs, which are likely to increase as the new Germany begins to flex its economic muscle.

Israel is, of course, not the only country worried about the rise of German might. The leaders of Britain and France are nervously consulting about the political and economic dangers that a new Germany would pose to the security of Europe and the stability of the European Common Market. They know full well that the Germans will be anxious to dominate Europe as they have done in the past.

But if Britain and France have reason to be worried, Israel should be even more concerned. After all, East Germany and West Germany may have disagreed on many things, but they had always seen eye to eye when it came to the Middle East. A newly reunified Germany aspiring to political and economic dominance will be sending its technicians, its expertise, and its weapons, including chemical weapons to every one of Israel's Arab enemies, in greater numbers than ever before.

Today's German menace should remind us of the terrible vulnerability of Jews in the face of yesterday's German menace when there was no Jewish State to protect them. And it illustrates, once again, the need for a secure, sovereign

Jewish State that will be politically, spiritually and militarily capable of standing up to all those who seek to destroy the Jews.

One can only hope that the German crisis will help bring would Jewry and Israel to their senses, and make them realize that the time has come to "just say no;" no to the Arabs who threaten Israel with annihilation, no to the Germans who arm the Arabs, and no to the Bush Administration's plan for a de facto Palestinian state that will allow the PLO to finish the job that the Germans began five decades ago.

January 26, 1990

A Tale of Two Gates

All the world is enraptured by the events surrounding the Brandenburg Gate, at the Berlin Wall, for four decades, the symbol of the division between East Germany and West Germany. In sharp contrast, the international community has had nothing to say about the gate that really deserves attention: The Mandelbaum Gate, which until 1967 symbolized the division between the two halves of the world's holiest city, Jerusalem.

During the first Arab invasion of Israel, in 1948, Jordanian troops seized the Old City of Jerusalem. For the next 19 years, the Jordanians illegally occupied the Old City, desecrated the Temple Mount and Western Wall, and used gravestones from the Mount of Olives cemetery as latrines. The Mandelbaum Gate at the entrance to the Old City, surrounded by barbed wire and sandbags, stood as a painful symbolic reminder that Holy Jerusalem was under enemy occupation.

In 1967, the Arabs invaded again (despite the absence of any of those so-called "Israeli obstacles to peace," like Jewish settlements in Judea and Samaria), and Israeli troops stormed past the Mandelbaum Gate and liberated the Old City.

The international community, which has never been particularly fond of victorious Jews, was not particularly happy at the Jewish liberation of Jerusalem, and neither the United States nor any of the other major Western countries ever formally recognized united Jerusalem as Israel's Capital. Indeed, the official U.S. position is that the final status of Jerusalem should be "negotiable," meaning that the U.S. expects Israel to negotiate the terms of its eventual surrender of the Old City to Arab control.

The vast majority of Israelis, like the vast majority of Jews everywhere would, of course, never agree to surrender Jerusalem to the Arabs. The Arabs, for their part, will never agree that Jerusalem should remain under Israeli control. It would seem to be a stalemate, which in this case, would be excellent since it would leave Jerusalem in Jewish hands. Unfortunately, however, the Israeli government has failed to emphasize the Jerusalem issue. As a result, the Bush Administration and its Arab allies have been able to promote a "negotiating" process, which will eventually produce quietly, and in stages Arab control over Jerusalem's Old City.

The Arab elections plan which Israel, Egypt, and the United States have been battling back and forth for the past year have stalled in part because of a dispute over whether or not Arab residents of the Old City Jerusalem should be allowed to participate in the vote. Israel is opposed to having Jerusalem's Arabs vote since it would clearly violate Israel's sovereign rule over the city. Egypt and the United States favor having them vote since it would hasten the process of returning the Old City to Arab control. Now the Israeli daily, Yediot Ahronot reports that Cairo and Washington are proposing a new gimmick designed to bypass Israel's opposition: Arab residents of Jerusalem would be allowed to register to vote as residents of Ramallah, a nearby Arab city just past the 1967 border.

Israel must use all of its resources to resist this Egyptian-American trick, and American Jewry must take to the streets, if necessary, to stop it. Otherwise, it will only be a matter of time before the barbed wire and sandbags return to The Mandelbaum Gate.

February 2, 1990

Three Lessons from Lebanon

The sad fate of Lebanon teaches Israel several important lessons.

Lesson #1: If Arabs cannot live in peace with other Arabs, they will certainly never be able to live in peace with Jews. Lebanon's Moslems and Christians share a common language and, in many respects, a common culture; their only meaningful difference is religion. Nevertheless, they have spent the last 14 years butchering each other with gleeful abandon. Is it conceivable that Arabs could live peacefully with Jews, with whom they have nothing in common?

Lesson #2: Democracy works well in the Middle West, but not so well in the Middle East. Lebanon was established in 1942 as a democracy, with a delicate parliamentary balance between the Christian and Moslem populations. But it soon became clear that democracy is a very fragile concept in a cruel region like the Middle East. The Moslems eventually attained a numerical majority, by their higher birth rate and an influx of Palestinians from Jordan. From their new position of strength, the Moslems demanded control of the country, and when the Christians resisted, a civil war ensued. If Israel gives in to Palestinian demands, how long will it be before the Jewish State is likewise swamped by the higher Palestinian birthrate and an influx of Palestinian "returnees" from Jordan?

Lesson #3: If the West is prepared to abandon its fellow Christians in Lebanon for the sake of political convenience, it will surely abandon the Jews of Israel when realpolitik demands it. France sponsored the creation of the modern state of Lebanon in 1913 and vowed to protect it, but has refused to lift a finger to defend it from the current Syrian onslaught. The French apparently regard their relations with Syria as more important than Lebanon's existence. The United States, supposedly the protector of the Free World, stood idly by white Lebanese and Palestinian Moslems, and their Syrian allies, ravaged the country from 1975 until 1982; the U.S. finally sent in a token battalion of marines in 1983 (and even then only to hasten Israel's withdrawal from southern

Lebanon. But the marines fled the minute they came under attack by Lebanese Moslem terrorists. If this is how the U.S. and Western Europe behave when their fellow Christians are endangered, it is not hard to imagine how the U.S. and Western Europe, with the latter's history of inquisitions, crusades, pogroms, and complicity in the Holocaust will behave if Israel's existence is endangered.

Supporters of Israel should pay close attention to the latest developments in Lebanon: the lessons to be learned and could be a matter of life and death for Israel.

February 9, 1990

Shamir's Real Blunder

There has been plenty of criticism of Prime Minister Yitzhak Shamir for declaring that "a big Israel" was needed to absorb the current wave of Soviet Jewish immigration. But most of the critics missed the important point.

Israel's right to the territories it liberated in 1967 is not dependent upon whether or not there are immigrants to settle there. Israel has a right to those lands because they are the biblical inheritance of the Jewish people and because their return to Arab rule would leave the Jewish State just nine miles wide at its midsection.

For Shamir to link Israel's "right to Judea, Samaria, and Gaza with the wave of immigrants is to distort the Jewish claim to that land. Shamir's remark was, of course, tactless. But its most serious implication relates to the question of just how steadfast Shamir will remain in the face of U.S. pressure to surrender Judea and Samaria. If he views those territories merely as real estate in which to settle new immigrants, how strongly will he stand up to U.S. demands to concede some of that real estate in exchange for "peace?"

The frightening possibility that Shamir will collapse in the face of U.S. pressure became evident again last week when Israel announced that it would give in to U.S. demands to freeze the deportation of Arab illegal aliens living in the territories.

How ironic that the controversy over Arabs living illegally in the territories should arise precisely at the same time as the controversy over Soviet Jewish immigrants who want to live in the territories. The State Department and the media howl in protest at the idea of Soviet Jews having the freedom to choose to live in their ancient homeland. Yet, they demand that illegal Arab aliens be allowed to remain in the territories.

Allowing members of one ethnic group to reside in a certain area while barring members of a different ethnic group from living there is racism. In

South Africa, it is called "apartheid." In Hitler's Germany, it was called the Nuremburg Laws.

Israel should not be afraid to call the Arab squatters by the same term the U.S. calls its squatters illegal aliens. And it should not be afraid to point out that opposition to Soviet Jews living in Judea and Samaria is racism. Shamir's blustering about "a big Israel" may have been a mistake, but his real blunder is his failure to speak to the West in language that it can understand. He should make it clear that Israel will tolerate neither illegal aliens nor racist discrimination. Individuals who have ever-stayed their visitor's permits should be treated precisely as the U.S. treats them by deporting them. And individuals who want to live in this or that neighborhood should have the right to do so, regardless of race.

February 16, 1990

Beneath Their Skins, Brothers After All

Why the fuss between Prime Minister Shamir and Minister Weizman? It is nothing more than dance by them.

As Minister of Defense (1977-1980), Minister Without Portfolio in charge of Israeli-Arab affairs (1984-1988) and as a Minister of Science (1988-present), Weizman has consistently used his position to undermine Israel's security, in the name of "improving Arab-Jewish relations."

It was Weizman who instituted the policy of allowing the PLO to send funds into Judea, Samaria, and Gaza. According to Mohamed Milson, formerly head of the Israeli Civil Administration in the territories, Weizmans's policy allowed the PLO to funnel $436 million to its local operatives during 1981-1986. Who knows what role that money played in preparing the groundwork for the Arab *intifada*?

It was Weizman who lobbied among cabinet ministers in a last-minute attempt to prevent Israel's strike against the Iraqi nuclear weapons factory. It was Weizman who blocked the scheduled demolition of thousands of illegally built Arab homes in Israel. It was Weizman who publicly criticized the assassination of PLO leader Abu Jihad, the mastermind of the Munich Olympics massacre.

And it was Weizman who by last February, denounced Prime Minister Yitzhak Shamir, Foreign Minister Moshe Arens, and Deputy Foreign Minister Benyamin Netanyahu as "squareheads on the borderline of fascist."

So, when Prime Minister Shamir recently announced that he was dismissing Weizman from the cabinet, he had plenty of justification. The incident that prompted Shamir's move, Weizman's contact with the PLO, was merely the icing on the cake.

That's why Shamir's reversal is so disturbing. It suggests that the firing of Weizman was not really based on Weizman's actions; after all, for years, Shamir had ample reason to fire him but was actually a cynical attempt by Shamir to bolster his position within the Likud by demonstrating that he is "tough on the PLO." In reality, Shamir's views are not different from Weizman's. Shamir himself, in a vain effort to satisfy the bidding of the U.S. Administration, dutifully brought to Washington the "Peace Plan" for elections in Judea, Samaria, and Gaza. His loud protestations opposing a PLO state, therefore, carry a hollow ring to them. In a personal meeting held on April 11, 1989, at the Park Lane Hotel in New York with Mr. Shamir, this columnist pleaded with Mr. Shamir not to advance such a plan and advised him that it could only lead to a 22nd Arab state, a PLO state, with dire consequences for Eretz Yisrael.

Forty-two days later, on May 21, 1989, a leading Israeli newspaper, Maariv, quoted former U.S. Secretary of State Henry Kissinger as making a similar warning: "The historical expression teaches that the nation who holds elections always achieves independence. Israel should determine in advance what borders it wants to have and to permit elections only subject to this. You can forget about any territory in which elections will take place. The people participating in elections in such territories will win their independence."

Many Likud activists are deeply concerned that Shamir is steering Israel down a slippery slope that will begin with "Arab autonomy elections" and will end in a de facto PLO state in Israel's backyard. Last year, the Likud Central Committee voted to amend the elections plan to ensure that it does not produce a PLO state. But to keep Labor in the national unity government, Shamir has ignored those Likud amendments and pursued his course.

Now, again motivated by his desire to keep labor in the government, Shamir has agreed to let Weizman off with just a slap on the wrist.

It was a bad move on all counts. The Likud activists are not fooled; they know what Shamir is up to. The Labor Party is convinced that it can reverse anything Shamir does just by threatening to pull out of the government. And

Weizman has been told, in effect, that he can continue to play the role Vidkun Quisling played during World War Two and still retain his cabinet seat.

March 9, 1990

Jews with Pride, and Jews who Lack It

There are Jews with pride. But is Efraim Zuroff one of them?

Zuroff, the Jerusalem representative of the Simon Wiesenthal Center, lives in the Jewish settlement of Efrat, which means that he and his family are the potential targets of Arab rock-throwers every time they leave home. Yet, in a recent interview with The Jerusalem Post, David Horovitz writes that Zuroff is extremely unhappy with "the stereotypical image of the settler with his bushy beard, his gun in his belt and his eternally pregnant wife."

Zuroff seemed to be echoing the sentiments of Shimon Peres, who declared in a 1988 outburst that "the appearance of the settlers, with their *kippahs* and beards, invites contempt, and ridicule."

"Self-hatred" may be too strong a characterization for such expressions, but it is clear that Zuroff and Peres share a sense of acute embarrassment, even shame, at the thought that the outside world might see such Jews as representatives of Israel.

What is not clear is exactly why Zuroff and Peres should be so perturbed. The *kippahs* and beards of the settlers are traditional signs of pride in one's Jewish identity. The settlers' guns are evidence that Israeli Jews have learned the bitter lesson of Diaspora Jewish history that it is better to be armed and alive than vulnerable and victimized.

And what in the world is wrong with a pregnant wife? Zuroff's profession involves documenting Nazi war crimes, so surely, he must appreciate the devastating impact on World Jewry of the Nazis' murder of two million Jewish children. Jewish settlers who choose to have many children are patriots who are fulfilling the Jewish religious obligation to replenish the shrunken ranks of our people. In this era of "me first" Yuppies and abortion-on-demand, we should welcome the sight of Jews who are prepared to sacrifice their material comfort for the sake of a higher goal. They deserve to be praised, not mocked.

If the Simon Wiesenthal Center wants to continue its worldwide reputation, and maintain its credibility, perhaps those in the leadership positions of the Simon Wiesenthal Center should give some in-service preparatory training to their representatives before sending them out to represent the Simon Wiesenthal Center.

The origin of the Zuroff-Peres line of thinking is no mystery. The ceaseless barrage of international criticism aimed at Israel has made some Jews excessively sensitive to world opinion. But being ashamed of the traditional symbols of Jewishness will not impress non-Jews. **One must have some self-respect before it is possible to win the respect of others.**

March 3, 1990

The Jerusalem Issue: A Golden Opportunity

The sudden injection of the Jerusalem issue into the Middle East discussions presents Israel with a golden opportunity to put a halt to the process that is leading to the nightmare of a PLO state. Will Jews seize the opportunity or squander it?

President Bush's statement denouncing Israeli "settlements" in the Old City of Jerusalem did not represent a change in American policy. It was merely a timely reminder that the U.S. has never recognized the Jewish right to Jerusalem. As far as the U.S. is concerned, the Western Wall is "illegally-occupied territory." The same goes for French Hill, Gilo, Ramot, and many other ordinary urban neighborhoods in the Holy City, each housing tens of thousands of residents.

It has always been part of the State Department's strategy to play down the Jerusalem issue. The reason is simple: Jerusalem is an issue that unites all Israelis and, indeed, virtually all Jews everywhere (except for an insignificant fringe element). On other issues, Israel may be divided. But not on Jerusalem. If Washington tried to pick a fight over the status of Jerusalem, it risks being confronted by a united Israel, unwilling to make concessions. The issue of Jerusalem is, therefore, a time bomb for the State Department, threatening to explode all of Washington's carefully laid out plans for engineering an Israeli withdrawal from Judea-Samaria and the creation of a Palestinian "homeland" in those areas.

At Camp David, back in 1978, the U.S. negotiators deliberately kept the Jerusalem issue on the sidelines, confining it to a series of side letters, one each from Begin, Sadat, and Carter, restating their government's positions on the status of the city. If the U.S. had insisted on negotiating the Jerusalem issue, the talks would have fallen apart.

U.S. strategy during the past 12 years has remained consistent with the Camp David precedent: keep Jerusalem on the back burner, pressure Israel to

31

gradually surrender all of the other territories, and then, at the very end, demand that Israel surrender the Old City.

The latest phase in this process is the inclusion of eastern Jerusalem in the Arab elections plan. If the U.S. were to openly demand that Jerusalem be part hi of the plan, Israel would strongly resist. So State Department strategists have cleverly tried to drag Jerusalem in through the back door by proposing that Arab residents of Jerusalem register fictitiously as residents of nearby Ramallah, and then be allowed to vote.

Including the Arabs of Jerusalem in the elections plan is the first step towards eventually surrendering the Old City of Jerusalem to Arab rule – just as allowing the Arabs to hold elections in Judea, Samaria, and Gaza is the first step towards eventually surrendering those territories to PLO rule.

But President Bush's attack on Israeli "settlements" in Jerusalem offers a golden opportunity to halt this whole dangerous process before it is too late. Bush's statement has lifted the veil of diplomatic deceit for just a moment and reminded Israel that today's demands for surrendering Judea and Samaria would be followed, and tomorrow, by demands for surrendering Jerusalem.

April 27, 1990

Pollard-Bashing: A Vile Sport

"Pollard-bashing" is a sport that has become rather popular among timid American Jews who are afraid of "dual loyalty" accusations.

Jonathan Pollard, the American Jew who provided Israel with U.S. intelligence data about PLO terrorist encampments and Syrian nerve gas production, is currently serving a sentence of life imprisonment in a maximum-security prison in Illinois.

There has always been a variety of views in the American Jewish community regarding Pollard's behavior. Some believe that Pollard's actions were justified because the Pentagon failed to honor the American commitment to provide Israel with intelligence data about Israel's enemies. Others question the property of Pollard's actions but are honest enough to admit that the information he gave Israel was vital to Israeli security. And then some are afraid of "dual loyalty" accusation and therefore insist on condemning Pollard and misrepresenting his actions.

Into the latter category, one must place the mean-spirited attack on Pollard, which appeared in a New Jersey Jewish periodical in April. The attacker was Shoshana Bryen, director of the Jewish Institute for National Security Affairs, and she claimed that the belief "that the information Jonathan Pollard stole was 'life and death' for Israel is based entirely on air and wishful thinking."

Bryan must have a very peculiar view of what constitutes "life and death for Israel." Even Wolf Blitzer, who is by no means sympathetic to Pollard describes in his book, Territory of Lies, how the documents Pollard gave Israel were vital to Israeli security. For example, Pollard provided the Israelis "with a large stack of documents pinpointing the exact location of Arafat's headquarters at Hammam Plage, a beach in the suburban outskirts of Tunis," information which was crucial to Israel's 1985 strike on the PLO in Tunisia, Blitzer writes (p.113).

Pollard also gave Israel "the exact U.S. gathered information about Iraqi and Syrian chemical warfare production capabilities, including detailed satellite pictures and maps showing the location of factories and storage facilities." Blitzer also notes, "The United States did . want to make such specific information available to Israel, fearing a pre-emptive strike. Pollard also gave the Israelis the exact details on all Soviet arms shipments to Syria and other Arab states including the specifics on the SS 21 ground-to-ground missiles and the SA-5 anti-aircraft missiles he also provided Israel with the U.S. intelligence community's most detailed assessment of the new Soviet MIG-29 fighter (P. 166)."

After an unmanned Israeli reconnaissance drone successfully made its way through the entire Syrian air defense system in 1985, Israeli Officials concluded: "that this remarkable achievement was possible only because of the information Pollard had provided (p. 168)."

Pollard also "collected documents on other potential threats facing Israel, including from Pakistan. Specifically, he gave the Israelis Information about Pakistan's program to build an atomic bomb, including huge satellite photographs of its nuclear reactor facility outside Islamabad," Blitzer wrote (pp. 168-169).

Whatever one's view of what Pollard did, one thing is clear: Pollard is a Jew who is suffering in prison because he tried to help Israel. That fact alone should be sufficient to enlist the compassion of the Jewish community. Those who are incapable of feeling such compassion should at least have the decency to remain silent.

May 4, 1990

Apartheid In Jerusalem 'Christian' Quarter

If a rioting anti-Jewish mob attacked Jews who were trying to move into an apartment building in Scarsdale or Beverly Hills, decent people everywhere would be outraged.

Fortunately, such behavior does not take place today in Scarsdale or Beverly Hills, but it is taking place in Jerusalem, the holiest city in Judaism, and the capital of the reborn Jewish State.

During Passover week, several Jewish pilgrims took up residency in a former hostel located in the so-called "Christian Quarter" of Jerusalem's Old City. Although the area bears the designation "Christian," the term actually has no historical validity. Jews lived in all quarters of the Holy City, including the so-called "Christian" quarter, until Arab pogromists expelled them in 1936. The Jews who moved into the former hostel were exercising the Jewish right to live anywhere they choose in the Land of Israel, and they were fulfilling the Zionist obligation to repopulate regions that were made *Judenrein* by Arab pogromists.

What happened in Jerusalem last week was the culmination of a simple, legal business transaction. Earlier this year, a private corporation entered into an agreement with Mardios S. Matossian, the "Master Tenant" of the hostel, which is owned by the Greek Orthodox Church. Matossian's lease with the Church gives him the explicit right to sublet portions of the hostel to pilgrims. Matossian chose to sublet a portion of the building (excluding a portion which is his residence) to the corporation, which in turn permitted the Jewish pilgrims to move in.

"Pilgrims" is a key legal term in the controversy. The lease permits "pilgrims" to live there. The Israeli judge who initially ordered the Jews to be evicted from the hostel assumed that the lease was referring to Christian pilgrims. But is that a fair assumption? Hasn't Jewish tradition always mandated pilgrimages to Jerusalem during the Jewish Festivals? Don't Jews have as much right as Christians to come to the Holy City?

The moral issue at stake is whether or not the Israeli authorities will tolerate apartheid in their capital. At a time when religious and political freedoms are being renewed in countries all around the world, and when even South Africa is beginning to reform its apartheid system, it is morally unconscionable that apartheid-like regulations should be implemented in Jerusalem itself.

Those American Jewish "leaders" who demand the right of blacks to live in all parts of Johannesburg but denounce Jews for wanting to live in all parts of Jerusalem are decades behind the times. The walls of apartheid and totalitarianism are crumbling around us, and it is time that they crumbled in Jerusalem as well.

June 8, 1990

The 'Two-Plus-Four' Talks: Something Is Missing

The Two Plus Four talks are a forum for the four World War Two allies; Britain, France, the United States, and the Soviet Union to help pave the way for the reunification of the two Germanys. Now they have been expanded to "Two Plus Four Plus One," following Poland's demand to be included. But while representatives of those seven governments meet, Israel, which is the party with the strongest moral claim to be present, is absent.

Every one of the seven countries represented at the talks played some role in the Holocaust: the Germans, who carried it out; the Poles, who eagerly assisted them, the Soviets, whose participation in the Molotov-Ribbentrop pact helped pave the way for the Nazi conquest of Europe; the British, whose "White Paper" shut the gates of the Holy Land to Jewish refugees; the French, who during the war years aggressively hunted Jews, especially children, and turned them over to the Germans for extermination: and the Americans, who not only stood idly by throughout the Holocaust years, but denied refugees entry. Meanwhile, other Jewish refugees beached at the shores of the United States, begging to be admitted were sent back to the death camps from which they were fleeing. Those who murdered, assisted the murders, or ignored the murders, have less right to be at the Two Plus Four talks than does Israel, the representative of the Jewish victims.

Poland demanded and was included in the talks because it wants to press for a guarantee that the reunified Germany will respect its borders. However, it was the Jews who were the primary victims of the old Germany and the Jews; that is, the Jewish State could easily become a victim of the reunified Germany if appropriate restraints are not enacted.

For the past 45 years, East Germany and West Germany disagreed on many things, but their approach to the Middle East was frighteningly similar. Both made fat profits at Israel's expense by selling billions of dollars worth of weapons to the Arab states.

37

West Germany's policy of paying "reparations" to Holocaust survivors can never atone for its deadly policy of selling arms to the Arabs. On the one hand, West Germany was paying measly reparations to survivors of the Holocaust, while, with the other hand, it was helping to pave the way for a second Holocaust by giving the Arabs every sophisticated weapons system under the sun. Meanwhile, East Germany served as a haven and training grounds for PLO terrorists, as well as an important source of Soviet bloc arms for the Arab regimes.

A strong, confident, reunified Germany means a Germany that is likely to flex its economic muscle by stepping up its arms sales to Israel's Arab enemies. Israel, therefore, has every right in the world to be present at the "Two Plus Four Plus One" talks, to ensure that the New Germany will be prevented from repeating any of the evils that the Old Germany perpetrated.

Israeli representatives at the talks could, and should, demand that Israel's borders be guaranteed against invasion by the Arabs whom the Germans have been arming. They could, and should, demand German recognition of Jerusalem as Israel's capital. They could, and should, demand that the Germans ever their economic ties to Israel's enemies and start giving the Jewish State some meaningful economic assistance. Vague premises are worthless. The oral promise made by West Germany's Helmut Kohl to Edgar Bronfman of the World Jewish Congress that young Germans will be educated about the Holocaust is nothing more than lip service. It's time Jews stop applauding and believing in lip service. What's needed is concrete, written guarantees that apply directly and specifically to German behavior in the Middle East.

Israel must be invited to join the Two Plus Four talks. If it is not invited, it should demand to be invited. This is no time to sit around and wait for the nations of the world to decide a matter that is crucial to Israel's fate. These nations felled the Jewish people before. This is a time for Jews to stand up and demand their rights.

June 15, 1990

American Jewish Congress Hires an Extremist

A veteran activist in the pro-PLO New Jewish Agenda has been hired as the new executive director of the Pacific Southwest Region of the American Jewish Congress. This could mean that the American Jewish Congress (AJC) is shifting to the left. Or it could mean that leftwing extremists are successfully infiltrating mainstream Jewish organizations. Either way, it's bad news.

The new AJC official is Laura Geller, the Hillel rabbi at the University of Southern California. Back in 1980, Geller was affiliated with a pre-Arab group called the "Committee of Americans for peace in the Middle East," which placed an ad in The New York Times demanding "Palestinian self-determination." Since 1982, Geller has been associated with the New Jewish Agenda, a radical-left group which has repeatedly attacked Israel and picketed Israeli consulates in the United States. As recently as August 1988, Geller was mentioned in Agenda, in Brief, an internal Agenda newsletter, as still being active in New Jewish Agenda's Los Angeles chapter.

Geller is also currently a member of the editorial board of *Tikkun*, the far-left magazine that regularly bashes Israel and champions the PLO cause.

Does the AJC embrace the views of New Jewish Agenda and *Tikkun*, or will it compel Geller to sever her ties with the radical-left upon assuming her new job?

And if Geller does sever those ties, will that simply enable her to hide her tree extremist views while using the A. J. Congress AJC as a vehicle to promote her agenda?

These are questions that must be answered, especially because of the A. J. Congress' recent hiring of another leftwing militant, David Twersky. Twersky, who has praised the PLO as "moderate" and publicly called for a reduction in U.S. aid to Israel, is now Director of Communications for the A. J. Congress AJC. No doubt, Twersky and Geller will feel very comfortable in each other's company. But how will the Jewish community feel, knowing that one of its premier defense organizations is filling its staff with extreme critics of Israel?

Through intelligence and knowledge, man comes to resemble the character of the angels.
(adapted from lbn Gabirol)

June 29, 1990

We Called You Mr. Baker, But You Didn't Answer

Secretary of State Baker has declared, in a voice dripping with sarcasm and venom, that the Israelis should call the White House switchboard "when they're serious about peace." Mr. Baker seems to have forgotten that the Jews have called the White House many times – but the White House didn't always answer.

In 1939, the German Jewish refugees aboard the St. Louis, hovering off the coast of Miami Beach, called out to the White House to grant them haven. The White House didn't answer. The Jews were sent back to Hitler's death camps.

In 1944, the Jews trapped in Hitler's inferno cried out to the White House to bomb the railway lines leading to Auschwitz. The White House didn't answer.

Six Million perished.

When the newly reborn State of Israel was fighting for its life, in 1948, it called the White House, begging for weapons with which to defend itself. President Truman didn't answer. The U.S. had declared an arms embargo on the Middle East, meaning Israel since the Arabs were being armed to the teeth by the British.

In the spring of 1967, as the Arabs tightened a noose around Israel's neck, as Nasser closed the Straits of Tiran, and as the Arab armies marched toward Israel's borders and the Arab armies marched toward Israel's Jewish State, the Israelis called the White House for assistance. President Johnson didn't answer. He had forgotten the promise that Eisenhower hade made to the Israelis back in 1957, the promise that the U.S. would ensure that the Straits of Tiran would stay open.

41

As the Arabs prepared to invade in 1973, and Israeli intelligence detected the imminent attack, Prime Minister Golda Meir called the White House for help. Henry Kissinger warned her that if Israel launched a pre-emptive strike, the U.S. would give it no weapons. Golda Meir succumbed to the pressure, Israel suffered devastating losses, and the U.S. refused to provide Israel with any weapons throughout the first ten days of the fighting Kissinger's way of making sure that the Israelis would not win too big a victory.

Near the end of the 1973 war, when Israel had the Egyptian Third Army trapped in the Sinai Desert, and Israeli troops were on the road to Cairo, the Israelis made the mistake of calling the White House to consult. Kissinger replied by pressuring them to halt their advances and release the trapped Egyptians.

What Nixon and Kissinger did for the Egyptians, Reagan and Secretary Alexander Haig did for the PLO, pressuring Israel to lift its siege of Beirut in 1982 and refrain from wiping out Arafat and his hordes.

In other words, Mr. Baker, we Jews have plenty of experience with calling your White House. Either they didn't answer, or they answered by pressuring us to surrender to our enemies. Pardon us for being suspicious, Mr. Baker, but a lot of us are afraid that you want us to "call the White House" now so that you can shove a Palestinian state down Israel's throat.

I have a suggestion, Mr. Baker: how about giving the Arab states Israel's telephone number and asking them to call when they are serious about peace? After all, they are the ones who have been invading Israel for the past 42 years, and they are the ones whom you should be pressing to make peace. Tell them that the area code for Jerusalem is 02, and the Prime Minister's number is 705555.

July 26, 1990

A Prophecy of Doom That Israel Should Ignore

Earlier this year, the Israeli ambassador to the United States, Zalman Shoval, courageously went public with the information that the Bush Administration was giving Israel a run around on its request for refugee housing loan guarantees. Bush's advisors were predictably outraged, but Shoval earned the respect of his countrymen and friends of Israel around the world for his willingness to cast aside diplomatic niceties and speak the truth.

Now, however, Shoval has tarnished his reputation for political courage by urging Israel to surrender its right to Judea and Samaria to obtain further U.S. loan guarantees.

In an interview on Israel Radio recently, Shoval declared that Israel would have to choose between allowing Jews to settle Judea and Samaria and/or receiving the loan guarantees. If Israel continues to permit Jews to live in those areas, Shoval predicted, the Bush Administration will not approve the loan guarantees.

Shoval's comments were immediately picked up by the international media and made into headline news. Israel's enemies in the media are eager to increase pressure on the Jewish State to surrender Judea and Samaria, and Shoval's remarks gave them yet another stick with which to bash Israel.

Delivering such prophecies of doom should not be part of Shoval's job. It would be more appropriate if Shoval spent his time exposing the double standard that Bush and Baker are using against Israel. After all, the same day that Shoval's remarks made headlines, it was also reported that Kuwait is continuing its massive deportations of Palestinian Arabs. Shoval could point out the Administration's hypocrisy in ignoring Kuwait's behavior while censuring Israel, particularly when Israel is permitting many of those Palestinian Arab deportees to settle in Judea and Samaria.

43

Nor should Shoval stop there. As Israel's ambassador to the U.S., it is Shoval's responsibility to point out that the $10 billion in loan guarantees is a form of aid that costs the U.S. nothing. It merely enables Israel to borrow money from private American banks. Only if Israel defaulted on its loans something it has never done before would the U.S. be liable.

Finally, Shovel should point out that America's moral debt to the Jewish State far exceeds a handful of loan guarantees. The American refusal to help save Jews from Hitler deemed the Six Million Jews who would have made Israel into a military, technological, and financial superstate. Can anyone put a price on a debt like that? One wonders what price tag could be put on the military intelligence that Israel has supplied to the U.S. over the years, the captured Soviet weaponry that it has turned over, the battle-testing of U.S. weapons in Arab-Israeli wars. America's investment in Israel has yielded returns whose worth boggles the imagination, as the distinguished Israeli editor, Aryeh Stav, discusses in the latest issue of *Midstream*. Stav's essay was written too soon to include another benefit that Israel gave the U.S: victory in the Persian Gulf War. By staying on the sidelines and absorbing Iraqi missile attacks, Israel allowed the U.S. to maintain its Arab coalition and press ahead with its military campaign.

Perhaps Ambassador Shoval could remind the public of that fact the next time the "Jewish settlements" issue is raised.

August 2, 1991

Syria's Reply Is No Reason to Celebrate

Syria's reply to the U.S. proposal for a Middle East peace conference is no reason to celebrate. President Bush's declaration that the Syrian reply is a victory for the peace process rings just as hollow as his February 27 proclamation of "victory" over Iraq.

Bush's foolish embrace of Syria suggests that this Administration is persisting in its dangerous habit of underestimating coddling Arab tyrants. The last beneficiary of Bush's errant judgment was, of course, Iraq. As we now know, on the very eve of the Iraqi invasion of Kuwait, the U.S. ambassador in Baghdad, April Glaspie, was telling Saddam Hussein with the approval of her superiors in Washington that the U.S. would not interfere in intra-Arab border changes.

Glaspie's gaffe was not an isolated incident. Several Iraqi defectors, as well as General Norman Schwarzkopf himself, have confirmed that U.S. intelligence failed miserably in its forecasting of Iraqi behavior. And the U.S. knowingly turned a blind eye to the sales by U.S. companies to Iraq of technology used for the development of nuclear and other weapons. Just last week, President Bush acknowledged the latest U.S. intelligence failure when he revealed that American bombers have failed to locate Iraqi nuclear weapons storage sites.

Bush's policy towards Syria is all too reminiscent of has informed behavior towards Iraq in 1988-1990. In return for Syrian participation in the coalition against Iraq, which was not exactly a courageous move by Syria, since Iraq is its longtime enemy, anyway, the U.S., via Saudi Arabia, rewarded Damascus with $2 billion and agreed to ignore Syria's annexation of Lebanon. Syria used the $2 billion to purchase new Scud missiles (much more effective than the version used by Iraq) and will use Lebanon as a new front in the next Arab invasion of Israel.

But that didn't deter Bush. Now, having "delivered" Lebanon to the Syrians, he is trying to "deliver" Israel.

Israel is expected to surrender strategically vital lands in exchange for vague U.S. "security guarantees," which are likely to be about as reliable as the American promises to defend South Vietnam and Taiwan. Indeed, in the wake, of the U.S. intelligence failures in the Persian Gulf, it seems likely that any "guarantees" for Israel will be worth even less than those made to America's former allies in Asia. Consider, for example, the problem of the chemical and nuclear weapons that Syria is currently developing.

The Bush Administration's declared policy of "no rewards for aggressors" in the Persian Gulf has been rendered worthless by its post-Gulf policy of rewarding the aggressor-state Syria, with its bloody track record of occupying Lebanon, invading Israel, and sponsoring international terrorist attacks that have claimed hundreds of American victims. Cuddling up to Syria will not produce peace, except, perhaps, the "peace" of the grave – Israel's grave. Is the American Jewish community prepared to organize Israel's friends, Jew, and non-Jew, for an around-the-clock vigil, to prevent such a scenario today before it is too late?

August 8, 1991

'Peace' Talks with a Predetermined Outcome

Will the proposed Middle East peace conference truly serve as a forum for Arab-Israeli negotiations, or will it turn out to be merely the framework for imposing Arab demands on Israel? The latest diplomatic developments indicate that the outcome of the proposed conference has been predetermined in accordance with the Arab agenda.

At a July 25th news conference in Damascus, Syrian Foreign Minister Farouk al-Sharaa revealed that President Bush had secretly promised Syria to support the Syrian demand for a total Israeli surrender of the Golan Heights. What is most alarming is that Bush and his sides have not even bothered to deny the Syrian foreign minister's claim. A "senior Bush Administration official" told the Associated Press that Bush's promise to Damascus was "not new," but simply reflected "an old U.S. position," which has not changed. That's not exactly comforting news to friends of Israel, who recall that in 1975 President Gerald Ford sent Israel a letter promising to give "great weight" to Israel's need for the Golan in any future negotiating process.

American presidents seem to have an unfortunate habit of contravening promises that their predecessor made, especially when those promises were made to Israel. To induce Israel to withdraw from the Sinai in 1957, Eisenhower promised Israel the U.S. would come to Israel's aid if Egypt blockaded the Straits of Tiran. In 1967 the Johnson administration refused to honor Eisenhower's promises. In August 1970, Nixon promised Israel the United States would not allow Egypt to take advantage of the Egyptian violations of the ceasefire agreement that was supposed to end the "war of attrition" by moving SAM missiles closer to the Suez Canal. But before the Yom Kippur War broke out, Nixon ordered Israel not to make preemptive strikes against the missile sites. The Ford administration promised Israel that the U.S. would not recognize the PLO; the Reagan administration recognized the PLO anyway. The Reagan administration declared Syria to be a "terrorist state:" The Bush Administration allied with Syria anyway. Perhaps the Bush

Administration will make various promises to Israel to induce it to surrender territories. Who knows if the next U.S. administration will honor Bush's promises?

In any event, nobody should be shocked that Bush and Baker have secretly promised to support the Arab position at the conference. Why else would the Arabs agree to such a conference? The Arab regimes have not had some sudden change of heart about Israel. They have not suddenly cast aside the Islamic principle of domination over non-Moslems, or the ideology of Arab nationalism, which leaves no room for a Jewish State. Arab newspapers are still filled with anti-Israel hatred. Arab television broadcasts still speak of "destroying the Zionist entity," and, most importantly, every Arab country is stockpiling massive quantities of sophisticated offensive weapons.

Given this atmosphere of undiluted Arab hatred of Israel and feverish Arab military development, the only reason that Syria or the others would agree to negotiations is a promise from the U.S. to pressure Israel into retreating to its indefensible pre-1967 borders. Such retreat would leave Israel ripe to be overrun by Arab armies.

Under intense pressure from the U.S., the media, and certain Jewish liberals, Israel is allowing itself to be dragged into a "peace process" that has been carefully choreographed according to a dangerous prearranged script. By dropping its traditional insistence on direct, one-on-one negotiations with the Arabs, Israel is slowly forced to agree to a conference at which every other party the Arabs, the U.S., the Soviets, the Europeans, and the United Nations will join hands to pressure Israel to surrender.

Each Israeli concession has only lead to demands for more Israeli concessions. Each retreat has set in motion events that will lead to further retreat. If Israel cannot resist the pressure to enter negotiations that have a prearranged outcome, how will it find the strength to resist the imposition of that outcome?

August 16, 1991

Israel Must Escape from the Trap by Saying 'No'

The most ironic aspect of Israel's step-by-step surrender to international pressure is that it is taking place precisely at the time when the Jewish State is in many ways at the peak of its strength. Alas, military strength cannot always substitute for self-confidence and national morale, those two crucial areas in which Israel so sorely lacks these days.

The initial results of the Persian Gulf War left Israel and world Jewry feeling more optimistic than ever before. And why not? Iraq, one of Israel's most dangerous military foes, had just been devastated by Allied bombers; Syria by itself did not pose an immediate military threat; Jordan and the PLO had been discredited because they supported Saddam Hussein. Most of all, hundreds of thousands of new Jewish immigrants were pouring in from the Soviet Union and Ethiopia, infusing the Jewish State with new hope, new skills, new manpower, and new life.

Then, in the twinkling of an eye, it all began to crumble. American Jewry stood by silently as the Bush Administration began focusing its post-war attention on the need to pressure Israel to make more concessions to the Arabs. Instead of putting an end to Baker's dangerous diplomacy, the Israelis thought that they could appear to be the 'good guys' by making 'confidence-building gestures' to the Arabs. But the gestures were not reciprocated, and the concessions that Israel made only whetted the Arabs' (and Baker's) appetite for more Israeli retreats. Because the Israelis failed to say 'no' right away, they were soon trapped into saying 'yes' again and again and again.

Israel's military strength has not sufficed to stem its erosion of morale. Pressured by Baker, harassed by the international media, all but abandoned by Diaspora Jewry, the Israelis have been left in psychological disarray. Feeling trapped and isolated, they are easily seduced by the illusion of Arab "moderation" and the lure of $10 billion in loan guarantees from the U.S.

Anyone familiar with Jewish history knows that Jews have often been trapped and isolated, but they didn't always surrender. In 1943, the Jews of the Warsaw Ghetto knew how to say "no" to the Nazis' demand that they surrender. With homemade guns and God-given courage, they answered the enemy in the only language that the enemy understood.

Israel today could use some of that courage in Warsaw. But it also needs the active assistance of its Jewish brethren around the world. Israel's leaders should not hesitate to ask Diaspora Jews to tighten their belts and contribute whatever is necessary to make up for those $10 billion in loan guarantees.

Turning the Jewish national home into a negotiable commodity to obtain some U.S. loan guarantees is morally unconscionable and strategically perilous. It will leave Israel subject to gradual dismemberment under the pressure of losing U.S. aid, leaving Jews as vulnerable as they were during the dark years of the Warsaw Ghetto.

August 23, 1991

The Enemy Within: Jewish Turncoats, Then and Now

The tragedy of individual Jews siding with their people's enemies is a phenomenon well known to anyone familiar with Jewish history. From the medieval Jewish converts to Christianity who became prominent anti-Semites to the pro-PLO Jewish radicals of our own time, those renegades have caused untold damage to Jewish interests. It is no wonder that the verse in Isaiah, "Your destroyers shall come from among you," is interpreted by most biblical commentators as refereeing to Jewish traitors who wreak havoc upon their people."

Time after time throughout Jewish history, Jewish turncoats have joined forces with the enemies of the Jews and played important roles in the formulation of anti-Jewish policies. During the Spanish Inquisition, some of the fiercest Christian fanatics involved in the torture and murder of innocent Jews were former Jews. They had converted to Christianity to escape their Jewishness and find material security in the Christian world.

In other European countries during the Middle Ages, individual "Court Jews" curried favor with the ruling authorities at the expense of the local Jewish community. In some instances, of course, Court Jews played a necessary and even valuable role as an intermediary between the Jewish community and the local king. But all too often, Court Jews misused their positions to gain personal advantages, while the rest of the Jews suffered from poverty and oppression.

Entire books have been written about the role of Jewish "Kapos" or collaborators during the Holocaust. There can be no doubt that local Jewish leaders were, in many cases, forced into impossible situations by the demands of the Nazi occupiers: nobody should be quick to judge or condemn them. In many cases, they truly did their best to assist their fellow Jews, despite the extreme circumstantiates in which they were trapped. Yet there can be no denying that some Jewish leaders went too far, becoming actual collaborators with the Nazi enemy to save their skins. Ben Hecht's powerful book Perfidy

51

(first published in 1962) told the horrifying tale of one such traitor. Rudolf Kastner, who deliberately hid news of the gas chambers from the Hungarian Jewish community in exchange for a promise by the Nazis to spare him and a handful of his friends and relatives. After the war, Kastner actually signed an affidavit on behalf of a Nazi war criminal with whom he had become friendly, resulting in the Nazi being set free by the Allies.

In this context, one cannot help but think of the role currently being played in the formulation of U.S. Middle East policy by President Bush's handful of Jewish advisers. The Administration's ferociously pro-Arab slant has been shaped to a large extent by Jewish turncoats like Dennis Ross, the Director of the Policy Planning for the State Department; Aaron David Miller, a senior member of the State Department's Policy and Planning Staff, and Daniel Kurtzer, the Deputy Assistant Secretary for Near East and South Asian Affairs.

These Jewish Arabists operate almost entirely behind the scenes, so the Jewish community is generally unaware of the nature of their actions. But two years ago, *The New York Times* revealed that it was Kurtzer who, more than anyone else, had been the architect of the U.S. decision to recognize and negotiate with the terrorist PLO. This past April, a stunning expose of Bush's Jewish henchmen, which was published in *Moment Magazine*, detailed how Kurtzer and the company have continued to push the pro-Arab line in U.S. foreign policy. The article is a must-read for every Jew who cares about Israel.

Kurtzer's background will no doubt raise some eyebrows. He claims to be an Orthodox Jew, and at one time he actually served as a dean at Yeshiva University. One might think that because of Kurtzer's anti-Israel activity, the Y.U. the administration would forcefully criticize him. Instead, however, Y.U. President Norman Lamm has been quoted in *The New York Times* as praising and defending Kurtzer.

Jewish turncoats who help plot the U.S. abandonment of Israel do not deserve to be praised or defended; they deserve to be condemned, forcefully and unequivocally, and be made persona non grata in the American Jewish community.

August 30, 1991

No Deals with Arab Stalinists

The short-lived Stalinist coup in the Soviet Union horrified the Free World. But it was greeted with joy by the leading Arab regimes, thereby demonstrating, once again, that they are not ready for sincere peace talks with Israel or anybody else.

The government-controlled media in "moderate" Jordan cheered the anti-Gorbachev coup. Spokesmen for the PLO declared their enthusiastic support for the red fascist revolt. Syria's leaders were already looking forward to fresh shipments of sophisticated weapons from their new Stalinist allies.

Are these the parties with whom Israel is expected to sign peace treaties? Are these the regimes with whom Israel is supposed to entrust strategically crucial territories? No logical person could urge Israel to do so. But the policies of the Bush Administration are not logical; they are the product of a cold, calculated plan to implement the Arab agenda at Israel's expense.

Secretary of State Baker and his Arabist aides (most of whom are, ironically, Jews) have used Israel's request for a $10 billion loan guarantee as part of their cruel carrot and stick game, holding out the possibility of the loan guarantee as to the carrot, while lashing Israel with the stick of anti-settlements criticism. Baker and his crew, using the American media as their voice, have cleverly employed contemporary euphemisms like "land for peace" and "peace process" for the same deadly purpose that our enemies used euphemisms like "*Arbeit Macht Frei*" and "resettlement in the East" 50 years ago to undermine any attempts by the Jews to resist the final "solutions" that are being planned.

Is it far-fetched to compare today's crisis in that of the Holocaust years? I think not. It was, after all, the ultra-dove Abba Eban who coined the phrase "Auschwitz lines" to describe the precariousness of Israel's pre-1967 borders the borders in which the Arabs, and the Bush Administration, are determined to confine Israel.

If Israel is to resist such a fate, it must make its move sooner rather than later. For Israel to break off its "engagement" to the Bush-Baker scheme now might be embarrassing, but to try and do so later will simply be impossible. Once Bush has succeeded in dragging Israel to the *chuppa*, it will be too late to say no. Bush will be in no mood to give Israel a get. Dimming Israel's fate from the peace conference scheme will be out of the question. Israel will be trapped and subjected to Bush's whims at the negotiating table. Resistance to any of Bush's demands will mean that Israel will be blamed for sabotaging "peace."

Certainly, Prime Minister Shamir is aware of these dangers, but the combination of American pressure and American Jewish silence has eroded his traditional firmness. Perhaps Shamir thought that the peace plan he presented in Washington in 1989 would take some of the heat off Israel. Instead, Baker took the Shamir plan, stripped it of those aspects that would insure Israel's security, and twisted the remainder into the phony "peace" conference scheme that new mow the Jewish State.

At this point, the honorable thing would be for Shamir to resign and turn over the reins of power to a colleague who has the money to stand up to international pressure. Anything fewer guarantees that Israel will be slowly dragged down the road to national suicide.

September 13, 1991

The Protocols of the Elders of Washington

My visit to Israel last week left me more worried than ever before about the future of the Jewish State. The headline-grabbing events in the Soviet Union have diverted the Israeli public's attention. At the same time, the State Department quietly continues pressuring Israel to make more dangerous concessions for the sake of the proposed "peace" conference.

Israelis with whom I spoke, people who are loyal Jews and usually alert to the perils that their country faces, optimistically predicted that Secretary of State Baker and his aides would now be too preoccupied with the events in Russia to spend time pressuring Israel. Unfortunately, such optimism is hopelessly unrealistic.

Baker, like any devoted secretary of state, is entirely capable of attending to several different foreign policy matters simultaneously, and the Middle East remains to top his agenda. One might say that during Baker's three years in office, he has displayed something of an obsession with Israel, an almost fanatical commitment to criticizing and harassing the Jewish State. The turmoil in the Soviet Union, however significant it may be, is not likely to jar Baker's Middle East fixation.

Indeed, fresh confirmation of this unfortunate *Ha'aretz*, which reports that despite the Soviet crisis, Baker is more determined than ever to convene some sort of Middle East "peace" conference, whether Israel likes it or not.

According to *Ha'aretz*, Baker is insisting that Israel agree to "accelerate the preparations" for the conference, by making new concessions on the Jerusalem issue. Baker is furious with Israel for refusing to negotiate with Jerusalem Arabs (whose presence would challenge Israel's claim to the city) or PLO representatives (who are committed to the annihilation of the Jewish State). The *Ha'aretz* report says that Baker has rejected Israel's request for a U.S. commitment to guarantee that Palestinian Arab delegates to the talks will not declare themselves to be PLO representatives. Get the picture? The Arabs will present a list of Palestinian delegates, the U.S. will pressure Israel to accept them, and then when the conference opens, the Palestinians will declare that they are at the talks as representatives of the PLO.

If Israel then withdraws from the negotiations, it will be blamed for "obstructing peace." And the U.S. will apparently join in the blame, according to *Ha'aretz*, which reports that the Bush Administration has specifically refused "to commit that they will be sympathetic to Israel's walking away from the negotiating table should the Palestinians take such a stance."

Recent Jewish history provides an eerie parallel to Israel's current dilemma. During the early 1900s, the Russian secret police forged a pamphlet entitled *The Protocols of the Elders of Zion*, which purported to reveal a secret Jewish plot to conquer the world. *The Protocols* became the rallying-cry for anti-Semites everywhere to rise against the Jews.

Today's "Protocols," the "peace process" scheme that has been cooked up in Washington, is being used to rally the international community against the Jewish State. Just as the old Protocols were used to spread the notion that the Jews were undermining Christian civilization, the new Protocols involve spreading the idea that the Jewish State is the "obstacle to peace," that the Israelis are expansionists who lust for a "Greater Israel," and so on. If the original Protocols helped stimulate anti-Jewish mob attacks in Russia, it would be no surprise if Washington's Protocols result in Israel being trapped by an international lynch mob at the "peace" conference in October.

September 20, 1991

Bush Picks Up Where 'Intifada' Left Off

The Palestinian Arab "intifada" may have dialed in its drive to strip the Jewish Suite of its heartland, but President Bush seems determined to succeed where the Intifada failed, and he is pursuing his unsavory objectives with a vigor that far outpaces previous U.S. presidents who dabbled in Middle East diplomacy.

The single most striking feature of Bush's Middle East policy continues to be its rank hypocrisy. Applying a grotesque pro-Arab double standard, Bush seeks to link loan guarantees for Israel to Israeli political concessions, even though he never made any such linkage when U.S. aid to Arab countries was at stake.

Bush went to war on behalf of Kuwait and Saudi Arabia. Yet, he never linked America's military assistance to any kind of political steps by the Saudis or Kuwaitis, such as recognizing Israel or ending their boycott of the Jewish State.

Bush urged the Saudis to give Syria $2 billion as a reward for joining the anti-Iraq coalition, but he never linked that aid to any Syrian political concession, such as making peace with Israel or freeing the 5,000 Jews that Syria is holding hostage.

Bush continues to pour billions of dollars worth of military, economic aid into Egypt each year, topping it with his decision to forgive Egypt's $7.2 billion of debt to the U.S. Yet he never linked that aid to any Egyptian policies, such as halting its hostile anti-Israel propaganda barrage, instituting democratic reforms, or ceasing the persecution of Coptic Christians.

Israel alone is singled out, Israel alone is prevented from receiving loan guarantees, which are not grants, and not even loans, which will cost the U.S. practically nothing until it declares that Judea and Samaria are off-limits to Jews.

Whatever the outcome of the battle over the $10 billion in loan guarantees, it is clear that Israel is being dragged into a dangerous political process from which it cannot emerge victoriously.

Now that Bush has clearly and publicly linked U.S. aid to Israel's policies in the territories, there can be no doubt that the subject of U.S. aid will hang like a sword of Damocles over Israel's head throughout the upcoming peace conference. Virtually every Arab demand will be backed up by the threat that Bush will reduce American aid to Israel unless Israel gives in. Since Bush's position is that all of the liberated territories, including the Old City of Jerusalem, are "occupied Arab territory," and Israeli attempt to resist surrender, those regions will be met by the fiercest U.S. counterpressure.

Israel will be faced with a choice of either making suicidal territorial concessions or walking out of the peace conference, being blamed for "obstructing peace," and facing a cut-off of U.S. aid.

Bush's deadly linkage has forced Israel's hand. Israel must pull out of the peace conference trap now, making clear that it is going not because of the $10 billion per se, but because the controversy has revealed the dangers of Bush's pro-Arab agenda. Pulling out now may be unpleasant, but it will be less unpleasant than the consequences of having Bush succeed where the Intifada has failed.

October 4, 1991

Bush Incites the Haters

Whatever President Bush may have intended when he launched his attack on the 'Jewish lobby,' one thing is clear: his characterization of himself as "one little guy" besieged by pushy Jewish lobbyists has warmed the hearts of Jew-haters everywhere.

In a desperate attempt to win the sympathy of the Congress and the American public, Bush inadvertently employed bigoted imagery that could easily incite anti-Semitic sentiment.

The president owes the American public an apology. He insulted the public's intelligence by resorting to the language of ethnic rivalry. At a time when anti-Jewish violence still rages in Brooklyn, should the president be declaring on national television that Jews are in effect manipulating U.S. foreign policy to America's detriment?

Bush's obsession with blocking Israel's request for loan guarantees has gone beyond all reason and threatens to erode America's long-standing friendship with the Jewish State seriously. Even friends can make mistakes, and if Congress goes along with Bush's crusade, it will have made one of the colossal mistakes of our era.

All Israel is asking for is a second-party guarantor so that it can borrow money from private banks to house refugees. That's not exactly what one would call a strain on the U.S. economy. In fact, it would cost the U.S. next to nothing. The idea that the U.S. would refrain from agreeing to the guarantee is preposterous when one considers that the refugees Israel seeks to house are those that the U.S. refused to take in! A report in the September 15 edition of the *New York Times Magazine* detailed how various European countries harshly expelled numerous refugees that have been trying to cross their borders in recent years. Israel, in contrast, stands with open arms to welcome every refugee at its gate. Yet the Bush Administration, instead of giving Israel the small help it so desperately needs, is talking about sending billions of dollars to the Soviet Union and the newly independent Baltic nations of Lithuania, Latvia, and Estonia. Wouldn't it be ironic if the Lithuanians, Latvians, and Estonians, all of whom eagerly collaborated in the Holocaust, become the beneficiaries of U.S. aid, while Israel the home of those who survived the Holocaust goes is left begging?

Bush has laid his cards on the table. He is determined to force Israel out of Judea and Samaria step by step, and he is fully prepared to use U.S. aid as the leverage with which to force such a suicidal withdrawal. Israel is getting an early taste of what is in store for it at the proposed Middle East peace conference.

The time has come for Israel to wash its hands of both the request for the loan guarantees and the proposed peace conference. If Israel needs financial help, it can turn to its many supporters around the world, explain the crisis in the bluntest of terms, and take the steps towards internal economic reform that will be necessary to win the confidence of foreign investors. As for peace, that will come when and only when the Arabs are at last convinced that Israel can never be defeated, neither on the battlefield nor at the negotiating table.

October 11, 1991

Bush and 'Zionism-Is-Racism,' A Cheap Trick

President Bush's appeal to the United Nations to rescind its "Zionism is racism" resolution is a transparent maneuver designed to undermine Israel's request for the $10 billion in loan guarantees.

Supporters of Israel in this country dare not be fooled by the administration's cheap trick.

Ordinarily, this sort of political wheeling-and-dealing is done with some subtlety. The Bush Administration, by contrast, has made its strategy painfully obvious. It is so obvious. In fact, it was broadcasted across the pages of the *New York Times* the morning after Bush's speech at the UN:

"Administration officials stud Mr. Bush's main purpose in appealing was to smooth his efforts to schedule the Middle East peace conference (and) to make amends with American Jewish groups. 'This shows our evenhandedness toward Israel and signals them that we can be trusted as an honest broker in the peace process to come,' an official said."

Far from demonstrating the administration's "evenhandedness," the President's speech, in fact, demonstrated how little respect he has for Israel's supporters. Bush and his aides seem to regard American Jews as gullible little children whose temper-tantrums over the $10 billion can be soothed with the lollipop of his speech against the "Zionism is racism" resolution.

American Jewish activists are too sophisticated for such nonsense. They know that the "Zionism is racism" resolution, as contemptible as it is, does not do any concrete damage to Israel. It is merely a symbolic expression of the international community's hatred for the Jewish State. Certainly, it should be rescinded. But when to rescind it, or how to rescind it, should have no connection to the life-and-death questions that Israel faces as a result of what Bush calls "the peace process."

Hundreds of thousands of penniless Soviet Jewish immigrants are pouring into Israel. They need housing. They need jobs. Reversing "Zionism is racism" will give them neither.

The Middle East peace conference, if convened as Bush's terms, will put Israel in grave danger. The focus of the conference will be pressure on Israel to retreat to the indefensible pre-1967 borders. Reversing "Zionism is racism" will not protect Israel from such pressure.

If President Bush and his aides are sincerely concerned about the "Zionism is racism" libel, if they really care about such international challenges to Israel's existence, they can demonstrate their concern by recognizing some of the real threats facing the Jewish State threats which they are encouraging.

Secretary of State Baker recently endorsed Syria's demand for Israel's surrender of the Golan Heights. That would leave all of northern Israel naked to attack by Syria's Scud missiles (which are far more deadly than those Iraq used).

President Bush has condemned the Jewish neighborhoods of eastern and northern Jerusalem as "illegal settlements." That raises the prospect that the U.S. will support stripping Israel of its capital.

American diplomats have been meeting in Israel for the past few weeks with three local Arab militants who describe themselves as PLO representatives. They're negotiating about how to force Israel to gradually allow the emergence of a de facto PLO state in Judea, Samaria, and Gaza.

Syrian missiles? Arab rule over Jerusalem? A PLO state in Israel's backyard? Those are the kinds of things that should truly bother anybody who is sincerely worried about the survival of Zionism.

October 18, 1991

Jews No Longer 'At Home' In America

Not a long ago, a prominent Jewish professor authored a history of American Jewry entitled *At Home in America*. Certainly, it is true that for most Jews, the phrase "at home in America" was precisely how they have felt about the United States. But now that an American president has, for the first time, openly attacked the American Jewish community, perhaps the time has come to reconsider just what that phrase "at home" really means.

Jewish tradition, of course, utterly rejects the concept that Jews could be "at home" anywhere outside of the Land of Israel. Judaism, in contrast to other religions, is very much a land-centered faith. Many of the Torah commandments are dependent upon Jews being physically resident in the land. Many of the prayers are for the reconstruction of the Temple in Jerusalem or the return of the exiled Jews to their homeland.

"At home" in Crown Heights or the Valley? Impossible, says the classic Jewish texts. The Diaspora, or more accurately, the Exile is depicted as a punishment, a curse, a tragedy not an opportunity to grow fast and comfortable.

Still, most American Jews have never paid a great deal of attention to those texts, and even some of the observant Jews who are familiar with them prefer to skip over those "Land of Israel" related passages whose implementation would be especially inconvenient.

So feeling right "at home" in America, Jews set to work contributing their talents and energy to making it a better country. They succeeded as no other ethnic minority group has ever succeeded. Their contributions have been unparalleled. Who can count the Jewish comedians who have made Americans laugh, the Jewish playwrights who have moved audiences to tears, the Jewish Hollywood producers who have entertained millions, the Jewish doctors who have healed, the Jewish lawyers who have pleaded, and the abundance of industries built by Jewish sweat and Jewish brains?

63

All of this was possible because anti-Semitism in the United States, while always present, never reached the levels of intensity that it reached elsewhere. Certainly, this country has had its share of "American First" rallies, Ku Klux Klan tiki torches, and neo-Nazi marches. But in American political life, they have always been the exceptions, not the rule. The governmental authorities always regarded anti-Semitism as illegitimate.

Now all of that has changed. For the first time in this country's history, a president has publicly attacked the American Jewish community for the "crime" of exercising its democratic right to lobby. Let nobody be fooled by his use of euphemisms like "the pro-Israel lobby." That phrase means **Jews**. He knows we know it, and they know it. The "they" I am referring to are the millions of potential anti-Semites in this country who will interpret the President's words as a declaration that it is open season on the Jews. These potential Jew-haters range from the editors who immediately filled their newspapers with wildly exaggerated stories about the amount of aid America has given Israel (read: the Jews) to the blue-collar workers in neighborhood bars who nodded and grumbled about "the Jews" getting $10 billion while other Americans struggle to make ends meet.

If Jews begin to feel like they are no longer really "at home in America," it is with good reason. It used to be that the only time one would discover anti-Semitism in the White House was long after the official in question had retired. For example, former Vice President Spiro Agnew's rantings about the "Zionist lobby," or former President Richard Nixon's taped remarks about Jewish anti-war protesters. How times have changed. Now even the occupant of the White House can go after the Jews, provided only that he uses the appropriate euphemisms.

G-d is a Pro-Israel Lobbyist

The hundreds of pro-Israel lobbyists who have been "besieging" the White House have the aid of an Ally who has sworn to give "the land which I promised to your fathers, to Abraham, to Isaac, and to Jacob," a territory that includes "every place whereon the sole of your foot shall tread, from the wilderness, and Lebanon, from the river Euphrates even unto the hinder sea." He is the same Ally who has promised to "bless those that bless Israel, and those that curse Israel I shall curse."

Those words are the words of the Almighty. The citations are from Deuteronomy 6:10 and 11:24, and Genesis 12:3, respectively.

In other words, those American Jews who recently exercised their democratic rights by expressing their opinions on Capitol Hill are not the only pro-Israel forces with which George Bush must contend; he must also consider the Divine legacy inscribed in the pages of the Bible.

Observant Jews are not the only ones who recognize the validity of Israel's Divine right to the Holy Land; so do many Jews who are not scrupulous in their religious observance but acknowledge their Torah heritage. Add to that total the tens of millions of Bible-believing Christians who know that G-d is on the side of Israel, not Ishmael. That's a pretty formidable body of citizens.

Like every American president before him, George Bush must carefully weigh the relevant factors before determining his Middle East policy. He must consider moral questions, such as the right of the Jews to one tiny homeland, within defensible boundaries, where they will be safe from future Holocausts. He must consider spiritual questions, such as the Biblical promises to the Jews and his own religious beliefs, such as how he will answer on the ultimate Day of Judgment. And of course, he will factor in cold political matters such as Arab oil, Jewish votes, and the like.

Bush and Baker pleaded with Israel to refrain from taking part in the coalition's war against Iraq, for the benefit of what they believed to be U.S. national interests. Israel agreed to do so, to the detriment of its national security policy of retaliation. Now Bush shows his "appreciation" by whipping up the anti-Israel sentiment with his Orwellian claims about American soldiers "risking their lives for Israel."

This administration has just sent a letter to the president of Lebanon, agreeing that Israel should withdraw from its narrow security belt along the Israeli-Lebanese border. Yet it remains completely silent about the Syrian occupation of the other 99 percent of Lebanon.

This administration has declared the Jewish neighborhoods in Judea, Samaria, Gaza, and the Old City of Jerusalem to be "illegal," a complete reversal of the Reagan Administration's position that the Jewish settlements were not illegal (even though Reagan did criticize the settlements policy).

This administration committed the sinister act of stopping Germany from sending promised financial aid to Israel until and unless Israel caved into the administration's pressure on the settlements issue.

These kinds of outrageous actions give those "pro-Israel lobbyists" every reason in the world to voice their concerns on Capitol Hill. One can only hope and pray that they and their chief Ally will continue to make their presence felt.

November 1, 1991

Israel Surrenders

Without firing a single shot, the Bush Administration has managed to subdue the strongest country in the Middle East completely.

No missiles or bombing raids were needed for Bush's conquest of the Israeli national will. Bush attained his victory simply by using verbal and psychological warfare, a carefully hatched strategy of leaks to the media, behind the scenes arm twisting, and cynical manipulation of the American Jewish community by alternately reassuring and denouncing it.

The fascinating aspect of this whole sorry process has been the extent to which President Bush and Secretary of State Baker have openly articulated their pro-Arab strategy. Unholy words by unholy people against the people of the Holy Book.

It was Baker who told *Newsweek* that the U.S. would have to corner Israel the way a hunter corners his prey during a turkey hunt.

It was Bush who declared that it was "illegal" for Jews to move into the neighborhoods of Jerusalem that Israel liberated in 1967.

It was Baker who testified before a Congressional committee that the presence of Jews in Judea and Samaria was "the single biggest obstacle to Middle East peace."

At every turn, Bush and Baker upped the rhetorical ante, barraging Israel with ceaseless criticism, pressure, and complaints, so that the Israelis (and their American Jewish supporters) were constantly on the defensive, unable to mount any kind of effective counter-attack.

And so, the Israelis, having been thoroughly intimidated by the one-two punch of the Bush Administration and its media allies, have now been cornered into participating in a Middle East conference whose agenda has been dictated by Yasser Arafat and Hafez Al-Assad

Nor is it hard to understand why Bush wants the conference. Focusing attention on Israel diverts the American public's attention away from Bush's failure to solve America's domestic problems, and the fact that he allowed the victory in the Gulf to deteriorate into the slaughter of the Kurds while Saddam Hussein remains in power.

But it is hard to understand why the Israelis have agreed to the conference when one considers that:

- the Bush Administration has declared in advance that it supports the basic Arab demands;

- the Syrians are refusing to discuss water rights and other vital issues until after Israel retreats to the 1967 boundaries; and

- despite Israel's objections, the PLO is openly orchestrating the process by which the Palestinian Arab delegates to the conference have been selected.

According to media reports, the PLO's list of 14 delegates has been given to the U.S. but will not be given to Israel before the conference. If those reports are correct in their listing of the names, Israel is going to find itself negotiating with some very unsavory characters indeed:

- Saeb Erakat, who on the "Nightline" program in June 1988, dared to claim that during the 1940', the Palestinian Arabs were just as many targets of Hitler as were the Jews. An allegation that was so outrageous that even the ultra dovish Leon Wieseltier denounced it was "obscene."

- Mustafa Natshe, who has said (in the Lebanese magazine **Al-Hawadith**, in August 1986) that "people under occupation have the right to use armed struggle to fight against their occupiers."

- Elias Freij, mayor of Bethlehem, who regularly meets with Yasir Arafat in defense of Israeli law because (as he puts it) "As long as I am

68

declaring that the PLO is the sole legitimate representative of our people, then it is my right to meet its leadership any time I wish."

Men like Erakat, Natshe, and Freij will not bring peace to the Middle East. But with the help of Bush, Baker, and American Jewish silence, they may yet succeed in bringing a deadly PLO state to the Middle East.

November 15, 1991

Israel Squeezed in Madrid, Scapegoated in Washington

The Bush Administration seems obsessed with the idea of achieving a phony "peace" in the Middle East, something that may produce a Nobel Peace Prize for George Bush or James Baker but will leave Israel in more danger than ever before.

Baker's bullying of Israel may keep the Middle East negotiations going for a while. When the Israelis said they wanted the next round of talks to take place in Israel and the Arab countries, Baker whispered to his media pals that he might invite to have the talks in Washington and "dare" the Israelis to refuse. Israel quickly began to discuss "compromise" Sites that the Arabs; would like.

But this kind of badgering and strong-arming will not produce a durable peace. At best, it will produce a temporary peace treaty that will have Israel trading strategically vital territories for a "piece" of paper that can be torn up by the Arabs at any time.

The "peaceful" Middle East that George Bush has in mind, will circa 1996, look something like this:

Three years of Arab "autonomy" in Judea and Samaria will have produced a de facto PLO state in those territories. Israel will be back in its indefensible pre-1967 borders. and the Arabs will already be talking about "liberating the rest of Palestine."

Iraq, rescued from destruction by Bush's vacillating Gulf War policy, will have rebuilt, reamed, and be pointing its new, more advanced Send missiles at Israel only this time they will be armed with those nuclear warheads that Saddam Hussein hid from the United Nations. Bush's failure to crush Saddam will come home to roost, but Israel will pay the price.

Iran will also have nuclear capabilities. While the U.S. was busy wooing Iranian "moderates," the Iranian regime has been busy developing atomic weapons. First, target the Zionist infidels occupying Palestine.

The history books will record all of the terrible, tragic ironies:

... How Bush forced Israel to absorb Iraqi missile attacks, and then "rewarded" the Israelis by shoving a de facto PLO state down their throats;

... How Soviet Jewish refuseniks launched the whole dissident movement that helped lead to the crackup of Soviet Communism, and how Bush "rewarded" them by refusing to guarantee a loan to help house Soviet Jewish refugees in Israel;

... How America repeated its moral failure during the Holocaust years, by paving the way for the Arabs to "finish Hitler's job" by annihilating the Jewish State in stages.

Above all, political analysts will look back to the pre-election year of 1991 and analyze Bush's clever but shallow strategy of seeking fame as the Middle East "peacemaker" to cover up for his countless domestic failures. The more Bush's domestic popularity dropped, the more vigorously he pursued his skewed vision of a Middle East peace until he became obsessed with seeking peace at any price, and Israel's survival became the price that he was prepared to pay.

November 12, 1991

You Can't Give Away Someone Else's Land

Public opinion polls regularly report that a substantial percentage of Israelis favor the concept of "land for peace." Such claims should never be taken literally; they reflect the political bias of whoever is sponsoring the poll, the vague wording of the questions that are asked, and the fact that some of those giving the answers are Arabs, or people who have not really thought out the issue, or people who are afraid to state their real opinion.

But the real problem with such polls is that they are asking the wrong question entirely. Asking Israelis if they are prepared to give up land for "peace" presupposes that the land in question is their property and that they have the right to decide to surrender that land to Arab rule if they so choose. That idea flies in the face of the most basic concepts of Zionism.

Zionism is based on the belief that the Land of Israel is the eternal inheritance of the entire Jewish people. It never accepted the notion that the fate of the Land of Israel was to be determined solely by those who were actually residing there. How could it have? When Theodore Herzl launched the modern Zionist movement in the 1890s, the Land of Israel had a large Arab majority. Certainly, there was an important Jewish community in the country, one that had clung tenaciously to the land despite countless centuries of misery and deprivation. But the Jews were a tiny minority at that time. The vast majority of Jews, having been expelled by the Romans 1800 years earlier, were still living in the Diaspora. Had the land been regarded as being only the business of those living there, Zionism would never have arisen, and the Jewish State would never have been reborn.

The modern Zionist movement regarded the Land of Israel in precisely the same way that Jews had always regarded it: as the property of the entire Jewish people, even if they were (temporarily) in exile. The entire *raison d'etre* of modern Zionism was to bring the masses of Jews from the Diaspora to the Land of Israel.

Whether they lived in Poland or France or even the United States, those Jews had the right to settle in the Land of Israel because the land belonged to them, as Jews.

The establishment of the State of Israel does not change the status of the Land of Israel. It did not suddenly become the exclusive property of those Jews who have chosen to live there. On the contrary, it remains the property of Jews everywhere.

That's why Israelis insist that Diaspora Jews should help Israel – because it's their land, too. That's why Israel gives automatic citizenship to Jewish immigrants (and not to non-Jews) because it's their land, too. That's why religious Jews still pray, three times daily, for Jews in the Diaspora to return to the Holy Land – because it's their land, too.

And that's why pollsters do not have the moral right even to ask Israelis if they are willing to surrender portions of the Land of Israel to the Arabs.

Because the fate of the Land of Israel cannot be subject to the whims of Israeli voters, neither Israel's leaders nor the voters who elect them have the right to surrender any part of the land. It is not their property alone. It is the property of the entire Jewish people, and it is the property of future generations of the Jewish people.

November 29, 1991

American Pressure, Arab Unity, Jewish Silence

Throughout the past two years of intensive American diplomacy in the Middle East, three factors have remained constant: U.S. pressure, Arab unity, and American Jewish silence. This deadly combination has forced Israel into a corner from which it may not be able to emerge intact.

In the face of unrelenting American pressure on Israel, American Jewish leaders have, for the most part, stood on the sidelines, leaving Israel to fend for itself in its hour of distress. The only ones who have not stood on the sidelines are those who have jumped in on the side of the Arabs, by heaping criticism upon the Jewish State.

Now contrast that cravenly Jewish behavior with the steadfast unity of the Arab world. Despite occasional tactical disagreements, the Arabs have consistently rallied around their one-issue agenda: get land from Israel, to soften it up before eradicating it.

A unified Arab world and a hostile Bush Administration have succeeded in pressuring Israel into concession after concession, while American Jews look the other way.

The reckless Israeli proposal for Arab "autonomy" is being turned into a plan for a PLO state – yet American Jewish leaders are silent.

Palestinian Arab leaders like Hanan Ashrawli are openly and illegally consorting with Arafat. At the same time, Israel, under U.S. pressure, hesitates to act yet American Jewish liberals, who are supposedly committed to concepts like "justice" and "the rule of law," say nothing about Ashrawli and her fellow-lawbreakers.

The State Department has suddenly buried all evidence of Syrian and Palestinian involvement in the Pan Am bombing and is trying to pin the blame on "extremist" Libya, yet American Jews refuse to protest.

A prominent *Chasidic rebbe* last week praised President Bush, and 32 Reform rabbis have just issued a statement calling Israel's prime minister a "terrorist" – yet their sheepish congregants are silent.

It's "business as usual" for American Jews, as they go about their daily routines, enjoying the many pleasures of life, oblivious to the danger that threatens their four million brethren in Israel. For American Jews, the word "cocktail" refers to a party or a reception, where the well-to-do gather to amuse themselves. For Israeli Jews, the word "cocktail" has a more sinister connotation; it refers to the deadly bottles of flaming gasoline that the rioting Arab *intifada* gangs hurl at defenseless Israeli women and children.

American Jews must strive to bridge this psychological gap. They must understand the perils that Israelis face, appreciate the sacrifice the Israelis make to preserve the existence of the only Jewish State, and devote themselves wholeheartedly to Israel's defense before there is no Israel left to defend.

December 20, 1991

What's in A Name?

The current Middle East "peace" process marks the first time in modern history that a conquering army that has been ejected from the land of its illegal conquest is being invited to re-occupy that territory by the victims of the original conquest.

The Arab conquest of Judea, Samaria, Gaza, and eastern Jerusalem in the 1948 war were illegal and immoral. It was Arab imperialism, plain and simple, comparable to the recent Iraqi conquest of Kuwait and the Syrian conquest of Lebanon.

Yet Israel, which was the victim of the 1948 aggression and occupation by the Arabs, now seems to be on the verge of accepting an "autonomy" plan that will give the Arabs de-facto control of those territories once again. The Arab aggression of 1948, and the more recent Arab aggression known as the "*intifada,*" are being rewarded: the Arabs who illegally conquered the region are being invited to reconquer it, although this time, through diplomatic treaties rather than marching armies.

How have the Arabs accomplished this feat? By using simple rhetorical deceit. In 1948, there were no "Palestinians." It was just a matter of Arabs attacking Jews, and the international community had little sympathy for that, especially so soon after the Holocaust.

Suddenly, in the 1970s, there were "Palestinians." The change in name gave the Arabs the "justification" for demanding the surrender of Israeli terrorists. Overnight, the Arabs in those territories were transformed into a separate "Palestinian nation," with a hastily-concocted "Palestinian history and heritage," and of course with a demand for "self-determination" and "legitimate national rights." At Camp David in 1978, Menachem Begin inadvertently aided the triumph of this historical farce by thoughtlessly agreeing to recognize "the legitimate rights" of the Palestinian Arabs.

All talk of "Palestinian" rights is a smokescreen. The reality is that only the name has changed; everything else is the same. It's the same old Arabs, predominantly Moslems, murdering Jews and demanding that the Jews surrender territory. As part of the long-range pan-Arab plan to destroy the Jewish State.

Golda Meir spoke words of wisdom when she said that there was no such thing as a Palestinian nation. She did not mean as her sillier critics have alleged that there were no Arabs in Judea, Samaria, and Gaza. Obviously, there were. She simply meant that the Arabs who were there had no legitimate "Palestinian" identity, that the entire concept of "Palestinians" was an Arab propaganda invention designed to stake a competing claim to the Land of Israel. "Throw the Jews into the Sea" was too crude a slogan. "Rights for the oppressed Palestinians" have been much more successful.

Israel is not entirely to blame for its failure to head off the Arab propaganda onslaught. A tiny, besieged nation preoccupied with defending itself against invasions and terrorism, absorbing waves of new immigrants, and coping with the devastating economic consequences of the Arab boycott, simply can't accomplish everything that is needed. When a country is forced to fight on so many fronts at once, something has to give; in Israel's case, it is the information front that has proved the most vulnerable.

While Israel's inability to win the propaganda war may be understandable, the failure of American Jews to come to Israel's defense is simply unforgivable. There are so many ways in which American Jewry could have helped and still can help to protect the Jewish State tram its enemies. There should be a truly forceful Jewish lobby in Washington instead of the current paper tiger "lobby," Which he lost every crucial battle from AWACs to the $10-billion loan guarantee.

There should be a properly-financed organization devoted solely to defending Israel's good name and aggressively exposing Arab barbarism – instead of the weak-kneed Establishment "defense" groups and the well-meaning but under-financed independents. Most of all, there should be an all-out effort to convince young, idealistic American Jews to settle yes, physically go, and settle in Judea and Samaria. It is nothing less than a scandal that 24 years after the liberation of those territories, only 100,000 or so Jews live there.

The relatively small size of the Jewish population in Judea and Samaria is what has persuaded the Arabs and the international community that it is still possible to tear those lands away from Israel and uproot their Jewish residents, Yamit-style. A massive Jewish settlement effort, spearheaded and financed by American Jewry, would have made and still could make Judea and Samaria physically non-negotiable.

With their physical presence and with their dollars, American Jews have the power to prevent the establishment of a PLO state in Israel's ancestral homeland. The U.S. administration knows that and is rushing furiously to force Israel from the Golan and Judea and Samaria and Gaza.

Unfortunately, our laid-back religious and secular leaders have not awakened to this reality nor taken action to prevent it. Unless they do, the creation of a Palestinian state, a defenseless Jewish nation, and the resultant decline of Jewish life will be laid at the steps of such leaders, not Bush or Baker, who cannot be expected to be more Jewish than our leaders.

December 27, 1991

An Open Letter to President Bush

Your policy of bullying Israel ignores the principles of decency and morality upon which American foreign policy should be based. It is unconscionable that Israel, the only democracy in the Middle East and our staunchest ally in the world, should be pressed to make concessions to the Arabs that would be mortally harmful to it.

We have only recently witnessed with pride the role of our great country in standing up to the evil empire of atheistic Communism and totalitarianism and hastening its downfall. Now our country is demeaning itself by embracing another evil empire, the fundamentalist Muslim empire that stretches {rem Algiers to Baghdad. There is not a single democracy In the Arab world; human rights violated daily; defenseless civilians are slaughtered with poison gas; women are treated as serfs.

We should not be allied With a Syrian regime that murdered 20.000 of its people in Hama, holds thousands of Jews hostage, sponsors international terrorism, and gave arms and haven to the hostage holders in Lebanon. We should not be allied with a Jordanian regime that slaughtered 10,000 of its Palestinian Arab citizens in 1970-1941 and continues to deny democracy to its citizens. We should not be allied with Palestinian Arabs who cheered from the rooftops as Saddam rained Scud missiles on Israel and American soldiers in the Persian Gulf. We should not be allied with those who applauded the pro-Stalinist coup in the Soviet Union last August.

Israel's valiant struggle for freedom and democracy in the Middle East over the past 43 years, and Its magnificent support of the United Statues at the United Nations during this period, is unsurpassed in the entire world. After all the suffering that Israel has endured and all the lives it has lost defending itself against Arab totalitarian aggression, it is unthinkable that the United States should now aid in the creation of a Palestinian Arab state that would become another bastion of Arab totalitarianism and Islamic fundamentalism.

The claim that the Arabs have become more "moderate" cannot be taken seriously. The Arabs' fundamental refusal to accept the legitimacy of the Jewish State in their midst has not changed. Even in the darkest days of the U.S. Soviet cold war, there was always a "hotline" between the countries to prevent an accidental confrontation; it is impossible to imagine that there would ever be a hotline between Baghdad or Damascus and Jerusalem. The Soviet Union was based on a political and economic ideology that could, and did, crumble; the Arabs' rejection of Israel is rooted in Muslim religious beliefs that will never change.

The time has come for the U.S. to stop supporting undemocratic states in the Middle East; to stop pressuring Israel for concessions; and to recognize united Jerusalem as the capital of the Jewish nation, Israel.

January 3, 1992

Bush Rewards Arab Aggression

One by one, the American hostages who were held in Syrian-controlled Lebanon have been paraded into the Syrian Foreign Ministry in Damascus, where, standing beneath a portrait of Syrian dictator Hafez Assad, they have dutifully sung the praises of Assad's evil regime for supposedly helping to bring about the release of the hostages.

In Washington, too, praise has been heaped upon Assad, by spokesmen for the Bush Administration. Bush and his aids know full well that Syria was largely responsible for the hostage problem in the first place. It was Syria that gave arms, training, and money to the hostage-holders. It was Syria that permitted them to keep the hostages in Syrian-controlled regions of Lebanon.

Bush and his aids know all that. They also know of Syria's role in the global drug trade and its sponsorship of international terrorism. But hostage-holding, drug-dealing, and terrorism are the kind of things that would hurt Syria's image. And if Syria's true face were revealed, it would undermine Bush's strategy of making Syria look "moderate" so that Israel can be pressured into giving up the Golan Heights to Assad.

It was less than a year ago that Bush was claiming to base his Middle East policies on principle or "no rewards for aggressors." Now, ironically, it seems that his policy is just the opposite reward for the aggressors. Reward Syria's aggression against Lebanon by ignoring it and building closer relations with Damascus. Reward the Jordanian and Syrian aggression against Israel in 1967 by pressuring Israel to surrender the territories that it won from Jordan and Syria in self-defense. Reward Jordan's support for Iraqi aggression against Kuwait, by renewing U.S. military aid to Amman. Reward the Palestinian Arabs' support for Iraqi aggression, by demanding that Israel let the Palestinian Arabs create a deadly, irredentist state in Judea and Samaria.

And what about Israel? Wasn't it supposed to be rewarded for absorbing Iraqi missile hits to preserve America's phony Gulf War Coalition?

Afraid not. While Israel is pressured to release Arab terrorists to bring about the release of the American hostages, it is Syria, not Israel, that has received all of the State Department's praise. Israel, which supported America's Gulf War effort, has been bullied, harassed, and pressured by the Bush Administration. In contrast, Jordan and the Palestinian Arabs, who supported Iraq, have been coddled and showered with favors.

American's alliance with the Arabs may produce short-term gains (although it is difficult to name them), but as a long-term strategy, it is pure folly. Bush's Arab friends are among the most unstable dictators on this planet. Mubarak, Assad, and King Hussein are corrupt tyrants who could be overthrown at any time, by anyone of a dozen different enemies. Radical, militant Islamic movement could put a speedy end to any friendship with "the Great Satan," as Iranian Moslems call America.

In that event, Israel's role as a stable, reliable ally in a chaotic region would be dramatized as never before. Today's conventional wisdom in Washington is that the end of the Cold War has diminished Israel's strategic value to the United States; In fact, there is no way of determining if the Cold War has diminished Israel's strategic value to the United States. There is no way of determining if the Cold War has truly ended. The Soviet Union is an upheaval, and the process may continue for years. Nobody can predict who will rule in Moscow next year, or even next week. This country needs stable, democratic allies like Israel more man ever. By punishing Israel, and rewarding its enemies, the U.S. is ultimately shooting itself in the heart.

January 10, 1992

How The Arabs Wrecked America's Economy

All of the economic problems that are strangling America the recession, the soaring unemployment rate, the ever-widening trade deficit can be traced to one simple, common source: Arab oil blackmail.

The Arab oil boycott of 1973, and the failure of the United States to take decisive action to counter it, stimulated a series of crises which have given birth to every major economic problem that currently besets America – intensified a variety of social ills, to boot.

Before the 1973 boycott, the price of oil was $3.89 per barrel. By the following year, it had nearly doubled. The price of a barrel of all today is 500 percent more than what it cost before 1973, and it still costs the Arabs less than 50¢ per barrel to produce.

The U.S. could have taken forceful action. It would have been entirely justified had it sent in troops either alone, or as part of a multinational force to seize the Arabian oil fields in 1973-1974. After the sneak attack by Egypt and Syria on Israel during Yom Kippur, the United States State Department Arabists should have anticipated the Arab oil boycott. After all, they were supposedly experts in an Arab mentality and allegedly representing U.S. interests.

In the face of the grotesque Arab economic boycott Israel, the normal reaction of the Arabists should have anticipated Saudi Arabian support for Egypt and Syria by using Arab oil as a weapon to bring the U.S. to heel. What can one suspect if not even one of the over 21 U.S. Ambassadors to the Arab countries did not urge the United States to seize the Arabian oil fields during the Yom Kippur War?

What was true then is still true now. Indeed, the fact that the U.S. and its allies sacrificed the lives of their soldiers to protect Kuwait and Saudi Arabia gave them plenty of additional justification for taking control of the Arabian Gulf all resources. Instead, American blood has been spilled to save the Saudis, yet the Saudis continue to Emma American consumers by charging artificially inflated prices for oil.

The idea of seizing the Arab oil fields does not seem to have ever been seriously considered by American policy-makers, either in 1973-1974 or during the recent Gulf Crisis. Successive U.S. administrations Nixon, Ford, Caner, Reagan, and Bush alike have preferred to pursue a policy of appeasing the Arabs, paying whatever outrageous prices the Arabs demand oil. And that's not all.

The Arabs insist on being paid both in cash and in Israeli concessions. So not only does the American government compel U.S. consumers to empty their pockets at the gas tanks, hut America relentlessly pressures Israel to make suicidal concessions to the Arabs. America's foreign policy is totally subordinate to Arab whims, structured around the need to keep the Arabs happy so that the oil will keep flowing.

What makes all of this even more peculiar is that American companies are the ones who are developing the Arab oil fields in the first place. Mobil, Gulf, and the rest of the huge American oil-production firms have a virtual monopoly on the development of the region's oil resources. One may wonder why it is that the Japanese, for example, have never attempted to take over any part of the oil production process. Given their enormous financial abilities, business acumen, and general resourcefulness, one would expect the Japanese to move into the Arabian oil production business just as they have moved in on everything else in the world economy. Yet they have refrained from doing so. Could it be that Washington and Tokyo have some kind of understanding, one which leaves Arabian oil in the hands of American companies in exchange for the U.S. tolerating the huge imbalance in American-Japanese trade...?

Such a deal would satisfy the gentlemen at Mobil, while at the same time victimizing the American public, by forcing it to suffer all the disastrous side effects of the trade imbalance with Japan. Outrageous? Certainly – but only one of the many outrageous results of permitting Arab oil to wreck America.

January 17, 1992

An American Jew In Hebron

American Jews have a long and proud history of successfully battling against anti-Jewish discrimination. One of the most important and least known of those battles was fought in the city of Hebron a few years ago, by a determined and courageous American Jewish immigrant to Israel named Yona Chaiken.

Chaiken's name is not well known in the American Jewish community, and that is how he preferred it. He was repeatedly propelled to the center of Jewish controversy despite his modest, almost shy nature. It was the sheer force of his principles that compelled him to go where Ether Jews had feared to go before.

In his native Springfield, Massachusetts, Yona Chaiken went to court to demand his right to wear a *yarmulke* while teaching in a public school. He could have taken the easy way out; rabbinical permission to go bareheaded while on the job was available. Instead, Chaiken fought for nine years until the courts upheld the principle of Jewish religious equality. His struggle cleared the way for other American Jews to observe their religion in peace and dignity.

Chaiken exhibited the same admirable qualities after he moved to Israel in 1984. He could have settled in a relatively safe city like Tel Aviv or Jerusalem. Instead, Chaiken took his family (he and his wife had five children at the time) to Hebron, where the right to Jewish equality had yet to be established!

To the surprise and consternation of local Arab bigots, Chaiken promptly applied for a membership card in the Hebron Public Library. The Arabs who run the library refused his request. Chaiken fought. And he won. Some people might regard the episode as a minor matter. But can you imagine the outcry if the public library of Miami Beach or Beverly Hills refused to give out library cards to Jews? The Anti-Defamation League of B'nai B'rith, the American Jewish Congress, and the American Jewish Committee would fight tooth-and-nail to win the right of Jews to get those library cards because they symbolize the equal right of Jews to live in the place of their choice. Every resident of any city has the right to belong to the local public library. The Arabs in Hebron reject the right of Jews to live in Hebron. The Arabs were rebuffed, and Jewish equality was upheld, thanks to Yona Chaiken.

The major struggle for Jewish rights in Hebron lies in the not-too-distant future. If the Hebron Arabs would not even give a library card to a Jew today, when they are under Israeli rule, imagine how they will behave if the dangerous plan for Arab autonomy is implemented. The Arab governing authority will trample Jewish rights. At the same time, the international community looks away, and before long the Jewish holy sites in Hebron will suffer the same fate that the Western Wall suffered under Jordanian rule, when it was used as a garbage dump, and when Jewish gravestones in the Mount of Olives cemetery were used for latrines in Jordanian Army camps.

Yona Chaiken would have been a valuable participant in the coming battle for Hebron and the rest of the liberated territories. Unfortunately, he will not be there. Last month, Yona Chaiken succumbed to cancer, leaving behind seven children and a wife who is pregnant. Tax-deductible contributions to help the Chaiken orphans may be sent to Central Fund of Israel, 1460 Broadway, Sixth Floor, New York, NY 10036, Attn: Chaiken Fund.

January 24, 1992

Israel Cans Stand Strong for Its National Security Interests

President Bush's sharp drop in the polls and his faltering attempts to reverse the American-Japanese trade imbalance have gravely weakened his ability to pressure Israel. Now is the ideal time for Israel's leaders to vigorously resist U.S. criticism and take whatever measures are necessary to insure their country's national security.

It is no secret that popular, politically strong presidents feel free to lean on Israel. A president who is confident of re-election imagines that he can ignore the feelings of Israel's many supporters in the United States. No doubt that was how President Bush felt in the wake of the Persian Gulf War. America's lightening military triumph over Iraq gave Bush a huge boost in the pools. Feeling politically invincible, he surged forward with this pro-Arab plan for an international peace conference to "solve" the Arab-Israeli conflict.

But during the months of pre-conference negotiating and continuing during these first weeks of the conference and its follow-up talks, Bush's popularity has vanished.

The Gulf War victory turned hollow. The Kurds were slaughtered, Saddam Hussein was allowed to remain in power, and Iraq's nuclear storehouse has yet to be fully uncovered. A foreign policy triumph has turned into a resounding defeat.

At the same time, domestic problems have multiplied. Economic woes have deteriorated into full-scale recession. Health-care issues remain unresolved. The public's confidence in the future of the country has eroded. Every opinion poll has shown that Bush's popularity is sinking.

The president's trip to the Far East will do little to reverse this trend. Bush's tough talk about resorting to the trade imbalances between U.S. and Japan will not impress the Japanese, who know full well that America needs them more than they need America. After all, if the U.S. slaps tariff on Japanese exports to America, the Japanese have plenty of options, including the ability to increase their competition with America for markets in Europe and Asia. Bush's hope that his trip to the Far East will aid America's economy, or help produce more American jobs, is merely wishful thinking.

Israel cannot afford to ignore this new political reality. Bush is struggling for political survival. His re-election is by no means assured. He is in no position to start pressuring Israel for dangerous concessions. Like every Republican presidential candidate since Richard Nixon, he will want to attract enough Jewish votes (and dollars) in key election states that can swing the November election. He won't be able to do that if he positions himself as Israel's enemy.

If ever there was a time for Israel to implement appropriate national security measures, this is it.

Why deport only 12 Arab terrorist leaders? There are many hundreds, indeed thousands, of convicted Arab terrorists, rioters, rock-throwers and inciters in Israel who are equally deserving of deportation.

Why go ahead with the dangerous autonomy talks? The latest wave of murders of Jews proves that the Arabs cannot be trusted with any kind of autonomy or self-rule.

In explaining such actions to the American public, Israel can point to America's behavior in the face of threats far less immediate than those posed by the Arabs to Israel. The latest revelations about the Cuban missile crisis have shown that even after the Soviets agreed to remove their missiles from Cuba, President John F. Kennedy refused to pledge that the U.S. would refrain from invading Cuba. Unlike the Arabs, who have repeatedly attacked and terrorized Israel, Cuba had not yet taken any openly belligerent actions against the United States – yet the mere threat posed by the presence of the Soviet missiles was enough to provoke Kennedy to persist in his implicit threats to invade.

Israel should also point to the recent Persian Gulf crisis, when the U.S. launched a full-scale invasion to reverse the occupation by one Arab country to another Arab country, despite the absence of any threat to the U.S. itself. If the U.S. was justified in its actions against Cuba and Iraq, surely Israel is even more justified in taking steps to eliminate the proven danger posed by Arab terror.

Israel's leaders must seize the moment; tomorrow, it may no longer exist.

February 7, 1992

Jeffrey Goldberg's Mother Has Reason To Worry

Writing recently in the **Jerusalem Post**, satirist Jeffry Goldberg presented a letter that he had written, from Israel to his mother in the United States, on the day that the Persian Gulf War began. Saddam Hussein had plenty of reason for "not attacking Israel, Goldberg reassured his mother, "he knows we'll destroy him. Can you remember a time Israel didn't react to an attack? Of course, you can't because Israel always strikes back, Mom. So don't worry."

Goldberg is a first-rate humorist, and his January 17 column was no exception. But this time, some tears accompanied the laughter, tears for the Jews who lost their lives, and for the thousands who lost their homes because the Israeli government chose not to respond to the Iraqi missile attacks.

It wasn't so long ago that nobody could remember a time when Israel didn't strike **first**, much less strike back, at its enemies. In 1956, and again in 1967, Israel struck first. The Israelis wisely calculated that preserving their national existence was more important than scoring points with "world opinion."

The illusion that Israel's leaders would always strike first rather than risk Jewish lives, burst like a pricked balloon in 1973. That was the year that Henry Kissinger warned Golda Meir not to launch a pre-emptive strike against Egypt and Syria, and Meir meekly obeyed, sacrificing hundreds of young Israeli soldiers to appease Kissinger.

After that, nobody talked much about pre-emptive strikes, but every Israeli remained secure in the knowledge that the Israeli Army would surely strike back if an enemy attacked. Anything less than that would be inconceivable.

In January 1991, the inconceivable became conceivable. Iraqi missiles rained down upon Tel Aviv. Bush warned Israel not to strike back, lest his phony alliance with Egypt and Syria become "strained." And Yitzhak Shamir meekly obeyed, sacrificing Jewish life to appease the White House.

Did Shamir's decision pay off? Hardly. Instead of being rewarded for its restraint, Israel soon became the target for unprecedented pressure by the U.S. government. To make things worse, Arab regimes that played only a token role in the Gulf War reaped huge benefits. Bush forgive Egypt's $7-billion debt. He pressured Saudi Arabia to give Syria a $3-billion gift (which Damascus is now using to buy weapons that it is aiming at Israel). Even Jordan, which sided with Iraq and against the United States, is again receiving U.S. aid.

I'm afraid that Jeffry Goldberg's mother does indeed have plenty to worry about. She can't count on Israel striking first when its enemies threaten its existence. She can't even count on Israel striking back when Arab bobs rain down on its major cities. And she has every reason to fear that her son will become the next to be sacrificed by the Israeli government in the next vain attempt to appease the State Department, or the United Nations, or the world media.

February 14, 1992

Jewish Fate and Jewish Land Are Inseparable

From the day that the Almighty first promised the Holy Land to Abraham, the fate of the Jews and the land of the Jews have been intertwined. The original Jewish kingdoms provided the cement of Jewish nationhood, while the long centuries of statelessness that followed dealt a crippling blow to Jewish life. The reborn Jewish State of our times has infused Jewish life with purpose and meaning. Will we voluntarily surrender it in the name of a false peace or under the pressure of fair-weather friends?

Jewish statehood has never come easy; great things never do. In the days of Joshua, the Jewish army was confronted by primitive Canaanite tribes that worshipped idols and sacrificed human beings. Today, the Jewish army faces Arabs who worship the idol of Jew-hatred and sacrifice their children on the front lines of their *intifada* thousand years have passed, but the enemies of the Jews have not changed, and the tasks that the Jews fulfill have not become much easier.

The key to the survival of Jewish nationhood has been tenacity. Had Judaism been constituted as purely a religion, it would have faded from the map of history soon enough. But the Jews were meant to be uniquely fashioned as a religious-nation. Their identity was rooted in religion, nationhood, and their attachment to a specific land. It was the tenacity of that attachment which preserved the Jews as a nation.

Never did the Jews relinquish their country voluntarily. When it was conquered, it was conquered by force, after a bloody struggle in which the masses of Jews died fighting rather than surrender their territory. Three times the Jews were expelled, but never did they leave of their own accord.

Consider, then, the horrifying implication of a voluntary Jewish surrender of portions of the Holy Land.

Forget for a moment that the present Israeli government is labeled "rightwing" and is assumed to oppose surrendering territory. Face the fact that this government is voluntarily facilitating a process that will lead to the surrender of the very cradle of our territorial birthright, Judea, Samaria, and eventually part of Jerusalem as well.

If the Israeli government's plan for Arab elections and Arab autonomy in Judea and Samaria goes forward, the gradual establishment of an Arab state in those territories will begin. What, then, will that mean for everything that counts in Judaism and Jewish life?

What meaning will be left to our Passover pledge of "Next year in Jerusalem," if half of Jerusalem – the half that includes the Temple Mount and the Western Wall – is under the authority of an Arab administration, because Jews voluntarily surrender Jerusalem?

What will be the point of reading the Torah portion about Abraham's purchase of the Cave of the Patriarchs, in Hebron, if Arabs rule Hebron and Jews are no longer welcome there because Jews voluntarily surrendered Hebron?

Can we sincerely recite our daily prayers, or the blessings after our meals, with their pleas for a "speedy return to Zion," if the land of Zion has been reduced to nine miles wide at its midsection and can be sliced in two by an Arab tank column in a matter of minutes because Jews voluntarily surrendered Judea and Samaria?

The religion of the Jews and the land of the Jews are inseparable. One without the other is like a hollow shell. Voluntary surrender of the Holy Land is no more permissible than the voluntary transgression of the Sabbath laws or voluntary consumption of swine's flesh. It will empty our prayers of meaning and render our Sabbath songs worthless.

It will even lend encouragement to the vilest of Church doctrines about the Jews. Remember: the Church has always regarded Jewish statelessness as "proof" that the Jews were receiving Divine punishment for having rejected Christianity. The rebirth of the Jewish State put the lie to the Church's claim, which is why the Vatican refuses to recognize Israel. An Israel that is weakened by Jewish acquiescence to territorial amputations, in preparation for eventual destruction, will be seen by the Church as proof of its claims.

What is needed to prevent such a catastrophe is an Ignited American Jewry's forceful support of Israel, including, but not limited to, political, economic, and aliya, and strong support of Jewish resistance to territorial concessions. This will bring about a resilient Israel that will accomplish everything that Jewish fate intended: the restoration of Jewish pride, the infusion of Judaism with renewed purpose, and the preservation of our complete Torah legacy for future generations of Jews.

February 21, 1992

Moslem Noise, Jewish Rights

The ruling by an Israeli judge to limit the blaring of loudspeakers from a prominent Jerusalem mosque has shed some much-needed light on the little-known phenomenon of Muslim extremists trampling on Jewish rights in the heart of the Jewish State.

The very idea that Je wish rights could be abused in the State of Israel might seem absurd. After all, one of the major reasons for the creation of a Jewish state in modern times was to give Jews a homeland where they would be able to live their lives and practice their religion, free of harassment.

Yet successive Israeli governments, Labor and Likud alike, have been so fearful of international criticism that they have preferred to restrict Jewish rights rather than risk even the perception that Moslem rights were somehow being limited.

The most dramatic manifestation of this deplorable phenomenon is the issue of the Temple Mount. Although the Mount is the holiest site in Judaism, Israel failed to assert full control over the area even after liberating it from the Jordanians in 1967. Instead of reclaiming the site for the Jewish people, the Israeli government chose to give exclusive control over the Temple Mount to the Waqf. This Muslim religious council is viciously anti-Jewish and anti-Israel. Not only were the Moslems given control of the area, but Jews were completely barred from praying anywhere in the Temple Mount compound.

A similarly disturbing situation prevails in Hebron. Before the Israeli liberation of Hebron in 1967, Moslems barred Jewish visitors from going past the seventh step leading up to the Cave of the Patriarchs, one of the most sacred sites in Judaism. After Israel captured the city, some Jewish religious rights were restored, but many restrictions remained in force to appease the Moslems. Thus, Jewish prayer times are limited by what the Moslems will accept, and Jews are prevented from making *Kiddush* in the Cave because the Moslems object to the presence of wine on the site.

The question of mosques blaring their speakers has been a thorn in the side of the Jewish communities of both Jerusalem end, Hebron, for some time now. Jews who live in the vicinity of the mosques know that the volume of the speakers is deliberately turned louder on the Jewish Sabbath, clearly in an attempt to impede Jewish observations of the holy day. It should also be obvious that there is a logical reason, in 1992, to use crude loudspeakers in the faithful to pray; the mosques could easily establish times for prayers, just as other religions do.

The Moslems have two very practical reasons for using loudspeakers. The first stems from Judaism in principle that the "truth of Islam" can be demonstrated. Moslems having some physical advantage over non-Moslems. That's why Jews living in Muslim countries are not allowed to build houses taller than those of their Moslem neighbors. That's why Jews are not allowed to ride horses or donkeys in Arab countries – lest they appear physically higher than Moslem passerby.

The second reason is that the loudspeakers are not handy for summoning rioters. The two Israeli government commissions that investigated the October riots on the Temple Mount both concluded that the Moslem religious leaders on the Mount had deliberately used the loudspeakers to gather the thousands of Moslem believers who then attacked the Jews praying at the West Wall below.

There is an important psychological dimension. Each time the Arabs can intimidate the Israeli government into letting them trample on the Jewish religious right, they become emboldened to go ahead further. The entire Palestinian Arab *intifada* is a product of the Arab perception that massive violence forces the Israelis into making concessions. Every Jew right that is restricted, every mosque loudspeaker not allowed to blare, every concession that is made is the prelude to the next Arab demand and the next Jew surrender.

February 28, 1992

From Wannsee To Washington, Jews Are the Targets

A senior State Department official reportedly met last week with American Jewish leaders, and bluntly informed them that the "special relationship" between America and Israel "is a thing of the past." The report, which appeared in Israel's leading daily newspaper, **Ma'ariv**, is another frightening indication that Israel is slated to be sacrificed on the Bush Administration's alter of political convenience

Any Jew who has a sense of history cannot help but shudder at the realization that Israel is being trapped in a web of international pressure and deceit at precisely the same time that the 50th anniversary of the Nazis' Wannsee conference is solemnly observed. Bush is not Hitler, and Baker is not Goebbels. Yet the fact remains that the Middle East "peace" strategy presently being implemented by Washington could lead to the destruction of the four million Jews of Israel just as the Wannsee strategy of 1942 led to the destruction of six million European Jews. So much has changed in 50 years, but one thing remains constant: the Jews are scheduled to be the victims.

At first glance, one might think that an analogy between Israel today and European Jewry of yesteryear is fanciful. After all, the Israelis have a sovereign state and a powerful army; the Jews whom Hitler targeted obviously had neither. But even a country with a mighty army can be made vulnerable through political pressure. Abba Eban understood this when he coined the term "Auschwitz lines" to describe Israel's pre-1967 borders. No matter how strong its army, Eban was saying, Israel could face another Auschwitz if political pressure by foreign powers forced a retreat to the pre-1967 lines. Once confined to that nine-miles-wide territory, Israel would be ripe for invasion and annihilation.

There can be no doubt whatsoever that Bush's agenda calls for an Israeli retreat to the pre-1967 borders. Don't take my word for it. Just consider the words of Israeli cabinet minister Ehud Olmert. He's no alarmist or extremist, Olmert is known as the spokesman for the "dovish" wing of the ruling Likud bloc. On February 10, Olmert told a visiting delegation of American Jewish Committee leaders that "the ultimate goal of the Administration is to force Israel to withdraw its forces to the old boundaries."

The facts on the ground confirm Olmert's statement. The Bush Administration has repeatedly said that it rejects the idea of Israeli control over Judea, Samaria, Gaza, and the Golan Heights. It rejects the idea of even individual Israeli Jews living in those areas. And it is equally adamant concerning eastern Jerusalem. State Department spokesmen have said on numerous occasions that they object to Israeli "settlements" in the eastern part of Jerusalem just as strongly as they object to "settlements" elsewhere. The Administration refuses to move the American Embassy in Israel from Tel Aviv to Jerusalem because it does not accept Jerusalem as Israel's capital. All of this has been U.S. policy since 1967. Bush, Baker, and the company have simply hatched a new strategy to implement it.

Like the conferees at Wannsee, Secretary of State Baker has a handful of Jewish helpers. Fifty years ago, Jews who played that role were called "*kapos.*" Today they are more charitably referred to as the "Jewish Arabists" in the State Department. A recent **Moment** magazine profile of four of those Jewish Arabists described them as "indifferent to what Israel claim(s) as vital interests and undiplomatically hostile to Israeli Prime Minister Yitzhak Shamir." Indifference would be bad enough, but these Jewish Arabists have gone considerably further, they have been cited by **The New York Times** (on January 13, 1989) as some of the key architects of Bush's pro-Arab policies.

This is hardly the first time in Jewish history that individual Jews have risen to high government positions and then bent over backward, ignoring the plight of their fellow-Jews, to prove that they were not too pro-Jewish. Just recall how many Jewish advisers Franklin Roosevelt had, and how few of them were willing to speak up on behalf of those destined for Hitler's gas chambers.

Imagine the shock waves that would ensue if these Jewish Arabists managed to shake off their "bend over backward" mentality and resigned en masse from the State Department, in protest against Bush's abandonment of Israel, his embrace of Arab tyrants, and his flirtation with anti-Semitism?

The holiday of Purim approaches. It recalls a time when a Jew, Esther, rose to the highest levels of government, then hesitated to use her influence when her fellow-Jews were threatened with destruction. Her uncle Mordechai, spoke words that should be posed to the Jewish Arabists in the State Department: "If you fail to act, then salvation for the Jews will arise from another source, but woe to you on the Day of Judgment, for you had the chance to do something, and failed."

From ancient Persia to Wannsee 50 years ago to Washington today, the Jews have been threatened by a catastrophe. In Persia, the Jewish queen risked her position to save the Jews, and they were saved. In Europe, too many Jews became "kapos," and millions perished. Which of those two patterns of behavior will the Jews in Washington today decide to emulate?

March 6, 1992

The War Against a Jewish Jerusalem

Many leading American media organs have overly cozy relationships with the State Department, allowing themselves to be used to promote the administration's policies in exchange for news leaks and exclusive interviews. **Newsweek's** (Feb. 10, 1992) latest assault on the Jewish community of Jerusalem seems to fit right into the pattern.

The State Department has been conducting high-profile diplomacy to link Israel's request for loan guarantees to the settlements issue. Articles blasting the settlements have appeared regularly on the front page of **The New York Times** (under the byline of James Baker's tennis partner, Thomas Friedman), and now it's **Newsweek's** turn.

The pretense for Newsweek's latest anti-Israel blast is the fact that a handful of Jews recently purchased homes in the mostly-Arab neighborhood of Silwan, which is near the Old City of Jerusalem. According to **Newsweek's** bureau chief In Israel, Theodore Stanger, those Jews "stormed six houses in Silwan" and "forced the (Arab) families out at gunpoint." Stanger forgot to mention that the Jews purchased the right to move into the houses. And at highly inflated prices, to boot. Israel's courts have already examined the papers and ruled that the Jews have every right to live there. It is hardly surprising that the Arab families suddenly refused to leave since any Arab who admits to having willingly sold his house to a Jew faces immediate and brutal execution at the hands of the "*Intifada*" death squads. ("Moderate" Jordan actually has a law which makes it a capital offense to sell land to a Jew).

But one wonders how Stanger or James Baker, for that matter, would behave if the tables were turned. What if he legally bought a house from somebody, and then the occupant of the house refused to leave? Wouldn't he call the police and demand that they "storm" the house anti evict the occupant "at gunpoint" ...?

The most important and revealing aspect of **Newsweek's** tirade was perhaps its most subtle point. As proof that "Old City Arabs are increasingly hemmed in," Stanger wrote that "Government officials have allowed construction of a vast new Jewish housing and commercial complex outside Jaffa Gate, just to the west. That squares with Sharon's current drive to build homes for 90,000 additional settlers in the occupied territories."

Read that sentence again. Note how Stanger cited a Jewish housing project in western Jerusalem, to complain about the treatment of Arabs in eastern Jerusalem (the Old City), and then linked to the establishment of Jewish settlements in "the occupied territories." This is not merely journalistic sleight-of-hand, but a revealing commentary on this political agenda of Theodore Stanger and **Newsweek** and the State Department. The article could have been written by any of Baker's top sides.

Why do so many in the media resort to this kind of Israel bashing? First: they take their cue from the State Department leaksters, who grant them the interviews, provide them with valuable tips, and always have plenty of anti-Israel tidbits to disperse. Second: they are swamped by Jewish leftists, who are only too willing to supply anti-Israel quotes in exchange for a chance to make the headlines and impress their liberal friends. Third: they expect that the American Jewish masses won't respond aggressively.

The reason the journalistic community treats African-Americans with kid gloves is a simple fear of boycotts, protests, and other militant actions by Jesse Jackson, his ilk. American Jaws has no Jesse Jacksons. When was the last time that wealthy Jews threatened to withdraw their companies' ads from **Newsweek** because of its anti-Israel reporting? When was the last time that Jewish subscribers to **The New York Times** organized a real boycott of the paper to protest its pro-Arab slant? Israel-bashers and would-be Israel-bashers know the answers to those questions.

March 13, 1992

The Jewish Choice: Destruction or Redemption

Two phenomena have shaped the history of the Jews during the past century: destruction and redemption. Today, the Jewish nation stands at a crossroads, with the opportunity to decide whether destruction or redemption, will guide the decades to come.

The rise of anti-Semitism in Europe during the late 1800s paved the way for the cataclysmic destruction waged in the Nazi era. In France, the Dreyfus affair stimulated waves of vicious anti-Semitism, and French Jewry's illusions of emancipation and assimilation were shattered, as mobs surged through the streets of modern, enlightened Parish, yelling "Death to the Jews!" In Germany, anti-Semitic political parties garnered hundreds of thousands of votes, and leading scientists lent the haters an air of respectability by propounding theories of Aryan racial superiority. In Russia, the "Black Hundreds" pogromists shed Jewish blood with impunity, and the name "Kiev" became synonymous with slaughter.

All that was needed for this orgy of Jew-hatred to reach its destructive potential was an economic crisis and a charismatic dictator. By the 1940s, "Kiev" was replaced by "Auschwitz," as the slaughter of the Jews – now made efficient through modern science and technology attained unimaginable proportions.

Yet destruction was intertwined with redemption.

Jewish tradition teaches that the Almighty always sends the cure along with the illness. If the illness was Jewish vulnerability, the cure was Jewish statehood. Thus, the persecution of Jews in Europe during the late 1800s was accompanied by the rise of the modern Zionist movement. Every Jewish casualty of a pogrom lent new impetus to the drive to redeem the Land of Israel so that there might be a haven from the pogromists. Waves of anti-Semitism produced waves of immigrants to the Holy Land.

Only the British blockade of Palestine during the Holocaust prevented the emergence of a Jewish State, precisely when it would have served its historic role as a haven for the oppressed. And only the hesitancy of the Zionist leadership prevented the launching of a full-scale revolt against the British before the Holocaust reached its awful climax. History's lesson seems obvious: Jewish meekness leads to Jewish catastrophe.

Jewish meekness today threatens Jewish survival once again. American Jewish leaders have meekly stood aside while the Bush Administration strangles Israel for one-sided concessions. I am not speaking only about the failure of U.S. Jewish leaders to lobby for the loan guarantees; that is obvious. I am referring to the silence of the American Jewish organizations in response to the Bush-Baker effort to force Israel into what is usually called "the peace process" but might fairly be called "the Auschwitz process."

Don't flinch at the analogy. Its author is the ultra-dovish Abba Eben, who once characterized Israel's pre-1967 borders as "Auschwitz lines," since those borders would make Israel vulnerable to total annihilation. Israeli Minister Ehud Olmert said, last month, that the Bush Administration intends, via the "peace process," to push Israel back to those deadly borders. At Auschwitz, the Jews were victims of a web of deception, serenaded by an orchestra, and led to gas chambers that were disguised as showers. Israel today faces equally elaborate deception, serenaded by talk of "peace" while being led to Auschwitz borders that are supposed to be "secured" with phony promises of demilitarization.

When the Allies liberated Auschwitz, and the gruesome details of the annihilation were laid bare before the eyes of the world, international sympathy was inevitable. Genocide was a shocking new concept. And there is no doubt that such post- Auschwitz sympathy helped the Zionist cause in some ways. But don't count on any such sympathy today, if Israel is destroyed. The international community has become jaded. Mass death is commonplace. Millions starve in Africa, millions were slaughtered in Cambodia, and the world was hardly moved.

If Israel is pushed back to the Auschwitz lines, and a Holocaust ensues, there won't be any second chances for Jewish national redemption. **It's now or never!**

March 20, 1992

America's 'Special Relationship' With The Saudis

The anti-Israel gangs, Jewish and non-Jewish, use every-angle to undermine America's "special relationship with the Jewish State." They exaggerate the benefits to Israel and relentlessly minimize the greater benefits to the United States from this relationship. Now it turns out that the United States has had a much longer and much more serious "special relationship" with one of Israel's foremost enemies, Saudi Arabia.

An investigative report aired by the Public Broadcasting System on February 17 revealed that in 1947, the Truman Administration pledged to commit U.S. troops to defend Saudi Arabia if the Saudis are ever threatened. During the next four decades, the U.S. Army Corps of Engineers "managed billions of dollars worth of military construction projects in Saudi Arabia, including a military city large enough to accommodate 50,000 troops," according to **Newsweek**, which co-sponsored the PBS documentary.

It gets worse: according to the PBS broadcast, in 1963, President John F. Kennedy dispatched a full squadron of F-100 fighter-bombers to Saudi Arabia in response to the Saudis' fear of a threat from Egypt. The U.S. bombers flew constant patrol missions along Saudi Arabia's borders for months, until it was clear that Egypt would not attack.

What did the U.S. get in return? "The Saudi-led oil embargo of 1973 may seem poor reward," **Newsweek** noted. That's putting it mildly.
Consider the contrasts.

Saudi Arabia violates every American principle in the book. It is a dictatorship; it had Black slaves until at least the 1960s, and women are treated as third-class citizens. Israel is a democracy with equal rights for all citizens. Yet it is Saudi Arabia, not Israel, which gets direct American military protection.

Saudi Arabia initiated the Arab oil embargo against the U.S. in 1973, wrecking the American economy and causing agony for millions of American taxpayers. Israel has consistently proven itself to be America's most reliable ally, sharing vital intelligence information, battle-testing U.S. weapons, and even risking the lives of its citizens by absorbing missile attacks last year all to prove its friendship. Yet it was Saudi Arabia that received countless billions of dollars' worth of US. Weapons from 1947 until today, whereas Israel did not receive any substantial weaponry from the U.S. until 1973. To make matters worse, the Saudis receive their aid without any strings attached. At the same time, Israel is famed Ito succumb to humiliating political dictates to receive loan guarantees that won't cost the U.S. a penny.

Saudi Arabia would not even exist if not for Israel it would have been overrun by its Arab neighbors long ago, if not for the Arabs' fear that Israel would intervene the same way it intervened to prevent Jordan from being gobbled up by Syria in 1970.

The American military commitment to Saudi Arabia will go down in history as one of the worst deals this country ever struck. The Saudis trample American principles and gouge American consumers. They should be treated like any other two-bit dictatorship, and Israel, America's only real ally in the Middle East should be treated like the reliable friend that it is.

March 23, 1992

The Uses and Abuses of Begin's Legacy

At a dinner party a few years after the establishment of the State of Israel, Bernard Baruch asked Winston Churchill what convinced the British to give up the Palestine Mandate. Churchill said that the British were forced out by the actions of Menachem Begin's Jewish underground army, the *Irgun Zvai Leumi*. Churchill pointed, in particular, to the episode in 1947 when the British hanged several Irgun fighters, and the Irgun responded by kidnapping and hanging two British sergeants. "If not for this, we would still be there," Churchill asserted.

It is fair to say that the Jewish State would not have come into being if not for the Jewish armed revolt against the British. The revolt was a glorious chapter in Jewish history that deserves to be taught, in rich detail, in every Jewish school in this country. Every Jewish child should learn the names of his people's martyrs, the Dov Gruners and Meir Nakars, who went to the British gallows along with the *alef-beis*.

Thom are those who may perceive a certain contradiction between Begin's heroic role as the defiant fighter for Jewish sovereignty in the 1940s, and his puzzling role as the [small lender who repeatedly compromised on Jewish sovereignty during the 1970s. The confusion arises because of the popular misconception that somebody who excels in one field should be able to excel in other fields as well. Clearly, Begin was destined to be the leader of the Jewish guerrilla war against the British. His leadership skills were superlative, his military strategy was brilliant, and the victory he achieved will serve as an everlasting model for legitimate revolutionary movements.

But that doesn't mean Begin was suited to be the political leader of the State of Israel 30 years later. Not many Israeli politicians had the will to stand up to the brutal Pressure of the Carter Administration. Not many could have withstood the darts of the international media and the behind-the-scenes harassment by prominent Diaspora Jewish liberals. Begin was not the man for the job. Those who thought he could stand fast were to be disappointed.

What a pity that Israel's enemies today have been able to seize upon Begin's actions and statements as prime minister to use as ammunition in their verbal assault on the current prime minister of Israel. The moment Begin was laid to rest, the vultures of the State Department and the media came swooping down. The "bad Begin," the "terrorist" of the 1940s, was contrasted with the "good Begin" of the 1970s, the ones who surrendered the Sinai to Egypt. That's the model that the world likes: total Israeli withdrawal in exchange for a piece of paper that is non-enforceable and essentially worthless. And that's the kind of Jew the world likes: the one who talks tough but then makes every concession that is demanded of him. James Baker's fondest dream is to twist Yitzhak Shamir into another Menachem Begin.

Begin's greatest lay not in his willingness to surrender portions of the Land of Israel, but in his leadership of the Jewish revolution against the British occupation of the Land of Israel. His record as a military leader should be enshrined in the hearts of every generation of young Jews. As for his record as a political leader, history will show that he left a legacy that haunts Israel today, the blunder of enshrining in the Camp David Accords, the principle of self-determination for Palestinians.

April 3, 1992

Himmler's Strategy Revived

It seems that each passing day provides graphic new evidence of U.S. hypocrisy in the Middle East. President Bush complains about Iraq's failure to comply with United Nations resolutions and then rolls out the red carpet for King Hussein of Jordan, the leading flouter of the international embargo against Baghdad. Bush complains about the escalation of the Mideast arms race and then falls to prevent North Korean ships from delivering deadly missiles to Iran and Syria. Bush Administration officials accuse Israel of dealing with China, and then Bush vetoes a bill that would have limited U.S. dealings with China.

By allowing the Arabs to re-arm, by embracing even those Arab leaders who supported Iraq, and by manipulating the press to publish anti-Israel reports, the Bush Administration is using diplomacy and public relations as parts of an all-out effort to put Israel on the defensive and soften up the Israelis in preparation for the final, deadly squeeze.

The State Department Arabists who shape America's Mideast policy are hardly the first to employ political and verbal deception as part of a strategy to harm the Jews. Two new biographies of Nazi henchmen Heinrich Himmler offer fresh historical insight on the masters of deception. Richard Breitman, in **The Architect of Genocide: Himmler and the Final Solution**, describes how, in 1939, Himmler angrily lectured a subordinate who had been speaking too openly about Nazi strategy: "Never tell a person something earlier than is absolutely necessary! ... Never tell more people than necessary!" Breitman comments: "This was not just an outburst; it was the real Himmler lecturing on the proper technique for administering and implementing sensitive policies. It very well defined how Himmler himself would handle his plans for the Jews."

And that was precisely how the Nazis went about annihilating the Jews, as Peter Padfield describes in his new work, Himmler. "As always, the smooth running of the action would depend on deception," Padfield notes with regard to Nazi plans for deporting Jews from Warsaw to the Treblinka death camp. Jews who were to be deported were told only that they were being taken "to the east." At the entrance to the camp, "the old and infirm were led off to the 'infirmary,' " thereby giving the impression that the place was some kind of labor camp or ghetto, with medical care for the sick. Actually, the "infirmary" was "an open pit of corpses where they were killed with a single shot in the back of the neck and thrown in." Those who were not old or sick were taken straight to the heavily camouflaged gas chambers.

The key factor was that the victims did not know, until the very last moment, what was in store for them. Had they known sooner, they might have resisted. By the time they become aware, it was too late.

The Bush Administration's policy toward Israel functions according to similar dynamics. The U.S. says that it is opposed to the creation of new Jewish neighborhoods in Judea, Samaria, Gaza, and the Old City of Jerusalem. What the U.S. tries to keep quiet is the fact that halting new settlements is only a short-term goal. The long-term goal is to evict the current Jewish residents of those territories to make those lands *Judenrein*, so the Nazis referred to territories from which they wanted to evict all Jews. Just as the U.S. supported Egypt's demand to expel Jews from their homes in the Yamit regions of Sinai, so too will it support Arab demands to dismantle the Jewish towns in Judea, Samaria, Gaza, and Eastern Jerusalem. Bush has repeatedly said that he views the Jewish settlements as illegal; if they are illegal, then the next logical step is to eliminate them.

The same sort of diplomatic subterfuge is at week with regard to the future political administration of the territories. The U.S. is careful to avoid talking about the fine status of the territories. Bush wants to concentrate on "interim steps" like elections and autonomy for the Arabs. If they are interim stages because they know that if they said it, Israel might back out. The final stage in their minds is the establishment of a PLO state in Israel's backyard.

The Bush-Baker Mideast strategy had evolved with remarkable consistency since that day in 1989 when Baker (in an interview with **Time** magazine) compared America's role in the Arab-Israeli negotiations to that of a hunter on a turkey-shoot. The idea, he said, was to patiently stalk the turkey until the animal was cornered and could no longer escape. In Baker's analogy, America was the hunter, and Israel was the turkey. In Hitler's day, the Nazis were the hunters, and the Jews were the turkeys. How much has really changed?

April 10, 1992

The precedents That Begin Set

Menachem Begin was a man of many accomplishments, the most important of which was his leadership of the Jewish armed revolt that forced the British out of the Holy Land and paved the way for the establishment of the State of Israel. Nevertheless, Begin's achievements during the 1940s should not prevent us from recognizing that the political precedents he set during the 1970s have left Israel vulnerable to a variety of national security hazards.

The shallow eulogies offered by western statesmen and newspaper editors upon Begin's focused on his decision to surrender the entire Sinai Peninsula in exchange for a treaty with Egypt. Those who are the least friendly to Israel fondly remember to Begin as the Israeli prime minister who could be pressured into accepting the most extreme version of the "land for peace" concept – total surrender of land in exchange for a superficial peace. That's what the Bush Administration would like Israel to do today, as well trade its strategically crucial heartland for a paper treaty with pro-PLO Arabs. It remains to be seen if the current Israeli prime minister will stand up to U.S. pressure any better than did his predecessor.

The dangerous precedent of the Sinai withdrawal is matched in its folly only by the precedent Begin set on the Palestinian Arab issue. The Camp David accords marked the first time that a government of Israel agreed to recognize "the legitimate rights of the Palestinian people." Begin, of course, insisted that his view of those "legitimate rights" was not the same as that of the Arabs or their allies. But the fact is that he assented to the historically fraudulent concept that there exist a separate "Palestinian people" who, as a people, have "legitimate rights." In fact, of course, the Palestinian Arabs had never been "Palestinian" except in the sense of individuals who happened to live in a country that the Romans had dubbed "Palestine." There was nothing uniquely "Palestinian" about their identity, religion, language, or culture until they invented the "Palestinian" myth to undermine Israel. Under seven U.S. pressure, Begin forsook history and embraced fiction.

112

Worse than merely endorsing a verbal formula, Begin also endorsed the practical proposal for Arab autonomy" in Judas, Samaria, and Gaza. He envisioned a limited autonomy that would enable Israel to retain control of those territories. But that vision was hopelessly unrealistic. He opened up a pandora's box of security risks and international pressure, which allowed the Bush Administration to turn his idea of limited autonomy into the formula that is now on the bargaining table, which would implement expanded autonomy in the first phase and de-facto PLO sovereignty in the second phase.

Finally, of course, Begin established the precedent for the dismantling of Jewish homes. From now until the end of time, Israel's critics will point to the rubble of Yamit disputed territory to make room for "peace." At Yamit, Jewish rights were trampled upon, and the most fundamental concept of Zionism was torn asunder; no wonder the Israel-bashers cherish its memory.

Let Menachem Begin be remembered for his glorious achievements against the British. But let the dangerous precedents he set at Camp David be wiped off the books and formally repudiated before they doom Israel.

March 17, 1992

Israel Must Be Doing Something Right

Secretary of State Baker and his gang of State Department Arabists are angry at Israel for refusing to make Judea and Samaria *Judenrein*.

The United Nations condemns Israel for daring to defend itself against terrorists.

The international press furiously leaps at Israel's throat at every opportunity.

The Arabs are mad at Israel for refusing to commit suicide.

My conclusion: Israel must be doing something right.

If this gang of veteran Jew-haters, cold-hearted political double-dealers, and assorted hypocrites are angry at Israel, then surely Israel is in the right. If these thugs, bigots, and back-stabbers ever start praising the Israelis, Jerusalem will have reason to worry.

There is occasionally good reason to be disposed at this or that aspect of Israel's behavior. There are legitimate reasons to disagree with this or that Israeli policy (although such disagreements should never be aired publicly if publicly could harm Israel in any way, shape, or form). But when one takes a look at the reasons that most of the world is hopping mad over Israel's actions, one can understand just what everyone is mad about and just why we Jews have reason to rejoice:

- Israel refuses to make its own heartland "Judenrein," Israel continues to bravely resist international demands that it post "No Jews or dogs allowed" signs in Judea and Samaria

- Israel is continuing the long-overdue process of making Jerusalem a truly Jewish city. After years of delay and neglect, and despite hypocritical pressure from around the world, the Israeli

114

government is allowing Jews to take up residence in parts of the Holy City from which Arab pogromists drove Jews in the 1930s.

- Israel instills fear in the hearts of its hostile neighbors. Every Arab tyrant in the region knows that the Jewish air force could bomb him into oblivion if necessary. Every Arab terrorist chieftain must live with the fear that at any moment, an Israeli helicopter gunship could swoop down and blast him to pieces.

- Jewish pioneers are making the once-deserted hills and plains of Judea and Samaria blossom again. Stagnant, spiritless Westerners secretly envy Israel's hardy settlers, knowing that they are the only Western people that still exhibit the adventurous, pioneering, frontier spirit.

- Above all, Israel has survived. In the face of invasions, terrorism, and economic boycott, in the face of a thousand different hardships that would have long ago done in any other country, Israel has survived and indeed prospered. In this post-Auschwitz era, that is truly a remarkable Jewish achievement.

None of this should be taken for granted. Assistance from Diaspora Jewry is crucial to every one of the extraordinary Israeli accomplishments noted above. Only a complete devotion of Diaspora Jewish resources to Israel's needs can assure the continued strength and success of that glorious phenomenon that we call Zionism.

April 24, 1992

Why Is the Ford Foundation Financing PLO Propaganda?

The Ford Foundation, one of America's most distinguished philanthropic institutions, has, in recent years, become an important source of funding for pro-PLO Arab propagandists and their Jewish allies.

Consider some of the recent grantees listed in Ford's records. "A1 Haq," also known as "Law in the Service of Man," an Arab propaganda agency headquartered in Ramallah (just north of Jerusalem), received $260,000 from the Ford Foundation last year. It distributes reports and memoranda attacking Israeli treatment of Arab rioters, but refuses to condemn the Arab death squads that have executed over 500 fellow Arabs in the territories during the past three years.

The El-Hakawati Theater, in Jerusalem, was granted $100,000. El-Hakawati stages anti-Israel plays and concerts and has frequently served as the site for PLO rallies, forcing the Israeli authorities to shut it down on several occasions.

The Middle East Research and Information Project, or MERIP, was awarded $47,250. One of the most extreme pro-PLO groups in the United States, MERIP, openly defended the Arab massacre of Israeli athletes at the 1972 Munich Olympics for having provided "a boost in morale among Palestinians in the camps."

A-Najah University. One of the worst hotbeds of PLO activity anywhere in Judea and Samaria was given $43,750 last year by the Ford Foundation. The students use its campus as a base for firebomb attacks on Israeli traffic in the region.

And don't forget the Arab Studies Society, of Jerusalem, which received a grant of $27,200. Its director is Faisal Husseini, the PLO explosives trainer who was jailed in Israel in 1968 for assisting an Arab terror cell. Husseini, who was once described by then-Israeli Defense Minister Yitzhak Rabin, "the

116

number one PLO representative in the territories," is presently an adviser to the Palestinian Arab negotiating mm. His Arab Studies Society tries to provide an academic veneer for its standard PLO propaganda. Another Arab propaganda gag, the Palestinian Academic Society for the Study of International Affairs, received $35,000.

Jewish groups also receive a grant from the Ford Foundation but only certain kinds of Jewish groups. The Jews that Ford likes are the ones that help further the same goals as the Arab groups listed above. The New Israel Fund, which finances Israeli groups that defend Arab terrorists, received $150,000. The International Center for Peace in the Middle East, which is the academic wing of Peace Now, was granted $72,100. Interns for Peace, which sends American Jewish youngsters to do volunteer work in Arab villages, got $50,000. Meron Benvenisti, whose anti-Israel "research" is regularly quoted by Israel-bashers abroad, was given $35,000 for his Fund for Free Expression, the purpose of which is to "prove" that Israel obstructs free expression.

But Ford's favorite Jews were the ones at the Givat Haviva Educational Foundation; they were awarded $300,000. Givat Haviva, a prominent Israeli kibbutz, claims to foster "Arab-Jewish coexistence" by bringing together young Israelis and young Arabs. But there is more to such get-togethers than meets the eye. An official of the Israeli Education Ministry said recently that he opposed such Arab-Jewish meetings because they involve "youth in a very sensitive stage of identity formation, and prevents them from forming a positive national identity by disparaging Zionism and encouraging collective guilt for the fate of the Palestinians." What Great Haviva calls "experiments in coexistence" can easily degenerate into forums for young Arabs to make anti-Israel accusations and young Israelis to wallow in guilt feelings. Consider the implications of the 1989 incident (reported in the Israeli newspaper **Ma'ariv**) in which a Givat Haviva staff counselor was arrested for raising a PLO flag in the Arab village of Dira Hana, in celebration of the Arab's "Land Day.

Givat Haviva was named after Haviva Raleh, a young Jewish heroine from the Holy Land who was parachuted behind enemy lines in Europe to rescue Jews from the Holocaust. In her memory served by programs that break down Zionist morale and undermine young Israelis' resistance to Arabs who dream of perpetrating a second Holocaust? And if the Ford Foundation chooses to give funds to Givat Haviva alongside Arab grantees who openly support PLO massacres of Jews, what does that tell us?

May 1, 1992

Jewish Left Aims Its Guns at Israel

The Jewish left has launched a new, all-out offensive against Israel. In Jerusalem, left-wing Israeli "human rights activists" are feeding anti-Israel propaganda to foreign correspondents. In Washington, Reform rabbis are signing petitions attacking the Israeli government. And in New York, wealthy Jewish liberals are raising unprecedented amounts of cash to finance the struggle to undermine Israel's security.

The Jerusalem gang goes by the name of *"B'Tselem,"* or "In the Image," taken from the Biblical verse about man being created in the image of G-d. The idea is that both Arabs and Israelis are created "in the image" of G-d, and, therefore, Israelis should be nicer to the Arabs than they have been until now. There's nothing wrong with being nice, of course, but in this case, what B'Tselem wants is for Israel to be nicer to Arab rioters and terrorists. When you look at B'Tselem's monthly reports, you get the impression that the only people they really think were created "in the image" are Arabs who are killed by Jews. B'Tselem publishes long, detailed reports about Arabs being killed by Israelis (always in self-defense or by accident). Yet they have virtually nothing to say about Jews who are attacked by Arabs. They also write almost nothing about that largest victim-category of all: Arabs who are killed by other Arabs.

So while the B'Tselem crowd would have you believe that they're interested in fulfilling a Biblical command, in fact, they are merely pushing the same tired old line of the Jewish left: Israelis are guilty, Arabs are victims. But that's no surprise when one considers the founders of B'Tselem. They are not merely "human rights activists," as Western reporters always will them. They are not merely "professors, lawyers and parliamentarians" us one U.S. newspaper recently dubbed them. They are the elite of the Israeli left, including Knesset Member Dedi Zucker of the ultra-left wing Citizens Rights Movement, attorney Avigdor Feldman (formerly active with Yesh Gvul, the group that urges soldiers not to serve beyond the 1967 borders), and Joshua Schoffman of the Association for Civil Rights in Israel, which provides legal aid to Arab terrorists.

Meanwhile, in Washington, the extremist "Jewish Peace Lobby" has been busy collecting Signatures from Reform and Reconstructionist rabbis (a handful of Conservative rabbis also signed) on a petition urging all U.S. presidential candidates to support the idea of banning Jews from living in Judea, Samaria, Gaza, and the Old City of Jerusalem. The good news is that, of the 3,000 rabbis approached by the Lobby, less than 10 percent signed the petition. The bad news, of course, is that 256 of them did sign the horrifying, anti-Jewish document. Can you imagine Reform rabbis signing a petition recommending that Arabs, or blacks, be prevented from living in some neighborhood? Yet they are eager to take such action when the victims are Jews!

Much of the activity of the Jewish left, both in the United States and in Israel, is designed to attract media attention. Signatures of 256 names on a piece of paper carry a lot more weight when they are featured in newspapers around the country, under headlines like "Rabbis Criticize Israel." Reports about alleged Israeli mistreatment of Arabs have much more influence when they appear in **The New York Times**, under headlines about "Israeli human rights activists" supposedly "documenting" Israeli barbarism.

It costs a good deal of money to run a well-oiled propaganda machine such as the Jewish left has. Such operations require office space, secretaries, salaried staff, and much more. In the case of B'Tselem, the money is provided by a handful of wealthy comrades in New York end Los Angeles, known as the New Israel Fund. Parading under the deceptive claim that it is merely working to promote "democracy, social justice, and peaceful coexistence," the NIF has successfully raised millions of dollars for extreme-left Israeli groups like B'Tselem. Ten years ago, it raised less than $500,000 a year; now, it raises in the range of $7 million.

Some Jewish liberals honestly believe that their actions will help promote "peace" in the Middle East. Some Reform rabbis sincerely think that their actions are in the spirit of "the prophetic tradition of social justice." And some are just cynical wheelers-and-dealers who use their money to pressure Israel to accept policies that the vast majority of Israel voter reject.

Whatever their motives, the result is the same: they gladden the hearts of those who seek Israel's destruction, they smear Israel's good name in the world media. They undermine Israel's ability to protect itself against its enemies.

May 15, 1992

Jewish Double Standards

During wartime, all of a nation's resources must be devoted exclusively to the war effort. That's how America won World War II, by rationing essential commodities and using everything else for the war effort. Americans stood in line with ration coupons to purchase meat, sugar, coffee, gasoline, and other essential items which were difficult to obtain. Price controls were instituted. The manufacturing of nonessential goods was halted so that all manufacturing could concentrate on producing the weapons needed for victory over Hitler.

Israel, today, is still in a state of war with its neighbors. World Jewry should be on a war footing, doing without non-essential goods to devote all Jewish resources to the survival of the Jewish State. The Arabs have been at war with the Jews in the Land of Israel for nearly 100 years, and they may still be 100 years from now. As long as this war goes on, Jews everywhere must behave accordingly.

We all know about the double standards practiced by Israel's enemies. The United Nations denounces Israel for defending itself but refuses to criticize Arab atrocities. The State Department opposes loan guarantees for Israel but lobbied hard to get loan guarantees for Iraq. Journalists foam at the mouth every time Israeli soldiers kill an Arab rioter, but they ignore Arab massacres of innocent civilians.

But now, the time has come to face up to some of the double standards that American Jews practice concerning Israel. Consider:

- American Jewish leadership was silent when the United States, with the help of the Jew, Dov Zackeim, working for the U.S. Department of Defense, led the fight to kill the Israeli development of the Lavi project, the most advanced fighter-bomber plane necessary for Israel's defense that would also have made Israel less susceptible to the whims of U.S. pressure. Israeli Defense Minister Moshe Arens has recently stated that given the present

122

U.S. administration's tilt to the Arabs, it is regrettable that the Lavi project was not completed. Yet this same Jewish leadership and Dov Zackeim would never consider (and rightfully so) leading a campaign to stop the U.S. development of the SDI Missile Defense program or other programs to strengthen America's defenses.

- Wealthy American Jewish real estate developers risk heart attacks from the strain and exhaustion of nonstop wheeling-and-dealing, going for days on end without sleep in the effort to score a big real estate gain (often against Jewish competitors). Yet many of them are prepared to leave the most priceless land on this earth, the Holy Land of Israel, in the hands of those to whom they would never trust their real estate. They stand idly by while Jewish establishment doves press Israel for concessions, and Labor Party politicians (who are only too willing to surrender large chunks of Israeli real estate) forge ahead with a well-financed election effort that may yet end in victory. Where are the voices of outrage over the activities of the Jewish establishment liberals? And where are the contributions needed to prevent a left-wing triumph in Israel, which could lead to the dismemberment of the state? Isn't the danger of losing the holiest land on earth as important as the possibility of losing out on some real estate deal in Beverly Hills?

- American Jewish writers, artists, and musicians devote their vast talents to the enhancement of Western culture, turning their backs on Jewish culture and Jewish nationhood. Israel is the lifeblood of the Jewish people; why should Jews be concentrating their energy on strengthening the lifeblood of others at the expense of Israel's survival?

- Jewish liberals urge Israel to surrender its historical rights to get loan guarantees from Bush while spending outlandish sums to live lavishly in the Diaspora money that could have been used to replace the loan guarantees in the first place.

- Jewish communal funds are still being used to promote the development and entrenchment of Diaspora life, constructing ever newer and bigger

Jewish institutional buildings here, while sending only crumbs to needier causes in Israel, such as the absorption and education of penniless immigrants.

- Jewish organizations complain about the Arab boycott of Israel. But not one of them has organized an effective Jewish counter-boycott of the products of American companies that adhere to the Arab boycott.

- Rabbis pay lip service to aliyah, literally, by reciting the Prayer for the State of Israel each Sabbath, with its characterization of Israel as "the beginning of the flowering of the Redemption," while taking no concrete steps to advance the arrival of that Redemption.

- New Holocaust memorials are built, seeking to spread the notion that because of past Jewish suffering, the gentile world should be nice to Jews today. It's a message that, for the most part, falls on deaf ears and indifferent hearts. Trying to convince the non-Jewish world to own up to its guilt is hardly the best way to defend Jewish interests today. Our only real defense is the Jewish State, and it should be receiving the financial aid from the Diaspora that it needs to maintain that defense against a second Holocaust.

- The Jewish establishment's "defense" organizations are overstaffed and over salaried, yet they still can't do an adequate job of defending Israel.

- When America went to war in 1941, American Jews were leaders in the purchase of war bonds and went out of their way to encourage other Americans to buy war bonds and contribute to the war effort in a thousand and one ways. Shouldn't they make at least an equal contribution to the Israeli war-of-self-defense effort...?

Instead of new synagogues and schools, let the old ones suffice, and let the finds be used to sustain the Jewish State. Instead of Holocaust memorials and slick promotional mailings and overpaid Jewish bureaucrats, let Israel be provided with the funds it needs to "ingather the exiles" from Russia and Ethiopia. Instead of building even more comfortable Jewish homes in the

Diaspora, let us learn to make do with what we have, and use the extra money to assist the Jewish **national** home, Israel.

May 22, 1992

No Honors for Israel-Bashers

At first glance, it might not seem surprising that Thomas Friedman, **The New York Times** reporter, was chosen to be the featured speaker at a Jewish banquet in Los Angeles on May 2. As a longtime Middle East correspondent and the author of a best-selling book about Israel and the Arabs, he might seem like an appropriate speaker to discuss matters of Jewish concerns.

But a closer look at Thomas Friedman's track record reveals him to be one of the harshest critics of Israel in the world of American journalism. It is simply dishonest for the New Israel Fund to present him at its May 2 banquet as some sort of "neutral journalist" or "Mideast expert," when the truth about Thomas. Friedman is that he is a biased journalist with a distinctly pro-Arab agenda.

The entire basis of Friedman's claim to fame is his "disillusionment" line. In his book, **From Beirut to Jerusalem**, and countless media interviews, Friedman had portrayed himself as having been a staunch supporter of Israel when he went to Beirut as a reporter in the early 1980s. It was only when he witnessed Israel's behavior during the 1982 Lebanon War that he "buried every illusion I ever held about the Jewish state." Thus, Thomas Friedman, the alleged Israel-lover, became an Israel-basher because of Israel's evil deeds."

The truth about Friedman is rather different. In 1974, long before he went to Beirut, Friedman was a leading Israel-basher on the campus of Brandeis University. He was one of the leaders of a radical-left campus organization known as the Mideast Peace Group. In November 1974, he and his fellow-radicals signed an "open letter" in the Brandeis student newspaper in which they apologized for PLO terror (claiming that act of terrorism were not really "representative" of the Palestinian Arabs), demanded "Palestinian self-determination" (that is, a PLO state in Israel's backyard), and denounced the

American Jewish community for holding a rally to protest Yasir Arafat's appearance at the United Nations.

The evidence about Friedman's background, and the fact that his whole "disillusionment" story is therefore false, is so strong that Dr. Daniel Pipes, the eminent Mideast scholar who is director of the Foreign Policy Research Institute, concluded (in **commentary** in 1990): "A rewriting of one's biography has devastating implications for anyone's integrity.. readers are forced to reconsider Thomas Friedman's continued credibility as a correspondent."

Friedman used his subsequent journalistic career to advance the agenda he had promoted at Brandeis. In his reporting for **The New York Times**, while stationed in Beirut and, later, in Jerusalem, Friedman used the deceptive, Israel-bashing techniques that biased journalists always use: the unnamed sources, the repeated quoting of only those "experts" with whom the reporter agrees, the obsessive focus on news that makes Israel look bad.

But in the interviews that he occasionally granted to the media, Friedman had trouble hiding his animus towards Israel. He told the **Detroit Jewish News** that Israel's own "megalomania" was to blame for the media's focus on it (when, in fact, it was his obsession with Israel that was largely to blame). He told **Moment** that he supports "the rights of the Palestinians to national self-determination." He complained to Israel Radio that Israel had "contributed" to the 1985 Shi'it hijacking of TWA airlines by failing to release 700 imprisoned Shi'ite terrorist suspects.

When Friedman decided to write about his experiences as a Mideast correspondent, in **From Beirut to Jerusalem**, his pen dripped with anti-Israel venom. Consider:

* Friedman rehashes the phony story of the Lebanese girl who supposedly lost her arms in an Israeli bombing and whose photo ended up on President Reagan's desk, Friedman repeats the story even though his newspaper publicly retracted the story because it was false.

- Friedman refers to "the idea of Jewish power" as "Begin's pornography."

- Friedman denounces Israel as "Yad Vashem an Air Force." At another point, he accuses Israel's leaders of the "Holocaust" the Israeli national psyche.

- Friedman says that terrorism was "functionally relevant" for the PLO during its early years; that Arab terrorism must be "understood" as a reaction to Israeli oppression; and that it is wrong to refer to Palestinian Arabs as "terrorists" since he claims 99 percent of them have never engaged in terrorism.

Thomas Friedman is entitled to his anti-Israel opinions, no matter how repugnant they may be. But he is not entitled to deceive the public as to how he arrived at those opinions. And he should not have been honored by being named the featured speaker at a prominent Jewish banquet In Los Angeles.

May 29, 1992

Don't Reward Syrian Cruelty

No sooner had the Syrian government hinted that it might relent on its persecution of Syrian Jews, than the new U.S. ambassador in Israel, William Harrop, was demanding that Israel make more concessions as a "confidence-building gesture" to Damascus.

Harrop does not speak for himself; he speaks for the Bush Administration. His remarks, made on Israel Television, represent another outrageous attempt by Bush and Baker to reward the brutal Syrians and squeeze more one-sided concessions out of America's only real ally in the Middle East.

To say that Bush is subjecting Israel to a cruel double standard is, to put it mildly. In no other walk of life would anybody demand that the guilty party he rewarded, and no other nation would ever be asked by an ally such a reward. It's outrage from beginning to end, and the fact that the Jewish State is being singled out smacks of anti-Semitism.

When a criminal is caught, he should be punished, not rewarded with "confidence-building measures." A criminal should not be forgiven for his past crimes simply because he pledges in this case, hints that he will stop his criminal behavior. Should Charles Manson have been set free if he promised not to carry out any more mass murders? Should Jeffrey Dahmer be let go if he pledges to stop killing and cannibalizing? Syria does not deserve any gestures, concessions, or rewards for halting its brutal persecution of Syrian Jewry.

Make no mistake about it. Even if Syrian Jews are allowed to emigrate, and that is far from certain at this point, it is no proof that Damascus has become "moderate." On the contrary, it is painfully clear that whatever change Syria institutes in its treatment of Jews is simply part of its strategy to be removed from the State Department's "terrorist state" list so that it can be eligible for American and European financial aid. What will it do with those dollars? It's not hard to guess. Just remember what the Syrians did with the $3 billion that the U.S. ordered Saudi Arabia to pay Syria for its token participation in the Persian Gulf War effort. As soon as the war was over, the Syrians rushed to spend that $3 billion in sophisticated missiles from China and North Korea missiles that will be aimed at Israel.

Get the picture? Syria relaxes a bit on its 5,000 Jews so that it can buy the missiles that can help destroy the four million Jews of Israel.

It is outrageous for Bush's ambassador to assume that freedom for Syrian Jewry qualifies as a "confidence-building measure" by Damascus, and requires reciprocation by Israel. Ending the persecution of innocent Jews is a simple matter of human decency that should be expected of Syria if it wants to be considered part of the human race. If Bush wants the Syrians to undertake a real "confidence-building measure" that would facilitate peace negotiations, he should tell them point-blank that the best way to strengthen Israel's confidence is for Syria to abandon its claims on the Golan Heights.

After all, the Golan is a piece of territory whose only purpose from the Syrian point of view, was as a launching pad for invading Israel. If the Syrians are sincerely interested in convincing Israel that they want peace, then they should be prepared to forsake that claims on territory that has only been used for war. That would be a true confidence-building measure.

June 19, 1992

Israel's 'Failing' Economy: The Big Lie

If the Labor Party and its leftwing allies are victorious in the forthcoming Israeli elections, it will not be because of issues of border, national security, U.S. pressure, or Arab terrorism; on those questions, the vast majority of Israelis side with the Likud. A leftwing victory will come about only because the left and its media allies have succeeded in falsely portraying the Likud as having failed to improve Israel's economy.

An important new study by a group of economists and social scientists affiliated with the Israeli journal **Nativ** explains indeed, explodes the myth of the faltering Israeli economy.

For many years, of course, the Israeli economy was faltering. During its three decades in power, the Labor Party chained Israel's economy to socialist theories that stifled free enterprise, productivity, and economic incentive. A government-controlled economy meant a government-controlled society. The notorious Israeli bureaucracy became the butt of many jokes, but for most Israelis, it was no joking matter; it was a nightmare of regulations, long lines, and inefficiency that bred hopelessness, despair, and, for all too many young Israelis, emigration. The monstrous Histadrut labor union was permitted to maintain a stranglehold over the Israeli industry, ensuring that incompetent employees would never be fired, and non-productive factories would never be closed down.

The rise of the Likud to power in 1977, offered new hope. Likud was committed to free-market principles; at last, there was light at the end of Israel's long, dark, socialist tunnel.

No doubt, it is true that Likud moved too slowly to break the chains of socialist enslavement. The spread of Histadrut control was halted but not reversed. Inefficient government-owned firms were sold, but not quickly enough and not in large enough numbers. Too many self-interest groups were allowed to have their way to buy political peace. This was especially true during

131

the period of the Likud-Labor national unity government when the Likud allowed Shimon Peres, as finance minister, to use taxpayers' Shekels to bail out failing Histadrut-owned companies and bankrupt *kibbutzim*.

That being said, the fact is that over the past 15 years, the Israeli economy has moved substantially away from the discredited theories of socialism and made dramatic gains in the process.

To measure some of the most recent progress, consider one of the most notorious of Israel's bureaucratic nightmares: waiting to have a telephone installed. It was not long ago that one could read in the Israeli press about citizens who had to wait eight or nine years to receive their first telephone. When it came to power in 1977, the Likud inherited the incredibly inefficient government-owned telephone company, with its incredible backlog of unfilled customer orders. So the Likud did the only sensible thing something that Labor would never have done; it sold the telephone company to private owners. Sure enough, productivity increase, slowly but surely. As the **Nativ** study points out, in 1986, some 130,000 Israelis, or 22% of the total number of telephone users, were waiting for phones, although that was already an improvement. "By 1991," the study reports, "the waiting list was eliminated, and now virtually everyone receives a new line within two weeks."

Consider another important measuring rod of the Likud Economic success: the purchasing power of average Israelis. Since 1986, the faltering study found, "there has been a per-capita increase of 17% in the purchase and ownership of new cars; 46% of new television sets; 126% in VCRs; 38% in air-conditioning units; and a 34% increase in the number of trips abroad."

Privatization has increased efficiency, which has increased wages, which has increased the average Israeli's standard of living. Free enterprise has allowed healthy economic competition, allowing Israelis to profit from their hard work, allowing people to enjoy more of what they earn from their labor.

This is the reality of Israel's economy today, but you wouldn't know it from the Likud-bashing journalists in Israel and abroad. They are determined to spread the "big lie" of Israeli economic problems to bring down the Israeli government and install a new socialist ruling party.

June 26, 1992

More Big Lies

Whenever there are signs of economic trouble in Israel, Israel-bashers try to pin the blame on the government's settlement policy. They accuse the Israeli government of spending "enormous" sums of money on settlements in Judea and Samaria while allowing new Russian Jewish immigrants to suffer from unemployment and lack of housing.

The truth, however, is that all of the gloom-and-doom pronouncements about unemployment, immigrants, and settlements are either exaggerations or outright fabrications. An important new study by a group of economists and social scientists affiliated with the Israeli journal **Nativ** has exploded the lies and set the record straight at long last.

Consider the question of unemployment, for instance. The total number for Israelis who qualify as "unemployed" amounts to 10.9% of the workforce. That sounds like a high number. But the figure that really counts is the number of citizens who are "unemployed and seeking work" that figure is only 6.4% of the population. Now add the 40,000 new immigrants who have not yet found jobs (out of a total of 400,000 newcomers between 1989 and 1991!), and the total national unemployment rate is about 8%. How had is that? Compare it to the unemployment figures in countries that have not had to absorb hundreds of thousands of new immigrants in just three years, and do not face Israel's huge defense and security burden in Spain, 16% are unemployed; in Italy, 11%; in England and France, 10%.

Now let's talk about the government funds that are spent on settlements. Do they really constitute some huge drain on the government's budget, thereby depriving new immigrants? Hardly. A total of 83,000 housing units were built throughout Israel last year. Of that number, only 8,100 less than 10% were built in Judea, Samaria, or Gaza. Had those 8,100 been built within central pre-1967 Israel, say along the coastal strip, they would have cost the government much more, because land in that region is so much more

134

expensive. Had the 8,100 been built in some outlying region within the pre-1967 boundaries, such as the Galilee or the Negev, a whole new series of employment and transportation crises would have been created, because those regions are so far removed from the major cities where more jobs are available. Building them in Judea and Samaria- within an hour's commute of Tel Aviv or Jerusalem made perfect sense from an economic point of view.

The experts associated with **Nativ** have performed a public service. They have demonstrated that the Israeli economy is in far better shape than most people assume; that there is no unemployment crisis; that the absorption of new immigrants has been, by all reasonable standards, a success; and that the construction of housing units in Judea, Samaria, and Gaza, does not constitute any kind of drain on the Israeli economy.

This is the reality of Israel today. **Don't let the Big Liars tell you otherwise.**

July 10, 1992

A Jew Defends Arab Terrorism

It's not often that a Jewish extremist who defends Arab terrorism manages to become the president of an American Jewish organization. But that is exactly what has happened to Mordechai Bar-On, the Israeli extremist who is the new president-elect of the New Israel Fund.

Bar-On is a veteran politician from Israel's far left, having served in the Knesset as a representative of the radical Citizens Rights Movement. That fact alone raises questions "hunt the New Israel Fund's decision to make him its president since the Fund has always claimed that it is "non-partisan" and "non-political."

But what makes the selection of Bar-On especially interesting is that the things he has said and done in recent years have been so extreme, that even many of the New Israel Fund's liberal activists are likely to be shocked when they learn the truth about him.

Consider, for example, Bar-On's apologies for Arab terrorism. Writing in the leftwing Israeli magazine **New Outlook**, in May 1989, Bar-On said that "not every act of violence on the part of the enemy is an act of terrorism." He asserted that Arab violence against Israelis who are part of the "regime of occupation" is "not an act of terrorism, but part of an ongoing struggle." And who decides which Israelis are part of the "regime of occupation?" The Arab terrorists, no doubt.

Consider Bar-On's attitude towards intermarriage between Jews and Arabs. In 1985, be sponsored Knesset legislation that would have legalized Arab—Jewish inter-marriages.

Consider Bar-On's attitude towards the activities of Christian missionaries in Israel. In 1986, he used his Knesset postal privileges to distribute a letter from a group of US. Congressmen to all 120 Knesset

Members, endorsing the construction of the Mormon missionary center on Mount Scopus, in Jerusalem.

These extremist positions actually dovetail with the activities the radical Israeli organizations that the New Israel Fund finances.

The Fund's largest beneficiary is the Association for Civil Rights in Israel (ACRI), which has granted $1.4 million during the past three years. The ACRI frequently provides legal assistance to Arab terrorists. It has gone to court to prevent the Israeli Army from departing Arab terrorists, and it has taken legal action to stop the Army from dismantling the homes of Arab terrorists. Then Defense Minister Yitzhak Rabin complained, in 1988, that the ACRI's actions had undermined the Army's deterrent capabilities and led to an increase in Arab firebomb attacks against Israelis.

The ACRI has assisted a Jews for Jesus-type group, known as "Congregation Hesed V'Emet," which engages in missionary activity in the Israeli city of Rehovot; it also endorsed the construction of the Mormon center.

On the subject of intermarriage, the ACRI has called for changes in Israel laws that would permit marriage between Jews and non-Jews. Similarly, the director of the New Israel Fund's office in Jerusalem has said that she doesn't see "anything bad" in Arab-Jewish intermarriage.

How many American Jews endorse Arab terrorism, intermarriage, or missionary activity? Not many. That's why I suspect that the leaders of the New Israel Fund will soon regret the day that they chose Mordechai Bar-On to be their leader.

July 24, 1992

One Country's Blunder Is Another Country's Doom

Congressional investigators have uncovered a virtual mountain of evidence indicating that the Reagan and Bush Administrations poured large amounts of financial and agricultural aid into Iraq during the 1980s, despite the knowledge that it was being used for military purposes. Congress and the media have appropriately denounced the Reagan-Bush policy towards Iraq as "a major policy blunder."

For the U.S., the Iraq fiasco has turned into an embarrassing blunder, nothing more. For Israel, it was a matter of life and death.

A large and powerful nation like the United States can afford to make a blunder now and again, without America's existence ever being endangered. Just as the Bay of Pigs invasion was a flop, just as the defense of South Vietnam turned into a hopelessly complicated struggle, so, too, the arming of Iraq can be added to the list of foreign policy errors that were unfortunate but not catastrophic.

State Department wags are probably looking back at their pro-Iraq period, chuckling over their mistakes, chalking it all up to "faulty intelligence information" or "Saddam's deceit" or "good intentions that were a little too optimistic." Senator Robert Dole, the Bush Administration's chief congressional tool, is probably a bit embarrassed when he recalls his April 1990 visit to Iraq, when he heaped praise on the "moderate" Saddam. The U.S. ambassador in Baghdad, April Glaspie, is probably discomforted by the revelations about her promises to Saddam that the U.S. would not object to an Iraqi attempt to "correct" Iraq's border with Kuwait. All in all, it added up to some bad press coverage, a little egg on a few faces, and a very brief war that the U.S. won with ease.

For Israel, it was an entirely different story. America's little "blunder" helped Iraq arm itself with weapons of mass destruction that Saddam hoped to use against Israel. U.S. aid to Baghdad set Saddam on the road to the

138

development of nuclear, chemical, and biological weapons that would have been aimed at Jerusalem. It was just a stroke of good fortune that Iraq "(as not yet capable of equipping its long-range Scuds with chemical warheads. If the Persian Gulf crisis had taken place a little later than it did, poison gas might have "doped Israel's cities.

Who knows what such "blunders" may emerge in the years to come? Surely Bush's policy of arming the Arab regimes provides plenty of fertile soil for new disasters that will be embarrassing for America but catastrophic for Israel. Bush convinced the Saudis to give Syria $3 billion as a reward for its role in the Gulf War, money which the Syrians immediately spent on dangerous new weapons. Bush also refused to prevent North Korean ships from delivering deadly new Scud missiles to Damascus. How long will it be before Syria's Hafez Assad turns out to be the new Saddam Hussein? And what about Egypt? Bush has approved the sale of European nuclear reactors to Egypt, supposedly for "peaceful purposes." What if the current Egyptian dictator is overthrown by Islamic fundamentalists and Egypt has plenty of those – and those "peaceful purposes" are converted for use in a new war to "liberate Palestine"? How many such American "blunders" can Israel survive?

July 31, 1992

Rabin's Distorted View of The World

In his first speech as prime minister of Israel, Yitzhak Rabin declared that "peace, reconciliation, and cooperation are spreading over the entire globe, and we dare not be the last to remain, all alone, in the station."

Meanwhile, Serbian nationalists marked the 100th day of their siege of Sarajevo by dynamiting the city's electricity and water sources; rival black factions continued to massacre each other in South Africa, and the African National Congress threatened to resume anti-white terrorist actions there; Sikh militants slaughtered 11 civilians in northern India, continuing a 10-year-old war for independence that has claimed 2,200 victims this year alone; and 21 Kurds were killed in a battle between Kurdish separatist and Turkish soldiers in southeastern Turkey, where the Kurds have been fighting for independence since 1984.

The idea that the world has been enveloped by peace is an illusion. The idea that Israel can join the "peace" trend by making widespread concessions to its enemies is a dangerous illusion.

Most average Israelis don't accept Rabin's gloomy, defeatist view of the world. They don't see Israel as some weak, cringing pygmy that must slavishly join the latest international trend. Of course, Israelis want peace, and they'd be delighted if "cooperation and reconciliation" came to their part of the world. But they know full well that the reason there is "cooperation and reconciliation" between the two superpowers is that one of the superpowers no longer exists; they know that the reason there is peace in Europe is the belligerent, Soviet-occupied countries of Eastern Europe are no longer belligerent now that they are no longer soviet-occupied. To produce a similar change in the Middle East, Arab dictators would have to abdicate their thrones, democracy (a foreign, Western concept to the Arabs) would have to be introduced, and the Arabs would have to give up both Arab nationalism and Islam.

Since the Arabs the Arabs have not changed, average Israelis are not ready for wholesale territorial retreat, and Rabin should not think that he has a mandate for such its concessions. Reminder: Labor and Meretz received only 56 Knesset seats; Likud and its allies won the majority of the votes, only to lose over 65,000 votes that were thrown out because four small rightwing parties failed to cross the 1.5% electoral" threshold."

The Israeli public is not likely to react with enthusiasm to concessions that lead to a de-facto Palestinian state in Israel's heartland. This is especially true of those Israeli voters who cast their ballots for Shas, the Orthodox Sefardic Party, which in exchange for favors and a ministerial post, has (at least for the time being) joined Rabin's coalition. Don't count on the Shas-Labor alliance to last too long. Polls of Shas voters have shown them to be consistently hawkish and deeply religious. Most backed Shas for reasons of communal loyalty, not because they endorse the dovish pronouncements of Shas leader Aryeh Deri. More than a few Shas backers winced in shame when they learned that Shas had decided to support Rabin despite Rabin's decision to award the Ministry of Education to Shulamit Aloni, a vehement critic of traditional Judaism. Deri's refusal to heed the warnings issued by Israel's three most respected rabbinical authorities further tarnished Shas's image.

In a rather crass political maneuver, the six Shas Knesset Members requested that during the vote to install the new government, the Arab MKs be allowed to vote before Shas, so that Rabin would already have his 61 seats when Shas voted. The idea was that Shas could then claim that it did not put Rabin into power, but was merely going along with what had already been decided. The reality, of course, is that if Shas had stood by its principles, Rabin's government would have depended on the five Arabs for its majority and might not have been established at all.

Neither Shas voters nor the Israeli public at large will accept a Rabin government that tries to stampede Israel into making foolish concessions out of fear that Israel will be "left in the station" while the rest of the world makes peace. The government of the Jewish State must make its decisions in accordance with Israel's genuine security needs and Israel's legitimate historical and religious rights. Anything less will deserve and surely will receive – the contempt of Jews everywhere

August 7, 1992

Judea And Samaria, 25 Years Later

It was 25 years ago this summer that the army of Israel liberated the Old City of Jerusalem and the regions of Judea and Samaria. Countless thousands of Jews flocked to the Western Wall, to Shiloh, to Hebron and Shechem. At long last, the heart of the land of Israel had been returned to its rightful owners.

That Israel's ruling Labor Party immediately offered to surrender those territories (in exchange for worthless peace treaties) says a great deal about how far the Labor Zionist generation of Dayan, Allan, and Meir had wandered from their history and roots, from the basic Zionist understanding of the sanctity of *Eretz Yisrael*. If today's Labor government, under Yitzhak Rabin, is likewise pledging to surrender Judea and Samaria, it is because the younger generation is likewise estranged from its Jewish roots.

But before Likud leaders start pointing their fingers at Rabin, they should reflect on the fact they failed to take the steps necessary to prevent Judea and Samaria from ever being surrendered.

The most obvious step would have been the formal annexation ("reunification" would be the appropriate term) of those lands to the State of Israel. That would have made the territories an integral, formal, inseparable part of Israel. Likud's leaders feared how the world reacts to annexation, so they backed off and established settlements instead. Certainly, the establishment of settlements was a big step in the right direction. But settlements were no substitute for annexation.

And even settlement activity was not always permitted. When the government feared international criticism, It blocked Jews from settling in Hebron, for example (until the famous *"Beit Hadassah"* women forced Begin's hand in 1979), and in Shechem.

143

In 1984 and again in 1988, the Likud could have formed a right wing-religious government, but instead, it chose to form a national coalition and agreed to slow down settlements as the price of the coalition deal.

Settlements, of course, are not the only factor in the equation. If the subject of Judea and Samaria is, today, on the negotiating table, it is also because pro-PLO Arabs were permitted to gain *de-facto* control over large segments of the region. The *intifada* was never stamped out; Arabs who were convicted of rock-throwing or mob violence were given slaps on the wrist; and hardened Arab terrorists who were set free in prisoner exchanges Were allowed to live in Judea and Samaria, providing the-leadership for the intifada.

These are grim facts to recall, but they are vital lessons to learn because if Likud returns to power a few years from now, these mistakes dare not be repeated.

August 14, 1992

Natural Borders Vs. Political Borders

Anybody who examines the terrain of Israel and its neighbors immediately understands why the borders established by Israel during the 1967 war constitute the country's natural borders. To the east, the Jordan River and the mountain ridges of Judea-Samaria afford Israel's ideal geographical protection. In the northeast, it is the Golan Heights, which, under Israeli control, protects the entire northern part of the Jewish State. To the south and west, it was the giant expanse of the Sinai desert that provided Israel with a crucial buffer zone. These are Israel's natural borders.

The borders to which the Arabs, the United Nations, the State Department, and even sections of the Israeli Labor Party, want Israel to retreat are not natural at all; they are political borders. They have nothing to do with what is best for the country's security; they have been determined by arbitrary political factors, hone of which work to Israel's favor.

The U.S. policy of demanding Israeli surrender of territory has never taken into consideration what borders Israel naturally needs to defend itself. When Eisenhower pressured Israel to retreat from the Sinai after the 1956 war, be disregarded the security value of the Sinai and adopted a stand that was politically suited to his desire to curry favor with the Arabs. It was politics, pure and simple.

The American position that Israel should surrender the territories it liberated in 1967 likewise has nothing to do with what Israel actually needs. Indeed, if Presidents Nixon, or Ford, or Carter, or Reagan, or Bush, had truly cared about "secure borders" for the Jewish State, they needed only to consult the study that their own Joint Chiefs of Staff carried out in 1967, which concluded that Israel needed to retain virtually all of the 1967 territories to defend herself against Arab fume attacks.

But successive U.S. administrations have adopted positions based on strictly political criteria chiefly, how to; appease the Arab world. Other U.S.

foreign policy moves in recent decades have likewise ignored the natural border requirements of America's allies. The decision to abandon South Vietnam, for example, was strictly political; U.S. officials knew full well that an American retreat would lead to a North Vietnamese conquest of the South. The U.S. break with Taiwan, too, was a cynical political decision; the threat to Taiwan from Communist China had not diminished.

For Israel to surrender to America's political demands, at the price of its natural security borders, would be catastrophic. Politicians come and go, presidents are elected and then defeated, political decisions are made and then changed. But once Israel retreats from its natural borders to some precarious new political borders, there can be no going back. Judea and Samaria, or the Golan Heights, cannot be regained. They will be in Arab hands, and they will be raided as launching pads for future Arab attacks on Israel. And political boundaries will offer little protection against enemy tanks, bombers, and missile launchers.

August 21, 1992

Autonomy: More Dangerous Than, 'Land-For-Peace'

One of the fascinating aspects of the recent Israeli election campaign was the appearance of an extraordinary videotape depicting what life will be like in Judea and Samaria if the plan for Arab autonomy ever goes through.

Terms like "autonomy," "self-rule," and "elections" are often bandied about in the media, as if they are abstract concepts, without any consideration of their real-life consequences. But as this compelling Israeli videotape made clear, the Jewish residents of Judea and Samaria will face real-life consequences of nightmarish proportion under an Arab autonomy regime.

The autonomy plan, as promoted by former Prime Minister Yitzhak Shamir and current Prime Minister Yitzhak Rabin, proposes to grant the Arabs in the territories control over a broad range of daily affairs, including policy matters and the supply of public utilities.

To understand what it will mean to have an Arab police force in charge in Judea and Samaria, consider the video's opening scene: an automobile driven by a Jewish couple has just been involved in a traffic accident. The wife is seriously injured and requires immediate medical attention. Long minutes pass until an Arab ambulance, and Arab police officers arrive on the scene. In theory, they should be neutral public servants who rash to aid those in need, Jew or Arab. But in reality, of course, they regard Jewish settlers as the energy, as their "oppressors," as imperialists who are trying to implant a foreign presence on the land of "Palestine." The Arab police officer calmly unfurls sheath of forms that must first be filled out before the ambulance can take the injured woman. The husband is on the verge of panic; his wife is bleeding to death before his eyes. But the Arab officer is in no rush. He must check their identity papers, their identity papers, their driver's licenses, and who knows what else. And if a Jew dies in the meantime, he won't lose sleep over it.

The supply of utilities is another vulnerable point. If the Arab autonomy government declares Jewish towns to be "illegal settlements" and cuts off their water or electricity, will Israel forcibly intervene? Will Israel risk international condemnation for the sake of some Jewish settlers? The video's grim final scenes offer the likely answer, as Jews are seen huddling in their cold, dark apartments.

When the Israeli government first proposed the autonomy idea, back during the Camp David negotiations of 1978, the chief Israeli negotiator for the autonomy plan, Yosef Borg, said that the plan would give the Arabs in the territories "80% of statehood." That was dangerous enough, but in 1989, a senior Israeli official was quoted in **The New York Times** as saying that the current autonomy plan (having been broadened under U.S. pressure) offered the Arabs "nine-tenths" of statehood. To go from 90% of statehood to 100% of statehood won't be hard for the Arabs. Israel, after all, has proposed to begin the plan with free elections in the territories. Since the PLO or Islamic zealots have won every local election in those areas until now, it's reasonable to expect that they will dominate the autonomy government. The victorious candidates will be recognized throughout the world as the official representatives of "Palestine." If, after a year or two, they proclaim the region to be "Palestine," Israel will be helpless to stop them. The idea that Israel will be able to maintain some kind of "security stations" in the territories is wishful thinking; Israel's pleas for its security will be no match for the unstoppable steamroller of world pressure that will force a PLO state down Israel's throat.

Ironically, then, one might say that the autonomy scheme is even more dangerous for Israel than the Labor Party's traditional "land for peace" offer. After all, Labor's offer does not include Jerusalem, the Golan Heights, or the Jordan Valley. No Arab leader will sign a permanent peace treaty with Israel that would exclude those areas from Arab control. Thus "land for peace" can never really succeed, can never produce an actual peace-treaty because the maximum Israeli concessions cannot satisfy the Arabs' minimum demands.

Autonomy, however, can succeed, because the Arabs will accept it as an interim stage. Hanan Ashrawi and Faisal Husseini, the leaders of the Palestinian Arab negotiating team, have repeatedly said that they regard autonomy as a "transition stage"; Yasir Arafat himself told French television's

"Network One" in July that autonomy is acceptable "because it will lead to the Israeli withdrawal, followed by full Palestinian self-determination and statehood." The Arabs have a clear, logical plan leading from elections to autonomy to statehood. If the Israelis think that autonomy will produce anything less, they are only fooling themselves.

August 23, 1992

Rabin's Deal: Worse Than the Louisiana Purchase

The decision by Israel's Labor Party government to halt most of the Jewish construction in Judea and Samaria in exchange for a few billion dollars in loan guarantees is likely to go down in history as one of the most lopsided real estate deals in modern times, worse even than the famous Louisiana Purchase.

Although it was called the "Louisiana" Purchase, the deal that the United States struck with France in 1803 involved much, much more than just the territory that was to become Louisiana. The huge tract of land was 828.000 square miles, stretching from the port of New Orleans in the south to the Canadian border, in the north. From the land would eventually be carved no less than 13 new states, including Louisiana, Arkansas, Oklahoma, Missouri, Kansas, Iowa, Nebraska, Wyoming, South Dakota, North Dakota, Montana, and parts of Minnesota and Colorado. The territory involved constitutes fully 23 percent of today's America – and France sold it for just $15 million.

The territory known as Judea and Samaria is even more significant to Israel today than the Louisiana Purchase area was to the United States. The 2,123 square miles of land in Judea and Samaria is equal to about 28 percent of the pre-1967 territory of Israel. In addition to its size, consider the region's unique geographical features. It boasts a mountain range that is 81 miles long and an average of 25 miles wide; whoever controls the mountain ridges has absolute command over the territory to the east (Jordan) and the west (pre-1967 Israel). The regions of the Louisiana Purchase meant nothing in terms of American national security; the young U.S. faced no threats from the west. Israel's very survival, by contrast, could hinge on who controls Judea and Samaria.

There is another crucial difference between the Louisiana Purchase territory and the Judea-Samaria territory. Americans had no historical or religious claims to' that territory; indeed, it was the Americans who were the newcomers on the continent. Judea and Samaria, by contrast, represent the historical and religious homeland of the Jewish people. Cities like Bethlehem, Hebron, Shechem, and Shiloh were centers of Jewish religious life long before the Arabs arrived on the scene.

Yet it is Judea and Samaria, despite its crucial security value and its sacred religious quality, that Prime Minister Yitzhak Rabin is now auctioning off. Make no mistake about it: the suspension of Jewish development of those territories is the first major step towards complete surrender of the area. The French may have gotten the worst deal of the 19th century when they sold the Louisiana Purchase for just $15 million. Still, the Israelis are making the worst deal of the 20th century by selling off the land that is their Torah heritage for a handful of loan guarantees. Indeed, one might even say that they are making the worst deal of many centuries to come because they are not only depriving our generation of its homeland but future generations as well. What is sold to Baker and the Arabs today will not be available for the Israelis to repurchase tomorrow.

Judea and Samaria, like all the Land of Israel, is the eternal property of the entire Jewish people, and Diaspora Jews have a right indeed, an obligation to protest any attempt to surrender it. But before they do, they will have to acknowledge their role in leaving those lands vulnerable to future retreats. Massive Jewish immigration to those territories would have established a Jewish presence so large that any surrender would be physically impossible. The Arabs have consistently put Jewish settlement activity at the top of their agenda precisely because they understand that in the Middle East, territorial claims are staked or uprooted. If American Jews had put Jewish settlement at the top of their agenda, how different things would be right now.

Instead, the very heartland of the Jewish State is about to be ripped from the Jewish people. The cities which are at the center of Judaism throughout the ages are to be surrendered to Arab rule. Israel is to be reduced to fragile borders, to a pale shadow of its former self. How will this shriveling and weakening of the Jewish State affect Jews and Judaism abroad? Israel and Zionism have come to place a central role in the formation and preservation of

Jewish identity throughout the world. Can Judaism as we know it survives the collapse of Israeli pride and strength? Will anything that is meaningfully Jewish remain for our children and grandchildren?

October 16, 1992

Arab Killers, American Victims

An employee of the United States Embassy in Sudan has been executed by the Sudanese government, in the latest of a never-ending series of attacks on Americans throughout the Arab world. It's the latest bloody evidence that no matter how hard the U.S. tries to appease the Arabs, in the end, the Arabs will turn on Americans and American interests with a vengeance.

Until three years ago, the Sudanese Arab regime was one of America's closest allies in Africa. But all of the military and economic aid that the U.S. poured into Sudan was of no avail. In 1989, Islamic fundamentalists came to power and reproduced the old U.S. – Sudan alliance. In the tradition of the late Ayatollah Khomeini, the Sudanese Moslems did not hesitate to arrest U.S. Embassy employee Andrew Tombe, convict him on trumped-up charges of "treason," and summarily execute him.

True to its policy of downplaying Arab atrocities to score points with Arab dictators, the Bush administration took no meaningful action on behalf of Mr. Tombe. It made no efforts to publicize Tombe's plight while he was under arrest. Even after the execution, all the State Department intends to do is file a mild complaint with the Sudanese Finance Minister, who happened to be in Washington last week on other business on the Sudanese government, he could have easily forced his Arab "allies," like Saudi Arabia, to intervene. But he chose not to.

Attempts by the Bush Administration and its predecessors to cuddle up to Arab dictators have never paid off. U.S. diplomatic support for the Palestinian Arabs didn't stop them from trying to blow up George Shultz's car in Jerusalem, murdering a handicapped American aboard the S.S. Achille Lauro, or actively supporting Iraq even as Iraqis were killing American soldiers during the Gulf War. U.S. friendliness toward Syria didn't stop the Syrians from carrying out the car-bomb slaughter of hundreds of U.S. Marines in Lebanon, murdering U.S. navy officer Robert Stethem, sponsoring the terrorists who

153

blew up Pan Am flight 183 and serving as one of the world's major suppliers of heroin to U.S. drug dealers.

U.S. support for Saudi Arabia didn't stop the Saudis from unleashing the oil embargo of 1973, continuing to jack up all prices whenever they feel like it, or running to the U.S. the minute they felt threatened by Iraq, and arrogantly expecting the U.S. to be grateful for the "privilege" of sacrificing American lives on their behalf.

The next arena for American generosity and Arab ingratitude will likely involve the Arab autonomy regime in Judea and Samaria, whose establishment the U.S. is so energetically urging.

For many years now, the U.S. Consulate in eastern Jerusalem (situated in an Arab neighborhood) has played an active role in paving the way for a PLO regime in the territories. It is common knowledge that the Consulate is virtually a PLO coffee shop, with leading Pro PLO Arabs regularly dropping by for friendly chats with senior US officials (Jewish visitors to the consulate, by contrast, are usually given ice-cold treatment). "when a Council of a foreign country actively conducts political talks behind the government's back with the residents of his host countries, he is engaging an objectionable activity," former Israeli interior minister Yoseph Burg wants to complain, with regard in the behavior of US consulate officials in Jerusalem. Even the ultra-dovish David Clayman, director of the Israel office of the American Jewish Congress, has charged that the US consulate "is he would be embassy to a PLO Palestinian state."

Consulate seems to have another function: to spy on the Jewish residents of Judea, Samaria, and Gaza. Over the years, counselor officials have repeatedly shown up, uninvited, at the homes of former Americans living on Jewish settlements in the territories. They subject the settlers to lengthy questioning about their political activities, the viability of the settlements, the cost of their houses, and more. Just last month, Rabbi

Zevulun Lieberman, a Brooklyn night who also owns a home in settlement of Elon Moreh, was grilled by counselor officials who want to know what it would take to persuade Lieberman and his neighbors to move out.

The consulates' agenda is plain to see. At the behest of the Arabists in the state department, the counselor officials are keeping track of the settlers and planning a strategy for getting rid of them to pave the way for Arab control of the region.

But if Bush thinks that giving such to the Arabs will result in Arabic gratitude, they'd better think again. History proves that appeasement and friendliness only emboldened the Arabs and encouraged them to become even more extreme. In addition to posing a mortal threat to Israel, an Arab regime in Judaism, Mary will quickly bite the American hand that fed it. If the US finds itself in another conflict with Iraq, that government of Palestine will not hesitate to slide with Baghdad against the "American devils." If the US refuses to endorse every pillow demand, Palestinian Arab terrorists will declare "open season" On American targets throughout the world. All the political and diplomatic aid that the US has furnished them over the years will be forgotten the moment America stands in the way of Arafat's agenda.

October 30, 1992

Time to Face Real Cause of U.S. Woes

The American economy is the main issue on the minds of most voters this year, and the three presidential candidates have offered a variety of proposals intended to improve this country's economic plight. Yet all three have shied away from facing the central reason for America's economic recession, the outrageously high price of Arab oil, and the ripple-effect crises that it has caused.

Think about how things were before the 1973 Arab oil embargo and how they have been since that time. Before 1973, the U.S. was the world's largest lender; today, it is the world's largest debtor nation. Before 1973, Arab oil was available for less than $4 per barrel. After the Arab embargo, it shot up to $20 per barrel and has fluctuated between $20 and $30 ever since. It's not hard to see that the American economy never recovered from the tremendous shock that the Arab price hike caused. That's because the oil crisis didn't take place in a vacuum. Such a huge increase in the cost of a commodity that so many people depend on has repercussions. It began with one huge shock, which sent out ripples of additional shock waves that helped produce the soaring unemployment rate, the ever-widening trade deficit, and the various other trademarks of the American recession.

Instead of confronting the Arab, instead of compelling them to charge reasonable rates (remember that a barrel of oil still costs the Arabs only about 50 cents to produce), the U.S. has consistently pursued a policy of trying to appease them. This shameful policy has its origins in Franklin Roosevelt's infamous meeting in 1945 with the Saudi king, Ibn Saud. FDR promised the Saudi tyrant that the U.S. would not make any decisions in favor of creating a Jewish homeland without the approval of the Arab regimes. Thus, America's new prominence in the Middle East, replacing the crumbling British Empire, began by echoing Britain's foolish pro-Arab policies.

156

One would think that Roosevelt and the State Department would have learned from London's mistakes. After all, the British anchored their policy in the notion that the Jews and Zionism should be sacrificed so that the Arabs would be pro-British, especially during World War II. The result? The Arabs all sided with the Nazis anyway, no British concessions were ever sufficient to satisfy the Arabs, and the fury of the armed Jewish underground drove the Union Jack out of the Holy Land anyway.

The policy of abandoning the Jews and rewarding the Arabs hastened the downfall of the British Empire. America could meet the same fate. It could also find its position as a world leader seriously eroded if it continues along the path of trying to appease the Arabs. Yet, none of the three presidential candidates has indicated a serious intention to take the steps necessary to break the Arab stranglehold. One candidate has proposed a huge tax on gasoline. That's right; he wants American consumers to pay even more when it's the Arabs who should be taxed, not hardworking American citizens.

Another troubling sign is that all three candidates have endorsed the proposed sale of F-72 jet fighters to Saudi Arabia. They claim that the manufacturing of the jets will provide jobs for Americans. That's a short-term and very short-sighted solution to a very small part of the nation's unemployment problem. It's like putting a band-aid on a broken leg. America's problems won't be solved until this country's leaders realize that it is Arab oil piracy that is destroying the U.S. economy and that the time has come to compel the Arabs to behave like civilized nations instead of like pirates and blackmailers.

November 11, 1992

Herzl, Rabin, And Jerusalem

Before Theodor Herzl began propagating the notion of a Jewish return to the Land of Israel, he had a very different idea about how to solve the "Jewish problem." In his diary, Herzl outlined a plan for having the Jewish masses gather in the Vatican, where they would be personally converted to Catholicism by the Pope himself. Herzl was not the first Jewish thinker to propose conversion, or assimilation, or some other form of Jewish self-abnegation, as the answer to anti-Semitism.

But Herzl was honest enough to abandon his plan when the Dreyfus affair in France, and the election of an anti-Semitic mayor in Vienna; demonstrated that Jew-hatred was alive and well even in the countries where the Jews were the most integrated.

Still, when Herzl embraced Zionism, he was embracing a relatively small movement in the Jewish world. Even in the decades following the publication of Herzl's seminal work, **Der Judenstaat**, most Jews were indifferent to Zion. Comfortable and acculturated in the Western world, most Jews looked upon the Land of Israel as some quaint religious artifact, perhaps a place which they might one-day visit, but not the site of a sovereign Jewish state, and certainly not a future home for themselves.

Indeed, for Jews who were determined to live in the Diaspora, the Zionist movement increasingly became a nuisance. These assimilated Jews were afraid that Gentiles in their countries would wonder if Jews were really loyal citizens, or secretly pined away for the Holy Land. Jews who became anti-Zionists did so as a way of "proving" to their Gentile neighbors that they were truly loyal. The most egregious example of such behavior was, of course, the creation of the American Council for Judaism, which at the height of the Holocaust devoted its energies to preventing the establishment of a Jewish homeland that could have rescued the Six Million from Hitler; impressing Gentiles was more important to them than saving Jews.

Times have changed, circumstances have changed, but that old diaspora mentality, also known as the ghetto mentality, relives and well in certain segments of the Jewish World. The yardstick of "what will the Gentiles say" still determines the behavior of all too many prominent Jews and not just Jews in the Diaspora. Consider last month's declaration by Israel's prime minister, housing minister, and police chief, that they will prevent Jews from moving into Arab-populated areas of Jerusalem because such Jewish behavior might "provoke" the Arabs. They are also keenly worried that it might "provoke" the State Department, the United Nations, and the world media.

There was a time when the only places in the world where Jews were prevented from buying property were the Soviet Union and the Arab countries. The Soviet Union no longer exists, but now we must add another region to the "no Jews allowed" list: parts of the Old City of Jerusalem and its eastern neighborhoods.

I think it's fair to say that Theodor Herzl would have regarded this phenomenon as an appalling betrayal of Zionist principles. Once Herzl gave up his "mass conversion" idea and realized that there was no hope of Jews completely melting into Western society, he also repudiated the idea that Jewish behavior should be determined by what will impress non-Jews. The irony of ironies that Jewish behavior today in the sovereign Jewish State of which Herzl dreamed in the ancient holy capital of Jerusalem itself should be determined by that reprehensible yardstick. This analogy between Herzl's early views and the behavior of some Israeli leaders may seem harsh. But let us put aside prejudices and judge actions as they really are. If it looks like a duck, walks like a duck, and quacks like a duck, well, then it's a duck. And if certain Israelis talk and act like the quivering ghetto Jews of yesteryear, then there is no reason to shy away from saying so.

November 13, 1992

Arab 'Revisionists' Not Better Than Holocaust-Deniers

Holocaust "revisionists," the hoaxers who claim that there was no Nazi mass murder of the Jews, are treated with appropriate contempt by world Jewry. Neither Jewish historians nor leaders of Jewish organizations will publicly debate the "revisionists." They correctly regard the no-Holocaust claim as beneath contempt and refuse to dignity that slur by treating it as a matter for serious discussion.

Why, then, are Arab extremists who make equally insulting and implausible revisions of history treated as a party with which to negotiate and, perhaps, be given a country of their own?

On July 19, Haidar Abdul Shafi, the leader of the Palestinian Arab negotiating team, met in Israel with members of a visiting Danish study group. Explaining the Arab claim to the Land of Israel, Shafi declared that "the international community needs to understand the position of the Palestinians as the descendants of various Semitic peoples who settled in the region before Abraham of Ur immigrated there." The Danes dutifully swallowed this Arab lie and went on their way.

Shafi's attempt to link the Arabs in Israel today to the ancient peoples of the area, that is, the Canaanite nations, is understandable. By fabricating a "link" between the Palestinian Arabs of today and the ancient Canaanites, these Arab revisionists seek to "prove" that the Arab claim to the Holy Land preceded the arrival of the Jews. Of course, the Arab revisionist claim has no basis in history, geography, or demography. Every serious historian knows that most of the Arabs in Israel are immigrants, or the children of immigrants, who came to the Holy Land during the 1920s and 1930s. They left Egypt, Lebanon, Syria, and Saudi Arabia for a simple reason: poverty. They came to what was then British Mandatory Palestine for an equally simple reason: prosperity. Jewish development of the Holy Land created employment opportunities.

But the Arab "revisionists" don't care about historical facts. They're not interested in what really happened. The only thing they're interested in is how to beef up their propaganda arsenal so that they continue their campaign to dismantle Israel. That's why they are ready to revise any aspect of history, no matter how absurd. Dr. Monam Hadad, of Haifa University, who monitors such Arab revisionist activity, reported a few years ago that Palestinian Arab folklorists had recently published" a lavish full-color book on Palestinian dress [that] went so far as to claim that the design for a new uniform for El Al air-hostesses... had been 'stolen' from traditional Palestinian dress."

Arabs who deny the Jewish historical claim to the Land of Israel are, ultimately, no better than neo-Nazi "historians" who deny the Holocaust. They seek to stamp out Jewish history so that they may, in the end: stamp out the Jews. These Arab revisionists should not be debated, nor should they be accepted as legitimate negotiating partners or offered autonomy, "self-rule," or statehood.

November 18, 1992

Who Controls Israel's Destiny?

Just who is running Israel, anyway? Consider these recent events:

"National Insurance payments, which are government grants given to all families whose sons have served in the Israeli Army (or who have performed an alternative form of national service), will now also be given to those Who have not served in the Army – that is, to Arabs. This was part of the deal that Prime Minister Rabin cut with the extremist Arab Democratic Party (an oxymoron if there ever was one) to win its support for the Labor coalition. Without the Arabs, Rabin would have been unable to establish his government; Likud and its allies won a clear majority of the Jewish votes, so the only way Rabin could attain power was with the backing of pro-PLO Arabs.

What are the consequences of giving National Insurance grants to the Arabs? To begin with, there are economic consequences. It will be a huge new drain on the Israeli economy, 1.7 billion Shekels this year alone. But there are even more serious consequences. This new policy establishes a moral equivalence between those who risk their lives to defend Israel and those who quietly (and sometimes not so quietly) pray for Israel's destruction. Even Arab families whose sons have engaged in terrorist activities will receive the National Insurance grants.

The Knesset, which has been on summer recess, convened in special session at the insistence of Ariel Sharon, who wanted to have a full discussion on the Labor government's attempt to prevent Jews from living in some sections of the Old City of Jerusalem. But Sharon's request for the discussion was defeated by a vote of 41 to 40, with the votes of the Arab MKs proving to be decisive. The Labor leaders were anxious to block an open debate because they prefer to implement their anti-Jerusalem moves behind closed doors. The glare of national publicity would have forced them to support (or at least refrain from opposing) a Likud resolution reaffirming the Jewish claim to Jerusalem. But the votes of the Arab MKs stopped that from happening. (In a display of perverse logic, the six MKs of the Orthodox Shas party were absent. Hoping to appease their nationalist-minded constituents, the Shas MKs said they would be absent to show that they do not always support the Labor government's position. But their "non-support" for Labor actually translated into an Arab victory. Had the Shas MKs shown up, they would have had to vote in favor of the Jerusalem resolution, and it would have passed, 46-41; instead, the Arabs and their Jewish allies won, 41-40.)

Forty illegally-built Arab villages in Israel will soon be declared "legal." This was another of Yitzhak Rabin's promises to the Arab Democratic Party. Of course, once they are given official government recognition as legal villages, they will have to be given government funds for schools, roads, and countless other social services. These Arab law-breakers will, in effect, be rewarded for their breaking of the law.

Meanwhile, Jewish towns in Judea, Samaria, and Gaza that were built legally, with full government permission and approval, are being denied government funds for even the most basic necessities, such as the construction of schools. Not only in Judea, Samaria, and Gaza but even in some parts of the Old City of Jerusalem - which Rabin supposedly considers to be part of Israel the government is using economic pressure to starve out the Jewish residents.

Will Diaspora Jewish supporters of Israel endorse this kind of blatant discrimination? Traditional Zionism rejected such distinctions. During the 1920s and 1930s, Diaspora Jewish donors did not discriminate according to political preferences. Diaspora donations were used to help leftwing Jewish settlers establish their *kibbutzim* in the heavily-Arab territory, and were also used to help the nationalist Betar movement create its settlements.

Those brave pioneers, of all political stripes, risked their lives to establish Israel's borders. Today, Jewish settlers in Judea and Samaria likewise risk their lives to establish Israel's borders. Yet, now Diaspora Jewish funds are being withheld from them (by both the Labor government and the Jewish National Fund) because they want to live in the historical heartland of Israel, Jerusalem, Judea, and Samaria. Instead of furthering authentic Zionist goals,

Diaspora Jewish funds will now provide National Insurance payments to Arab families whose members may include terrorists; provide social services for illegally-built Arab villages that encroach on Jewish land, and serve as a means of pressuring Jews to leave Israel's Biblical heartland.

The next time that fundraisers for Israel Bonds and the United Jewish Appeal come knocking, Diaspora Jews will have the right to make it clear that they don't want their money to be used to help Arabs control the destiny of the Jewish State. That's not a controversial request. The idea that Jews should control their destiny, and not Arabs, is an old and time-honored concept: it's called Zionism.

November 20, 1992

U.S. Decline Due To Pro-Arab Tilt

When one examines some of the meet notorious episodes of government corruption in this country in recent years, it becomes evident that a disproportionate number of the scandals involve attempts by U.S. leaders to appease Moslem dictators.

The entire Iran-Contra scandal, which so badly tarnished the Reagan Administration, revolved around a duplicitous and sometimes illegal effort by U.S. officials to shower the Iranians with weapons in the hope of making them "moderate" and leading to the release of hostages held by Iranian-backed Arab terrorists.

The current "Iraq gate" scandal, which has done much to tarnish the Bush Administration, operated from the same premise. Bush decided that the U.S. should shower Iraq with weapons, in the hope of making Saddam Hussein more "moderate." The problem was that U.S. law prohibits giving weapons to countries that sponsor terrorism, and Iraq is one of those countries. So, according to congressional investigators, senior Bush Administration officials proceeded to secretly provide Saddam with "dual-use technology" that was disguised agricultural products but could be converted to military uses, or battered to other countries for military items. One top Bush aide has already admitted that, on orders from his superiors, he deliberately altered a list of such items that were given to Congress, to hide the military nature of the exports to Iraq that the administration had approved.

A third, and related, scandal, known as the "B.N.L. affair," concerns attempts by an Italian bank, Banca Nazionale del Lavoro, to provide loans to Iraq via its Atlanta affiliate illegally. What makes this episode even more sordid and what forced the Attorney General to appoint a special investigator recently is evidence that Bush aides interfered with the initial F.B.I. Investigation of the case to protect Iraq from embarrassing publicity.

Now we must add a fourth Arab-related case of possible U.S. government corruption. Leslie Gelb of **The New York Times** charged in a recent column that one of the secret motives for the U.S. invasion of Grenada in 1983 was to distract attention from the failed Reagan policy in Lebanon that had led to the catastrophic Arab terrorist attack on the U.S. Marines there. The charge is serious, and one presumes that Gelb would not have made it without some basis.

At the time, the Marxist-provoked turmoil in Grenada seemed reason enough for U.S. action. But looking back, it seems clear that it was the Lebanon quagmire, not the chaos in tiny Grenada, that was the much more significant episode in U.S. foreign policy. The problem began when the Reagan Administration tried to appease the Arab states and the PLO by pressuring Israel to refrain from destroying the PLO in Beirut. Then Reagan demanded that the Israelis withdraw from most of the rest of Lebanon, and offered to replace the Israeli forces with a U.S.-led international force. The Arab terrorists who had remained in those areas regarded the U.S. Marines as just as much of an unwanted "occupier" as the departing Israelis, and they promptly blew up the Marine barracks, murdering hundreds of Americans. That left Reagan with a dilemma. The appropriate response would have been an all-out U.S. military campaign against the terrorist encampments in Lebanon. But they would have angered the Arab regimes. So Reagan surrendered to the terrorists, and meekly withdrew the Marines from Lebanon. It was a shameful day for America. In retrospect, it doesn't seem so farfetched that the administration would have sought out a convenient foreign policy adventure to distract attention from its poor performance in Lebanon. Grenada was the perfect solution, especially on the eve of an election year.

The key to a revival of American might is a reversal of Middle East policy. Siding with the Arabs has proven catastrophic; siding with Israel fully, unconditionally, whole-heartedly is the cure. The time has come to treat Israel like the valuable ally and fellow-democracy that it is, and treat the totalitarian, corruption-inducing Arabs just as we treat the petty dictators of Latin America.

November 25, 1992

Jewish Rights Under Siege

It was one year ago this week that President Bush made his outrageous remarks describing himself as "lonely little guy" under siege by a thousand Jewish lobbyists. In the space of just one year, Bush has succeeded in turning the tables, so that today it is not Bush who is under siege (as if he ever was) by the Jews, but rather the Jewish right to the Land of Israel that is under siege by Bush – with help, ironically, from Israeli Prime Minister Yitzhak Rabin.

The Bush-Baker assault on the Jewish right to Israel shifted into high gear in the spring of 1990 with a double-barreled blast. First, Secretary of State Baker, speaking at the annual conference of the America-Israel Public Affairs Committee, demanded that Israel "give up the unrealistic vision of a Greater Israel." Then, President Bush went out of his way to characterize the Old City of Jerusalem as "Occupied Arab territory" from which Israel will have to withdraw eventually.

Baker's call for Israeli surrender of the Zionist dream, and Bush's call for Israeli surrender of Jerusalem, have now been reinforced from the unlikeliest of places – the office of Israel's prime minister: "We must cut ourselves off from the religion of the Greater Land of Israel," Rabin declared last week.

What Rabin derisively calls "the religion of Greater Israel" is, of course, nothing less than the Jewish religion itself. The callous ultra-secularists who dominate Rabin's governing coalition may be indifferent to their Jewish roots, but the majority of Israelis know full well that the Jewish right to all of the Land of Israel is indelibly enshrined in every single sacred Jewish text, and cannot be erased by politicians seeking to curry favor abroad.

It is, indeed, the pursuit of international approval that motivates Yitzhak Rubin. Nothing else could move an Israeli minister to befriend a president who has incited anti-Semitism with his attacks on Jewish lobbyists and a secretary of state who has been reliably reported to have said: "F – the Jews" on several occasions.

And so, once again, it all comes down to Arab oil. The Bush-Baker policy of embracing Arab dictators and harassing Israel is based on the perception that such a policy will promote American access to Arab oil. Rabin, in turn, offers concession after concession in the perception that Israeli surrender will improve his standing in international public opinion.

Bush's appeasement of the Arab oil barons is to be sealed with the spilling of Jewish blood and Jewish curtailment rights. Jews who reside in Judea and Samaria are being starved out, as Rabin outs off all economic assistance to them (even while he funnels huge amounts of money to the bankrupt *kibbutzim* and non-productive socialist companies owned by the Histadrut). Over 600 Arab terrorists are being set free on Israel's streets. Concrete barriers that protected Israeli motorists Arab rock-throwers and firebomb-throwers have been dismantled in the Bethlehem region and the Gaza Strip

Jewish rights today are under siege as never before. The Jewish right to be protected from Arab terrorists has been eroded. The Jewish right to travel on Israeli highways without being stoned or burned to death has been undermined. And the Jewish right to the Land of Israel, the most fundamental tenet of Zionism now faces perhaps the most determined attack that it has ever encountered.

December 11, 1992

An Open Letter to President-Elect Clinton

The overwhelming majority of Israelis are delighted by your election victory, and they look forward to an era of strengthened relations between their country and the United States. Those relations have been built on common strategic interests, on shared values, on an appreciation of our common Biblical heritage (something that you know well from your religious faith), and on Israel's role as the only Mideast bulwark against the rising tide of Islamic fundamentalism. But even more than that, Israelis are hopeful that you will recognize the extraordinarily precarious position into which previous U.S. administrations have forced Israel.

I am referring to the fact that Israel has been cornered into negotiating with Arab dictators in accordance with the flawed "land for peace" concept and pressured to offer territorial concessions that clearly endanger Israeli national security. The Bush administration treated Israel like a child (indeed, one of Bush's top Mideast advisers, Aaron Miller, was quoted earlier this year as saying, "I speak to Israelis the way I speak to my children), using threats and withholding economic aid in a primitive reward-and-punishment system. But if Bush and Baker were the parents and Israel the child, then one must conclude that Israel resembles an abused child, and Bush and Baker with their obsessive need to appease Arab dictators were addicted to Arab oil like an alcoholic parent is addicted to whiskey.

Israelis accept the terms for the current Mideast talks not because they really wanted to, and not because they really believed peace would emerge, but because they were forced by their abusive "parent," the Bush administration. Trapped in a dependency relationship, where Bush dangled aid like a carrot before a horse, the Israelis were unable to say "no." How could Israel refuse? How can an abused child pull himself up out of the abusive dependency atmosphere of its home?

In a recent court action in the United States, a child who was abused by his mother sued, successfully, to "divorce" her and live elsewhere. But Israel has no court to which it could turn for relief from the smothering, aid-and-pressure tactics of the Bush administration. In the court of world opinion, it found precious little sympathy; on the contrary, most nations urged Bush and Baker not to "spare the rod" when the Israelis behaved in some "naughty" manner, such as defending itself against neighborhood bullies.

The truth is that Bush's carrot-and-stick treatment of the Jewish State was not just bad for Israel but bad for America as well. By focusing all of their anger on the Israelis, Bush and Baker failed to deal with their problem, their fatal addiction to Arab oil. Like abusive, alcoholic parents, they couldn't see that they were on the road to self-destruction. U.S. dependence on Arab oil is an abyss from which there is virtually no escape. To appease the Arabs, America finds itself paying outrageous prices for oil, pressuring its only real Mideast ally for suicidal concessions, and, ultimately, sacrificing the lives of its sons and daughters on the battlefields of the Persian Gulf.

It was all too easy to ignore the problem. Instead of facing his oil addiction, Bush spoke of "international coalitions" and "a new world order." Instead of facing up to his abuse of Israel, he covered it up by talking about a "window of opportunity for Arab-Israeli peace," and "Israeli settlements blocking peace."

As a candidate, you appropriately criticized the Bush administration for helping to build up Iraq before

the war, for coddling the Syrians: and for falsely blaming Mideast tensions on Israeli settlements. Now, as president, you have the opportunity to put those words into action, to put an end to the abuse of Israel, to free America of its deadly addiction to Arab oil, and to invigorate U.S.-Israeli relations in preparation for the Islamic fundamentalist and terrorist threats that are sure to emerge in years ahead.

Israelis wish you well and are united in their desire to help you restore the U.S.-Israeli relationship to one of maturity, mutual respect, and independence.

January 1, 1993

Ein Breira: A Slogan of Survival Becomes an Excuse for Surrender

The Hebrew phrase *ein breira*, meaning "there is no alternative," has traditionally served as a brief but incise summary of Israel's spirit of survival. Incredulous foreigners watched the events of the Six-Day War or the Yom Kippur War unfold, as Israel snatched glorious victory from the jaws of catastrophic defeat, and wondered in amazement how Israel accomplished such feats; Israelis calmly replied, "ein breira." There simply was no other choice for Israel but to triumph. Defeat meant the destruction of Israel, the equivalent of a second Auschwitz. Israelis had "ein breira," and so they emerged victorious, no matter the odds.

When Israel's friends wonder how the Jewish State manages to survive each day, in the face of the vicious Arab economic boycott, the hostile international atmosphere, the daily knifings and bombings Israelis reply, "ein breira." They tighten their belts, they ignore the critics, they bandage the wounded, and then they go about their daily business, because of "ein breira," there is no alternative.

Some of this steely determinism had been eroded in recent weeks, thanks to a mood of despair that is being encouraged by certain Israeli politicians and how the slogan "ein breira" is being heard in a disturbing hew context. Prime Minister Yitzhak Rabin, who

during the election campaign promised that he would never surrender the strategically-vital Golan Heights now says that he does intend to give up much of the Golfing because there is "ein breira." There is "no alternative to surrender, according to Rabin, because it's too unpleasant to face "international isolation" and because Israelis have grown "tired" of the conflict with Syria. Rabin seems to have forgotten the fact that Israelis are "tired" of fighting Syria does not mean that the Syrians are no longer interested in fighting Israel. But instead of leading his nation in a proud affirmation of its

172

historical rights and security needs, Rabin has opted to encourage their sense of weariness and desperation.

Rabin's twisted new version of "ein breira" has also surfaced in his attitude towards the Gaza Strip. Not long ago, he declared that he wished that territory would fall into the sea, but, since that was not likely to happen, Israel should be anxious to surrender it, since it has such a large population of hostile Arabs. From Israel's security interests, keeping Gaza is vital; it has been the historic route of invasion of the Holy Land from the south, and who can be certain that Egyptian dictator Hosni Mubarak will not one day be overthrown by Islamic fundamentalists eager for a *jihad*? The obvious way to fortify Israel's southern defenses is to establish Israeli settlements in the region since every town and village can serve as a military in the event of warfare. But Rabin says that no such settlements can be built "ein breira," he insists, there is no budget for settling Gaza. This deadly "ein breira" means, in effect, that there is no budget to defend Israel. (Yet Rabin has made room in his "restricted" budget to bail out ailing Labor Party-affiliated industries and bankrupt *kibbutzim*, even though they are a drag on the economy and in any sane country would be compelled to become productive or shut down.)

Rabin is also saying "ein breira" to the directors of the Israel Military Industries. They have been forced to fire 3,000 workers because the Rabin government is buying more U.S. weapons instead of having the IMI manufacture weapons at home. "They say the factory isn't cost-efficient, but when we established IMI, was it for economic reasons?" asked IMI official Shalom Habshush, at a recent protest rally by the workers. "Is the atomic reactor cost-efficient? We established this firm with our sweat to defend the State of Israel." Rabin's response: "There is no alternative ... where will I get the money from? Where will I find resources to continue operating a plant with such great expenses?" The obvious answer is that he could get the money by not bailing out a few of those bankrupt Histadrut-owned companies, or some of those inefficient kibbutzim which neither make money nor do anything to defend the State of Israel. To do that, Rabin will have to muster the courage to defy his political cronies and put the national interest above the Labor Party's interests.

The ability of the Jewish State to maintain any degree of political and military independence rests on its ability to produce at least some of its weapons. If the production of the Israeli Military Industries is slashed, Israel will be left completely at the mercy of its main arms supplier, the United States – the same United States which withheld arms as a means of political pressure at the beginning of the 1973 war, during the 1975 "reassessment," and after the 1978 strike into Lebanon. (Not to mention the withholding of satellite spy data during the Gulf War, and the withholding of the loan guarantees.)

All of this points to another frightening possibility: that the new "ein breira" of the malaise-ridden Rabin era may alienate American Jewry from Israel. Will American Jews will write checks for Israel if they see their money being thrown away on unproductive Histadrut projects? One wonders how American Jews will respond when they learn of the letter Rabin sent to MK Abd El-Wahab Darawshe, the Knesset's most outspoken PLO supporter, guaranteeing that Arab youth will henceforth receive the same monthly social security payments as young Israelis even though the Arabs do not serve in the Army or preform any land of national service, while the Israelis give three years of their lives and sometimes lose their lives, or their limbs to the defense of their country; will American Jews want their donations ending up in the pockets of pro-PLO Israeli Arabs? Will American Jews be inspired to mount the barricades for Israel when Israel's present leaders are mired in defeatism, ready to risk Israel's survival by letting Syrian guns return to the Golan Heights and letting PLO supporters establish a de-fact state nine miles from Tel Aviv...? What are American Jews supposed to think when they read that Shimon Peres has still hotly denied the Evans and Novak report that he urged President-elect, Clinton's advisers, to "go easy" on Syria...?

When Israel's economy suffers severe new setbacks because of Rabin's socialist policies, when Israel faces new security dangers because it surrendered its territorial buffers, when American Jewry's faith in Israel's leaders has been shaken by the misguided policies of the Rabin government, then it will be one-minute past midnight for Israel and Jews everywhere.

174

January 8, 1993

From Israel To Somalia, Soldiers Under Stress

Soldiers are standing at a roadblock in a part of the country filled with hostile, heavily-armed gangs. Suddenly a speeding vehicle defies the soldiers' warnings and crashes through the barricade. The soldiers react instinctively. They know it might well be a carload of terrorists, and their choice is to shoot, or possibly be shot. They open fire, killing two of the passengers. It turns out that the passengers were members of an innocent civilian family; they didn't stop because their rickety old vehicle had no brakes.

Imagine what would have happened if the soldiers were Israelis, and the passengers were Arabs. Of course, the Israeli soldiers would have been completely justified in shooting, since they have had too many bitter experiences with carloads of terrorists ramming roadblocks to escape or to run over Israelis. But that wouldn't make any difference. Newspaper headlines all over the world would shriek about "trigger-happy Israelis murdering innocent Arabs." The United Nations Security Council would meet in an emergency session to pass a resolution condemning the Israeli army. State Department officials would blast the Israelis for being "reckless." Israeli leftists would demand that the soldiers be punished. And the nervous Israeli government, unable to withstand the criticism, would quickly cave in. The soldiers would be demoted, publicly humiliated, put on trial, and sentenced to jail terms. This isn't just an imaginary scenario; it's happened many tunes in recent years.

But the roadblock incident described above, which really did happen, did not involve Israelis, but rather American and French soldiers in Somalia. Their commanding officer explained that the soldiers were "just following the standing rules of engagement" when they fired. And that was all. There was no international outcry, no UN resolutions, no nervous American politicians running to denounce American soldiers.

And that's how it should be. When soldiers are put in dangerous situations, they must be free to take whatever action is necessary to accomplish

175

their goals and to protect themselves against the enemy. That's true for Americans in Somalia, and it's even more true for Israelis soldiers facing hostile Arabs. Whatever threats the Americans may face in Somalia, the Israelis face tenfold and hundred-fold when dealing with armed PLO gangs and rioting Arab mobs whose goal is to kill as many Jews, soldiers or civilians, as possible.

Avraham Burg, the leading dove in the Israeli Labor Party, declared recently that a soldier should "hesitate seven times before he pulls the trigger." That would make sense if Israel's top priority were to protect the lives of Arab terrorists and rioters. But since more Israelis believe that their top priority should be the protection of Israeli civilians and soldiers, Burg's recommendation is nothing less than a recipe for the spilling of Jewish blood. A soldier who hesitates seven times gives an Arab terrorist seven chances to murder him.

The issue of when to shoot is not the only area, but which the Israel-Somalia double standard has an appearance. Consider the question of the behavior of foreign journalists. Secretary of Defense Richard Cheney has strongly criticized the Western television crews for interfering with the landing and deployment of the American troops in Somalia. Turning a humanitarian military effort into a media circus, the TV crews brazenly use powerful camera lights even though that revealed the soldier's positions and obstructed their vision. Cheney apparently intends to restrict the journalists' freedom action in the future, just as the British put a strict limitation on media coverage of the Falkland Islands U.S. media coverage of the Grenada invasion. ("We never let the enemy join us on our missions," a senior U.S. army officer said, explaining the barring of journalists from the Grenada landing.)

The Israelis, however, become the targets to worldwide criticism if they dare to take action against foreign journalists, even though the very presence the journalists incites Arabs to attack Israelis, even though the journalists take advantage of Israel's liberal policy to smear the Jewish State, and even though there have been cases of journalists actually assisting Arab rioters (the most notorious was the case of a **Village Voice** photographer who was caught throwing rocks at Israelis.)

Israel should let its soldiers do whatever they have to do to defend themselves, and if the world screams, Israeli spokesmen can reply that they are simply doing what the Americans are doing in Somalia. Israel should keep foreign journalists far away from the scene of clashes with violent Arabs. If the world screams, Israeli spokesmen can reply that they are simply doing what the Americans are planning to do in Somalia. Let the word "Somalia" become the rallying cry for a new Israeli policy of sane, rational, self-preservation.

January 8, 1993

Weinberger Goes Free as His Victim Rots in Jail

The man who helped Israel combat Iraq's nuclear development is rotting in prison. The man who helped put him in jail was indicted for various criminal offenses but has now been given a Presidential pardon. And a man who spied for Iraq against the U.S. during the Gulf War has received a slap-on-the-wrist punishment. In this strange world of fours, where injustice triumphs all too often, there may be no more grotesque injustice than the tragic saga of Jonathan Pollard, Caspar Weinberger, and Albert Sombolay.

Pollard was sentenced, in 1987, to life imprisonment without parole for the "crime" of giving Israel several U.S. intelligence reports about the nuclear and chemical weapons development of Syria and Iraq. That information was crucial to Israel's efforts to undermine Arab nuclear activities. Pollard, an intelligence analyst, was moved to take that action when he discovered that his superiors were deliberately withholding that data from the Israelis despite a U.S.-Israeli agreement, which obliged the Americans to share such information. When Pollard complained about his bosses' refusal to give Israel a report about the Arabs' development of poison gas, the reply he received was cold and cruel: "The Jews are too sensitive about gas," they said.

Those who later crusaded to put Pollard behind bars – most notably, Defense Secretary Caspar Weinberger – angrily denied that crucial data was withheld from the Jewish State. But Bruce Brill, a former Middle East analyst for the National Security Agency, says otherwise. He recently revealed that on October 5, 1973, some 30 hours before the You Kippur invasion of Israel, he was shown a U.S. intelligence report disclosing the Arabs' invasion plans. "I naturally assumed that Israel, America's publicly declared friend, would have been notified immediately through proper channels about the imminent attack," Brill writes with remorse. Of course, the U.S. did not notify Israel, an "now I live haunted by the possibility that, somehow, I could have discovered the intelligence was not being forwarded, gotten it to the Israelis, and saved some measure of the anguish that become known as the Yom Kippur War."

178

After encountering precisely the same kind of anti-Israel bias that Brill witnessed, Jonathan Pollard acted upon his conscience.

Pollard knew that what he was doing was illegal, and knew that he would be punished if he was caught. What he could never have imagined is that the penalty he would be given for passing data to an ally of the U.S., in peacetime, would be worse than that given to individuals who passed data to enemies of the U.S., in wartime.

John Walker, for example, passed U.S. intelligence data to the Soviet Union over 17 years. That included the period of the Vietnam War, and the information he gave the Soviets included details about U.S. troop movements in South Vietnam, making them easier targets for the Soviet-backed Vietcong. To make matters worse, Walker recruited his brother, his son, and one of his friends to join in the espionage. He was convicted of treason much more serious than what Pollard was charged with yet received an ordinary life sentence, unlike Pollard, who received life with a recommendation of no parole. Walker's son, Michael, received a sentence of 25 years, will only hate to serve a maximum of 16, and could even be paroled after serving just eight years.

Or consider the case of Abdel Kader Helmy, an Egyptian-American rocket scientist who tried to smuggle U.S. war materials to Egypt. Acting on the orders of Egyptian Defense Minister Abdel Abu-Ghazala, Helmy tried to illegally smuggle 420 pounds of materials needed for developing the Stealth aircraft. He was sentenced to 46 months in prison and given a modest fine; he will be free in three years at the latest. Egypt may be temporarily friendly with the U.S., but it cannot be considered an "ally" of America as Israel is. Yet Helmy was treated with kid gloves, while Pollard was treated with an iron fist.

But the most outrageous case – and the one which most highlights the Pollard injustice – is that of Albert Sombolay. He was convicted, in 1991, of having spied for Iraq during the Gulf War. He gave Baghdad vital U.S. intelligence data, including information on the deployment of allied troops in the Gulf. He even gave Iraq samples of the protective equipment that the allied troops used against chemical weapons, so that the Iraqis could figure out how to penetrate it. Yet even though he spied during wartime, and despite the severe damage he caused, Sombolay was sentenced to just 19 years in prison.

What accounts for the cruel and unusual treatment meted out to Jonathan Pollard? There can be little doubt that Caspar Weinberger had a great deal to do with it. Perhaps because of his deep-rooted connections to the oil industry and its pro-Arab mindset, perhaps because of personal anxieties arising from the fact that he had one Jewish grandfather, Weinberger displayed an animus towards Pollard that is hard to fathom. On the day of Pollard's sentencing, Weinberger submitted a letter to the judge, claiming that it was "difficult to conceive greater harm to national security than that caused by [Pollard]." He urged that Pollard be given the maximum penalty, in violation of a promise by government prosecutors not to request the maximum penalty. On another occasion, Weinberger even privately told reporters that Pollard "deserved to be hanged."

Everyone who was outraged by the miscarriage of justice in the Pollard case had a right to feel satisfied when Weinberger was indicted earlier this year on a variety of criminal charges related to the Iran-Contra affair. At last, the would-be hangman might get a taste of his own medicine, but then George Bush decided to top off his four years of Israel-bashing by granting a presidential pardon to a fellow Israel-basher, and Caspar Weinberger is a free man again.

That would leave Jonathan Pollard back at square one – except for one thing. After years of silence, the American Jewish community is, at last, raising its voice on behalf of Pollard. The Weinberger indictment and pardon have only served to ignite Jewish anger over the Pollard affair further. One final, mighty, united push by American Jews – in the form of rallies, telegrams, and tireless lobbying – can win freedom for Pollard, whether from the outgoing President or the incoming one. It can be done; it must be done.

January 29, 1993

Martians, Jews, And Arabs

In a recent column (printed elsewhere, but quoted in this paper on page 20, January 15, 1993), I reported with tongue in cheek that a recent international conference of Moslem leaders, moved by the persecution of their fellow-Moslems in Bosnia, had resolved to acknowledge their historical treatment of the Jews and beg forgiveness from the Jewish people. Recognizing the vulnerable position in which Bosnian Moslems had been placed because of their statelessness, these Moslem leaders "saw the light" I wrote facetiously and admitted their error in opposing Jewish statehood, apologized for collaborating with the Nazis, expressed sorrow over having waged *jihad* against Israel, and urged that Jordan be made the future Palestinian Arab state.

Some newspapers published the article together with a note from the editor explaining that it was satire. Some newspapers did not, and, I am told, they have been deluged with telephone calls and letters from readers anxious to know more about this "Moslem change of heart."

I never dreamed that anybody could take such an article as anything but a satire. It is simply inconceivable that Moslem leaders could ever give up their war against Jews and Judaism. They would have to first abandon their religion for intolerance of non-Moslems is an integral part of the Islamic faith, and the Koran mandates the violent persecution of anybody who stands in Islam's way. As Dr. Yohanan Friedman, a leading expert on the Middle East wrote in the academic journal **Jerusalem Quarterly** (September 1979): "Jihad [holy war] is an essential commandment of Islam. It is a permanent war to be waged until the day of Judgment. An armistice may be permitted for limited periods only and may be concluded when facing the danger of defeat. Armistices may be broken, for permanent peace with the infidel in out of the question. The struggle must go on until the entire world comes under the sway of the one true faith."

Ironically, many Jews are so quick to believe that Arab od Moslem leaders have become "moderate" and so slow to realize the depths of Arab hostility towards Jews, Israel, and Zionism. Despite 100 years of Arab violence against Jews in the Land of Israel; actual Arab collaboration with the Nazis; five wars started by the Arabs; decades of terrorism sponsored by the Arab states; a boycott that is nothing less than economic warfare; a ceaseless international propaganda campaign designed to portray the Israelis as Nazis; and a PLO Covenant that to this day vows to carry out the phase-by-phase annihilation of the State of Israel – despite all this, there are many Jews who are ready to believe that the Arabs have changed their ways and will now live in peace with a Jewish State.

Such Jewish *naivete* is, to a large extent, the fault of Jewish leaders, who have utterly failed to educate the Jewish public as to the enduring nature of Arabs belligerence. The leaders of the major Jewish organizations have ready access to translations from the Arabic media and other important sources of information about the Arab world. They know the kind of anti-Israel and anti-Semitic rhetoric that dominates Arab newspapers and television broadcasts. They know about the thousands of Nazi war criminals still being given shelter in Arab countries. They know about the massive buildup of nuclear, chemical, and biological weapons by the Arab regimes. Yet they rarely, if ever, share this information with the Jewish public at large, thus leaving the Jewish Public at the mercy of the American mass media, which constantly pushes the idea of Arab "moderation."

Frankly, I feel a bit like Orson Welles. His famous "War of the Worlds" radio broadcast, on Halloween night, 1938, was obviously fictional. In fact, at the beginning of the broadcast, the radio announcer specifically said that that it was a work of fiction. But anybody who tuned in after that announcement heard only what sounded like a news report about Martians invading the earth.

The idea that Moslems would give up their Islamic dreams of destroying Israel and eventually imposing their religion on the entire world is even less likely than the possibility that Martians would invade. I feel confident when I say that if the day ever comes that Martians invade earth, then – and only then – will it be possible that the Moslems are ready to stop invading Israel.

Until then, Israel must stand firm, realizing that no amount of gestures, compromises, or concessions can ever satisfy the Moslem appetite. Only a militarily invincible Israel, with impregnable borders and the full support of Diaspora Jewry, can hold off the raging Islamic tide.

February 5, 1993

Kids Play House, Israel Plays Country

The Los Angeles radio station KNX, the local CBS affiliate, recently broadcast an interview with the American army officer whose unit was involved in killing seven Somali gunmen. The American officer did not show even the slightest remorse over what had happened. There were "snipers" in the area, he said, so there was no choice but to use heavy firepower. The reporter treated the officer gently, asking him respectful questions and never challenging his replies. The officer was given plenty of time to explain himself, and the CBS radio network made sure to broadcast the entire segment.

When Israeli officers are involved in such actions, CBS and the other television and radio news programs behave rather differently. Suddenly the reporters are aggressive and critical. The soldiers themselves are rarely allowed to speak at all. Instead, some government spokesman is given a few brief seconds to speak, while the reporters pepper him with hostile questions. When the segment is broadcast, there's always plenty of footage of Israelis shooting an Arabs bleeding. The hundreds of rock-throwing and firebomb, throwing Arabs who attacked the Israelis, are nowhere to be seen. The bleeding Israeli soldiers are not considered newsworthy. The possibility that the Israelis were acting in self-defense is irrelevant to the reporters and their editors, whose news coverage of Israel begins with the presumption that the Jews are guilty and the Arabs innocent, and nothing the Israelis do can change that perception.

It is precise because there is no hope of impressing the media, or the international community, that Israel's behavior is so perplexing. Israeli soldiers are under orders to refrain from shooting at rioters in the mistaken belief that such restraint will impress foreign journalists. The Israeli army shrinks from confrontations with rioters in the naive belief that fewer Arab casualties will make a good impression at the United Nations. The Israeli government departs terrorists, but then immediately starts making concessions: the terrorists can come back in two years, some of the terrorists were deported "by mistake"

184

(since when can it ever be a mistake to deport an Arab inciter of violence?), Red Cross visits are allowed, negotiations and the PLO are hinted at. All this in a vain attempt to score points with the State Department or **The New York Times**. But it just won't work.

When I was a child growing up in Milwaukee with nine siblings, and I often "played house." Make-believe "parents," make-believe "neighbors," and make-believe "children" would act out their respective roles. But when it was time for school, or chores, or shul, we would "dismantle" our fictional house and go back to real life. We knew when it was time to stop playing house.

But Israel sometimes seems as if it is "playing country." It doesn't observe the real-life rules of life and death in the Middle East. It doesn't deal with its enemies in the language that they understand. It doesn't let its soldiers defend themselves against attacking. Instead, Israel pretends as if it is living in some kind of fantasy world, where kindness begets kindness. Israel leaders act as if Israeli restraint will merit international praise. They delude themselves into thinking that Israeli gestures will result in Arab gestures. It takes a "tough" step, just for a moment, but then right away starts backtracking and 'hesitating and making concessions, fantasizing that Israeli concessions will produce Arab concessions and impress world opinion.

The last time Israel acted like a real country and fought like a country that wants to survive in the Middle East was in 1967. That was a long time ago. Since then, Israel's leaders have been steadily retreating in a make-believe world, increasing the danger that they will not survive in the real world. As children, my brothers and sisters and I would dismantle our pretend house, piece by piece. Israel, however, is a real country that is now in the process of being dismantled, piece by piece. And it will not be long before the process is complete the Arabs and the United Nations will make sure of that.

Ultimately, Jews in Israel and the Diaspora are fecal With a choice: either act as tough as necessary to survive and prosper in the Middle East or allow Israel to wither away, physically and spiritually, surrendering so much of its territory and independence that it becomes little more than a sad vassal-state, where Jews reside without real sovereignty, preserving their religious rites but little else. Of course, those Jews who have assimilated, who find Israel embarrassing and annoying, would like Israel to continue down the path of weakness and surrender. Their excuse is that Israel is surrounded by hostile forces so great that it must succumb to Arab demands. Still, their real motivation is to do away with Jewish nationhood altogether. Strength or surrender. Fortitude or collapse. The choice is momentous, and the hour is late. Truly it is one minute to midnight for World Jewry.

February 19, 1993

Demographics and Geographics

The United Nations is threatening sanctions against Israel. The U.S. supported the UN's condemnation of the Jewish State and is implicitly supporting the threat of sanctions. Headlines scream about Israel really deporting Arabs, and the front pages are filled with sympathetic-looking photos of shabbily-clad Arabs, shivering in cold southern Lebanon. The honeymoon between Israel's Labor government was brief indeed; again, Israel is being blamed, and Diaspora Jews are nervously squirming in their chairs. How, one wonders, did we reach this point? Why can't anything ever be right? Why is it that Israel and the Jews always need to be in the docket?

The first step in finding the answer is to recognize where not to look for the answer. There's no sense in pointing an accusing finger at the UN or the State Department or the media. Sure they're guilty of hypocrisy. But focusing on them distracts attention from the real culprit: the Jewish leadership, whose silence is what paves the way for the UN, the State Department, and the media to launch their assaults on Israel.

The leaders of the major American Jewish organizations have a record of colossal failure in every major crisis that has engulfed world Jewry during the past 60 years. During the 1930s' they were afraid to demand that German Jewish refugees be permitted to enter the U.S. They were even afraid to speak out against British restrictions on Jewish immigration to the Land of Israel, fearing that isolations would accuse them of dragging America into overseas problems.

By 1942, American Jewish leaders knew, in gruesome detail, about the annihilation of Europe's Jews. But they were afraid to demand that Roosevelt help save the Jews, this time, they feared that they would be accused of being more interested in European Jews than in the war effort. Millions of Jews were gassed in Nazi death camps while U.S. Jewish leaders went about their daily affairs, issuing bland press releases that had no chance of moving FDR to act.

During the 1950s and 1960s, the leaders of these same Jewish organizations – American Jewish Congress, American Jewish Committee, B'nai B'rith = sat silently by while Soviet Jews were persecuted and forcefully assimilated. These Jewish "leaders" claimed that demonstrations for Soviet Jewry would only "make things worse."

What they were really worried about was making things worse for themselves; they were afraid that their non-Jewish friends and neighbors would accuse them of provoking tension between America and the Soviet Union. Brave Jewish student activists defied the Jewish leadership, and took to the streets, staging a variety on-page on and forced open the Iron Curtain.

The same Jewish organizations that were silent during the Holocaust and inactive during the persecution of Soviet Jewry are today leading Israel down the path of disaster. When Israel faces world criticism, these Jewish "leaders" are afraid to speak out. They don't want to say unpopular things. So, they stand idly by white State Department Arabists and Israel-bashing journalists have a field day. Instead of defending Israel's deportation of 415 Hamas terrorists, the American Jewish Committee issued a mealy-mouthed statement saying that it "respects Israel's sovereignty," which was interpreted by the press, correctly, as **far less** than an expression of support for Israel's action.

These same Jewish "leaders" have, in recent years, begun clamoring for Israel to surrender Judea and Samaria. Henry Siegman of the American Jewish Congress, for example, has repeatedly cited Israel's so-called "demographic problem" as the reason that Israel should withdraw from those territories. Because there are so many Arabs in Judea and Samaria, according to Siegman's reasoning, Israel will be stuck with a huge Arab population if it doesn't retreat. But the irony is that it was Siegman's own American Jewish Congress, which helped create that demographic problem In the first place.

The AJ Congress's *"sha-shtil"* attitude during the Holocaust left millions of Jews trapped in Hitler's Europe. If there are more Arabs than Jews in those territories today, it's because millions of Jews who would have escaped to Israel and helped populate Judea and Samaria were, instead, murdered by the Nazis. At the same time, the AJ Congress and other Jewish organizations refused to lift a finger. **They** helped create the demographic problem; then **they** use the demographic problem as a stick with which to **beat Israel over the head.**

Of course, even if Israel is ever foolish enough to give up Judea and Samaria, the "demographic" problem will be simply be replaced by a much more dangerous "geographic" problem. Stripped of those land, Israel will have no eastern buffer zone to protect it from attack by a PLO state. How could Arafat possibly resist the temptation of sending tank units to slice Israel in half at its midsection, where it would be just nine miles wide?

February 25, 1993

Deception as Strategy

The initialing of the Peres-Arafat accord on February 9 was announced with great fanfare. It was the lead story on the evening news, the front-page headers in newspapers around the world. It was hailed as the beginning of peace in our time. Those who read the fine print, however, discovered that Peres and Arafat had only agreed on some issues, while other points remained to be settled. And the very next day, Prime Minister Rabin and his aides were saying that it would be weeks, perhaps longer, before all of the differences were actually resolved. Strangest of all, this sequence of events, with grand announcements followed by more conservative follow-up assessments, has happened again and again during the past year – and not by chance.

From the very start, Rabin and his asides knew that the concessions they intended to make to the PLO and Syria were too radical for the Israeli public to swallow. After all, Rabin ran on a platform that promised no negotiations with the PLO, no creation of a PLO state, and no surrender of the Golan Heights. As he began the process of abandoning those pledges, Rabin knew he would have to break the news to the public slowly, in small doses, lest he faces a full-scale citizens' rebellion.

Thus, during the months before he recognizes the PLO, Rabin permitted various Labor Party Knesset Members to meet openly with PLO officials in Europe, and even at PLO headquarters in Tunis. Each time, Rabin would deny that he had approved the meetings – yet he never took any action to punish those who had done so. Then, rumors began circulating that government ministers, including Foreign Minister Peres, had a net with PLO officials. Again, Rabin denied knowing or approving the contacts (which, of course, were illegal). Next, Rabin permitted his Labor Party to submit a bill abolishing the law that prohibited meeting with PLO terrorists. He did not vote for the bill, but he made sure that enough Labor MKs voted in favor, and the bill passed. All the while, Rabin, with the aid of the Israeli media, continued to cultivate the image of himself as a reliable "hawk" on security issues, in contrast to the more "dovish" elements of his party.

Rabin's negotiating strategy with the PLO has followed the same pattern. Each time Israel makes a concession, it is Peres who plays the "dove," announcing the concessions and taking the political heat. At the same time, Rabin's aides tell reporters that Rabin himself is not necessarily happy about the concession. Thus, the Israeli public is deluded into believing that Rabin is still a "hawk" and can be trusted not to make too many concessions.

Each time the Rabin government is close to agreeing to the final terms for PLO self-rule, it plays the same game: the announcement is made, then Rabin expresses reservations. A few days or weeks later, another announcement, then another expression of concern from the prime minister. The Israeli public thus becomes conditioned to the inevitability of an agreement in which Israel makes numerous concessions, while at the same time being lulled into thinking that Rabin is cautious and careful when all the while, Rubin is merely pursuing a carefully-calculated strategy of deceptive public relations.

By the time the final agreement is actually announced, the public's resistance and suspicion have been worn down. The repeated media announcements and fanfare have created an aura of expectation and hopefulness. Desperate for peace, and desperately wanting to believe that Rabin would not surrender vital Israeli security interests, the public has been conditioned for surrender. When the surrender comes, the public puts up little or no opposition.

Those who are familiar with Jewish history will immediately recognize the frightening parallels to other times when enemies of the Jews used strategies of deception so that the Jews would be gradually conditioned to worsen circumstances until they were too weak, confused, and divided to fight back when the final catastrophe came.

Don't kid yourself. Yitzhak Rabin is no fool. He knows exactly what he's doing. The tragedy is that so many Jews seem to have no idea what he's doing.

March 5, 1993

Is U.S. 'Shielding' Israel Or the Other Way Around?

Israeli Prime Minister Yitzhak Rabin rationalized his shocking reversal on the Hamas deportations by listing the supposed "benefits" that Israel would receive from the United States in exchange for permitting the return of hundreds of terrorists. He named two such "benefits." First, that the Clinton Administration will henceforth "shield" Israel from United Nations sanctions and international criticism, which, ironically, came about because the U.S. voted in favor of the UN Security Council resolution "strongly condemning" Israel. Second, the U.S. will become more actively involved in the Arab-Israeli negotiations, which, far from being good for Israel, will inevitably result in more U.S. pressure on Israel for one-sided concessions.

The problem, however, is that it is the exact opposite of historical reality. Throughout this century, it has been Israel and world Jewry. They have shielded the U.S., Britain, and the rest of the democratic world, by sacrificing Jewish interests for the sake of Western political convenience.

How was this pattern established? It began when England issued the Balfour Declaration, in 1917, promising to create a Jewish national home in the Land of Israel but world Jewry was guided by weak leaders who insisted that the Diaspora was safe, and who were unable or unwilling to recognize the great opportunity at hand to rebuild the Jewish nation in the Jewish homeland. Only a tiny minority of Jews contributed money and manpower to the Zionist movement. From that point on, the pattern was set: Jewish weakness and/or indifference, exploited for political advantage by the British, until 1948, and continued by the U.S. thereafter.

Thus, when the English promised thrones to two Arab rivals in 1922 and then found that they had only one throne to award Syria, it was the Jews who were made to pay the price. Two-thirds of the Jewish National Home was lapped off the Palestine Mandate, renamed Transjordan, and handed over to Arab rule. The Jew refrained from protesting; they wanted to be helpful to the

192

British, so they shielded London from Arab wrath by allowing their homeland to be dissected.

During the Holocaust, the Jews again tried to be "cooperative." Both the American Jewish leadership and the Labor Zionist-dominated leadership in the Land of Israel promised not to fight the British so long as the British were at war with Germany. When Jewish refugees escaping from Hitler tried to reach the Holy Land, and the British stopped them, world Jewry maintained its silence. England wanted to have the Arabs on its side during the war, and the only way to do that was to sacrifice the Jews by closing the doors to Palestine. So, once again, it was the Jews who shielded the British from Arab hostility.

Israel's victory over the Soviet-backed Arab states in the 1967 war shielded the U.S. and the rest of the Western Free World from the strategic danger that would have arisen if the Kremlin's Arab allies ruled the entire Mideast. But the Nixon administration responded by pressuring Israel to surrender the territorial buffer zones that it had just captured.

Even while pressuring Israel, the Nixon Administration had no qualms about asking Israel for favors. In 1970, the U.S. asked Israel to shield Jordan from the threat of a Syrian invasion. Israel complied; it sent troops to its border with Syria as a warning, and Syria backed off.

Later that same year, the U.S. needed Israel's help again. Egypt was badly losing its War of Attrition with Israel and begged the U.S. to arrange a ceasefire. Nixon wanted to improve American-Egyptian relations and impress the Arab world in general, to ensure U.S. access to Arab oil. Israel was expected to pay the price. The U.S. compelled the Israelis to accept a ceasefire that was supposed to limit the movement of missiles on both sides, but which the U.S. had no intention of enforcing. Sure enough, on midnight of August 1, when the ceasefire went into effect, Egypt immediately violated it by moving missiles into the forbidden zone, and Israel. The U.S. scored points with the Arabs, while Israel's defense against Egyptian SAM missiles in the Yom Kippur War to come were crippled.

On the eve of the 1973 Yom Kippur War, it was Henry Kissinger who demanded that Israel shield America's friendly relations with the Arabs. Israel was warned not to launch a pre-emptive strike; because that might result in an Arab oil embargo against America. The Israelis foolishly heeded that warning, absorbed the first blow, and countless deaths, and there was an oil embargo anyway. During the disengagement negotiations that followed the war, Kissinger repeatedly demanded that Israel farther "shield" America's relationship With the Arabs by making concessions, releasing the Egyptian Third Army that they had trapped; giving up Kuneitra in the Golan Heights, and withdrawing from the Suez Canal area and, later, in 1975, surrendering one-third of the Sinai, including vital mountain passes and oil fields.

Naive Israelis and Diaspora Jewish leaders called all of this "peace" and rejoiced at the thought that the U.S. was "shielding" Israel by stationing handfuls of American observers in the Sinai and promising Israel access to Iranian oil. Four years later, the Shah of Iran was overthrown, and the Iranian oil that Kissinger had promised was no longer available, but by then, there was a new president in Washington who could disclaim all responsibility for Kissinger's promises.

At Camp David in 1978, Jimmy Carter pressed Israel to shield Egyptian-American relations (and U.S. access to Arab oil) by handing over the entire Sinai, against the advice of Israel's military experts.

The Israelis thought that such sweeping concessions would put an end to U.S. pressure. But just four years later, when the Israeli army had the PLO surrounded in Beirut, one phone call from Saudi Arabia to President Reagan produced a fresh barrage of U.S. pressure that forced Israel to shield Arafat as he sailed triumphantly from Beirut to the accompaniment of a 21- gun salute.

And who can forget how Israel shielded the U.S. during the Gulf War? To shield Bush's phony alliance with the Arabs, Israel was told to absorb Iraqi missile strikes. It meekly complied. The reward? New U.S. pressure for concessions. American hints that the Saudis would soon drop the Arab boycott turned out to be nonsense. Private U.S. assurances that the loan guarantees would be forthcoming after the war likewise turned out to be hollow promises. Again, Israel shielded the U.S., and again Israel's reward was more suffering.

Today Prime Minister Rabin speaks of the U.S. "shielding" Israel. Once again, Israel is being asked to take life-and-death risks in exchange for fleeting promises. And it can expect, once again, that those promises will not be fulfilled. Every time that Israel has made gestures or concessions, its enemies have simply demanded even more gestures and concessions. Every time that Israel's friends have promised to "shield" it, Israel has ended up doing the "shielding." Repeatedly, Israel has been used as a sacrificial lamb to preserve the narrow interests of western political expediency. There can be little doubt that today's Hamas controversy is headed for a similar conclusion unless Israel, and its Diaspora supporters, finally wake up and recognize the catastrophe that is waiting just around the corner.

March 12, 1993

Anti-Israel Anchorman Targets Jewish Audiences

Tom Brokaw, the anchorman of the NBC Nightly News, was invited to speak at a prominent Conservative synagogue in Miami the evening after Purim and is likely to appear before other Jewish audiences around the country soon. He will be hoping against hope that his Jewish listeners have short memories. Because if they don't, he should be in for some tough questions.

Brokaw has never been friendly to Israel. But it was his key role in NBC's grossly distorted coverage of the 1982 Lebanon war that is especially hard to forget. Unabashedly departing from his role as anchorman, Brokaw let loose with two sarcastic attacks (on June 23 and June 24) on Israeli "censorship" of some film footage from the battlefront. That's right the same Brokaw who was scarcely bothered when the British blocked media coverage of the Falklands War, or when the U.S. interfered with coverage of the Grenada invasion. But when it came to Israel trying to protect itself against PLO exploitation of the media, Brokaw insisted that the pictures Israel was blocking "had nothing to do with Israeli national security," and then blasted Israel's prime minister for complaining about "the corrupt media" (Brokaw's phrase, put into Begin's mouth).

The language Brokaw employed in his reading of the news was thickly coated in pro-Arab bias. The Syrian occupation forces coated in Lebanon were a "peacekeeping army," Brokaw asserted, while the Israeli troops striking back at terrorist bases were part of a "war machine" (June 16). Terms like "Israel's aggressiveness" were a regular part of Brokaw's script (for example, on August 12).

Naturally, Brokaw refused ever to consider that the PLO might be a terrorist group, despite its decades of massacring defenseless Israeli civilians, and despite the mountains of evidence uncovered by the Israelis when they captured PLO bunkers in Lebanon. Thus, when Israel offered the media a chance to meet some of the terrorists from all parts of the globe that were being

196

trained by the PLO, Brokaw referred to the Israelis as offering "what **they** called evidence of an international terrorist ring" (June 30). And when he interviewed Israel's foreign minister on August 6, Brokaw referred "the PLO, or the terrorists, as **you** call them."

But Brokaw's sarcastic tongue was nowhere in evidence on July 26, when he interviewed the veteran Israel-bashing congressman Pete McCloskey. As far as Brokaw was concerned, it was major news that McCloskey had gone to Beirut to meet Yasser Arafat; of course, McCloskey's claim that Arafat had recognized Israel was a total lie, but that didn't stop Brokaw from giving him red-carpet treatment. And, just to dig the knife a bit deeper into Israel's back, Brokaw concluded by noting that the "debate" over Arafat's non-statement (a debate that existed only in McCloskey's and Brokaw's mind) "didn't keep Israel from pounding West Beirut for the fifth straight day."

While Israel was fighting a desperate war of self-defense against PLO terrorists in Lebanon, Tom Brokaw and NBC-TV were waging a mean-spirited television war against Israel in America's living rooms. In recent weeks, two other victims of NBC-TV's dishonest journalism have been the recipients of public apologies by the NBC top brass. Israel and world Jewry, however, are still waiting for Brokaw's apology.

March 19, 1993

Arab Terror in The U.S.: How It Could Have Been Prevented

With each passing day, evidence mounts that the bombing of the World Trade Center was not the work of some lone fanatic, but rather was carried out by a Moslem fundamentalist terror network that was responsible for a variety of crimes, including- the murder of Rabbi Meir Kahane. The question that needs to be answered is why the U.S. authorities made no effort to investigate these Islamic extremists before they began their murder-and-bombing spree.

The Federal Bureau of Investigation has known for years about the activities of various Arab extremist groups in the United States. A 1990 Congressional Report about FBI activities mentioned a case in which the FBI was monitoring an American Moslem extremist. Group that met in a certain mosque and was involved in sending money to Arab militants in Israel. According to the report, the investigation ended because the group "moved to another mosque." Does that sound like a logical reason to stop monitoring a potentially dangerous group? Or could it be that the FBI has only minimal interest in pursuing Arab terrorists because the White House is afraid that a crackdown on Arab terrorists in America would anger the Arab oil suppliers to whom the U.S. has become addicted?

Consider the handing of the Kahane murder. The man arrested for the killing, El-Sayyid Nosair, was a Moslem fundamentalist whose spiritual leader – Sheik Omar Abdel Rahman was previously indicted in Egypt for his role in violence there. In Nosair's apartment, the police found weapons, large amounts of ammunition, and a list of other Jewish leaders that he was planning to attack. A thorough investigation of Nosair's associates would have turned up the various extremists now under arrest or under suspicion for bombing the World Trade Center. But the authorities didn't want to pursue Nosair's connections; they were afraid that a full investigation might offend the Arab lobby. A low-level official in the District Attorney's office was assigned to handle the case; Nosair's hit list was ignored; and during the trial itself, the prosecution itself refused ever to say that Nosair was motivated by Arab or Moslem nationalism

198

– they were afraid that Arabs might be offended if they stressed the "Arab angle." As a result, Nosair was acquitted of the most serious charges against him, and Nosair's buddies were free to start plotting their attack on the World Trade Center.

But now, even before the smoke has cleared from the World Trade Center bombing, the U.S. authorities are rushing to make sure that the Arab world is not offended by the latest developments. President Clinton went out of his way to declare that "nobody should draw any broad conclusions" about Arab and Moslem terrorist activity; Clinton and his secretary of state are still pressuring Israel to take back the 400 expelled leaders of the Hamas terror group, to which the World Trade Center bombers are ideologically allied. There is still no sign from the U.S. government that it intends to prosecute El-Sayyid Nosair for violating Rabbi Kahane's civil rights – because, in such a trial, the prosecutions would have to explain Nosair's religious and nationalistic motives, and that might mean "offending" some Arab groups.

In the Rodney King case, the acquittal of the four police officers accused of beating King were immediately put on trial on a civil rights violation charge, because of demands by the African-American community. In the Rabbi Kahane case, however, most Jewish leaders have refused to demand that Nosair be re-tried – because sad to say, some of them were privately glad that Kahane is no longer around to get in their hair. **Israel Horizons**, Journal of the leftist "Americans for Progressive Israel" (*Hashomer Hatzair*), actually published an editorial back in 1984 (in the November/December issue), which expressed the hope that "someone would put a bullet into Mr. Kahane and be done with him." Most average Jews regard such sentiment as revolting and support a re-trial for Nosair, and if they would make themselves heard (in telegrams to the White House), something might get done.

So Israel is pressured to take in Moslem killers, Kahane's Moslem assassin will soon go free, and the Moslem terrorist network was left virtually untouched, all to appease the Arabs.

From the Jewish point of view, this is all just part of the same old story; **Israel and the Jews are made to pay the price so that the U.S. can keep the Arabs happy**. Israel was pressured not to strike first on the eve of Yom Kippur, in 1978, because Kissinger wanted to appease the Arabs. Israel was pressured to let Yasir Arafat escape from Beirut, in 1982, because the Saudis leaned on the Reagan Administration to rescue the PLO chief. Israel was pressured not to retaliate against Iraqi Scud missile attacks, in 1991, because the Bush Administration wanted to preserve its phony "alliance" with the Arabs.

And despite Israel's painful sacrifices, all U.S. has to show for its foolish appeasement policy is the graves of five Americans who happened to be in the World Trade Center that tragic day. It was a tragedy that could have been prevented, and many such future tragedies could be pre-empted – if America would wake up and realize that there can be no compromise with Islamic terror. There can be only victory or defeat, and right now, America is on its way to a bitter, bloody defeat.

April 2, 1993

NBC And General Motors: A Lesson for The Jews

The weekly television program "Dateline NBC" several weeks ago aired an investigative report claiming that certain trucks produced by General Motors are, because of their faulty design, likely to explode upon impact with other vehicles. Then, an investigation by GM found that a filmed demonstration of such an explosion was, in fact, rigged by the NBC staff, prompting GM to file a lawsuit against NBC for having broadcast the "Dateline NBC" report.

At first, NBC refused to acknowledge that it had done anything wrong. GM promptly announced that, in addition to the lawsuit, it would shift some of its ads on NBC from the high-priced nightly news to other NBC shows, and rumors began circulating that local GM dealers might withdraw their ads from local NBC affiliates. Twenty-four hours later, NBC capitulated, admitted their fraudulent behavior, and issued a public apology.

What does all of this have to do with the Jews and Israel?

Plenty.

For many years now, NBC Television has been engaged in a virtual org of Israel-bashing. What NBC did to General Motors is nothing compared to what it has done to Israel. When the Lebanon War began in June 1982, it was NBC that circulated the monstrous he that 600,000 Arabs had been made homeless, and 10,000 killed during the initial Israeli incursion (the actual numbers were a few thousand homeless and a few hundred dead). Another NBC monstrosity from that period was its broadcast of footage showing Yasser Arafat kissing babies in besieged Beirut.

NBC's coverage of the Arab *intifada* has been equally horrendous. Part of the problem with NBC's version of the "intifada" has been the egregious pro-Arab bias of Martin Fletcher and other NBC news correspondents in the Middle East: They call PLO killers "guerrillas" rather than "terrorists" because they really perceive the PLO's war against Israel as a heroic struggle by guerrillas against evil occupiers.

Another part of the problem with NBC's version of the intifada has been the fact that NBC's Israel bureau relies in part on biased local sources according to the Israeli newspaper **Yediot Ahronot** (May 5, 1989}, NBC supplies video cameras to local Palestinian Arabs to supply footage of events in territories, and it's not hard to imagine what kind of film they come up with.

But the major problem with NBC's version of the intifada, in particular, and the Arab-Israeli conflict, in general, is that its top executives harbor an anti-Israel bias that has its roots in a murky swamp that includes both "politically correct" sympathy for the "underdog" Palestinian Arabs and the weighty influence of Arab oil money. Arab petrodollars are invested in such a wide array of American industries that, for the sake of advertising dollars alone, a network like NBC has all too much reason to slant the news against Israel.

Yet, it is also a fact that the issue of ads influencing media coverage can cut both ways. If the Arabs can persuade NBC to lie about the Middle East, **why can't Jews persuade NBC to tell the truth about the Middle East?** It's no secret that many of the businesses that advertise on NBC and CBS and ABC and in the **New York Times** and the **Washington Post** – are Jewish-owned. If those Jewish owners displayed an ounce of concern for Israel's survival – if they would put aside their financial interests for just a moment and show some conscience about the **media's abuse of the Jewish State,** there would be a veritable revolution in media coverage of the Middle East.

And don't underestimate the impact of that media coverage. Newspaper and television portrayals of the Arab-Israeli conflict go a long way towards shaping public opinion, which in turn affects government policy. Sometimes, media coverage affects the White House directly. In early 1988, for example, President Reagan a personal commitment.

Pogrebin is also a member of the National Advisory Board of the pro-PLO New Jewish Agenda. to get an idea of Agenda's attitude towards Israel, consider the conclusion of a 1989 study of Agenda that was undertaken by the

American Jewish Committee: "Although NJA policies and platforms speak of a commitment 'to the existence of Israel,' there is a paucity of literature and activities that would reflect such commitment." Like Pogrebin, New Jewish Agenda often uses Jewish historical events or religious to support the Arab cause.

Agenda leaders have held Passover *seders* in which the *Haggadah* included writings by PLO officials; lit Holocaust memorial candles for the Palestinian Arabs outside the Israeli Consulate in Philadelphia; conducted *Tisha B'Av* services in which the destruction of the Jewish Temples is compared to Israeli 'brutality;' and issued a *Tu B'Shevat* (New Year of the Trees) leaflet which called the Jewish National Fund's afforestation effort in Israel "an instrument of war" against the Arabs. This is the organization in whose leadership Letty Pogrebin continues to take part, even as she serves as co-chair of Americans For Peace Now.

Letty Pogrebin, unlike many of her Peace Now colleagues, has not tried to hide her extremist opinions or associations. Pogrebin's openness contrasts with the behavior of her colleague Gail Pressberg, the president of Americans For Peace Now. He claims that the pro-PLO groups of which she was a leader for 14 years were not really pro-PLO (even though both the Anti-Defamation League and AIPAC have asserted that they were). But the activities and associations of both Pogrebin and Pressberg pose the same dilemma for the Conference of Presidents. Now that the member-organizations of Conference know that the two top leaders of Americans For Peace Now are veteran extremists who have consistently shown more sympathy for the PLO's cause than for Israel's, how can such a group be admitted to their Palestinian Arab militants with sophisticated video cameras to get the "right" kind of footage about Israel and the Arabs? So just as GM went all out to defend itself, filing a lawsuit and threatening to shift its advertising, the Jewish community can and should do likewise to defend the Jewish State.

In Brownsburg, Indiana, where that phony NBC truck-crash was filmed, a fireman who had witnessed the staged crash asked a reporter from the **Wall Street Journal:** "When was the last time you saw a major network saying they have screwed up to that extent?" The answer is self-evident. But I would ask: when was the last time that any leader of major American Jewish organization dared to use GM-style tactics to combat Israel-bashers like NBC? That answer, too, is sadly self-evident.

April 9, 1993

Only the U.S. Can Wipe Out Arab Terror

Like the contagious disease that it is, Arab terrorism has spread from its birthplace in the Middle East to the very heart of the West, New York City. Arab terrorists have claimed many American lives before – tourists, diplomats, bystanders in airport terminals, but when they struck at the World Trade Center, they shattered the illusion that the State Department has always fostered the idea that Arab terrorism was "an Israeli problem." As investigators continue to dig through the charred rubble of the World Trade Center parking garage, one thing has become painfully clear: Arab terrorism has become very much an American problem, too.

It has become an American problem in large measure because successive U.S. administrations have deliberately avoided undertaking any serious counter-terror effort. Worse, they have actually encouraged the spread of Arab terrorism by giving aid and comfort to the Arab dictatorships that sponsor terrorists. Iraq, for example, despite its role in sponsoring international terrorist groups received billions of dollars worth of military and economic assistance from the Bush Administration, much of it hidden under the guise of "agricultural equipment" Syria, which is the single most important sponsor of terror in the world, was eagerly courted by the Bush Administration, and the Clinton Administration is doing likewise. James Baker was too busy trying to improve American-Syrian relations to ask any questions about the more than one dozen terrorist groups headquartered in Damascus or Syrian-controlled Lebanon. Warren Christopher, on his recent visit to Syria, likewise ignored the terrorist issue.

While turning a blind eye to Iraqi and Syrian sponsorship of terrorism, the U.S. actively sought to prevent Israel from combatting the terrorists. When Israel struck at PLO bases in south Lebanon in 1978, President Carter threatened to cut off U.S. arms shipments unless the Israelis pulled back. When the Israelis were on the verge of destroying the PLO in Beirut in 1982, the Reagan Administration pressured Prime Minister Begin to withdraw.

205

Whenever Israeli soldiers shoot back at Arab attackers, the State Department complains about the Israelis "overreacting." Whenever Israel tries to deport a few terrorists, U.S. Officials accuse Israel of violating international law. And when the Israelis warned the U.S. a few months ago that there was a dangerous network of Moslem fundamentalist terrorists in the U.S., American officials told **The New York Times** that they were not convinced that the Israeli information was accurate. No doubt, the widows and orphans of the World Trade Center victims lie awake at night, wondering why Washington officialdom was so skeptical and cynical about something so desperately important.

Israelis, who have been made into widows or orphans by Arab terrorism, have spent time wondering why the U.S. has, for so many years, neglected to use its economic might to crush Arab terrorism. It could have done so years ago. It could still do it today. All that is required is an all-out economic quarantining of Arab regimes that sponsor terrorism. The U.S. would take the lead, and if it insisted, then its allies, the other major Western economic powers, would have no choice but to follow suit. All economic relations with the terror-sponsors would be severed. Their offices in the West would be shut down. Their accounts in Western banks would be seized. Bereft of Western imports, deprived of Western cash for their goods, lacking any alternative superpower to whom they could turn (now that the Soviet Union no longer exists), the Arab totalitarians would crumble in no time.

At that point, the U.S. could step in and put a permanent end to Arab terrorism by doing to Syria, Iraq, and the others exactly as MacArthur did to Japan after World War Two: overhaul their political systems, their economies, and their entire way of life, imposing democracy and forcibly ending the rampaging war of Islamic fundamentalism against the rest of the world. That's the only way to prevent future World Trade Center-style atrocities. Arab extremism and violence have to be pulled out by the roots, or they will grow back and strike again.

It is American Jewry's task to bring this unpopular but vital message to the U.S. public. American Jews, unlike most other Americans, are keenly aware of the dangers of Arab terrorism, because they closely follow events in

Israel and because all too many of them have friends or relatives who have been harmed by Arab terrorists. American Jews are therefore uniquely qualified to help the American public realize that the germs of Arab totalitarianism and terrorism can only be defeated by the medicine of American economic might and American political courage. The American people must be made to understand that there simply is no other way.

May 21, 1993

Squeezing Israel Into A Socialist New World Order

At the heart of the Israeli Labor government's foreign policy lies a fundamental inconsistency which boils down to this: if the Arabs really want peace, why not just give them everything?

If the Palestinian Arabs have really become "moderate," as the Laborites claim, why not just hand them Judea, Samaria, and Gaza on a silver platter? If the Syrians have really "changed," as Shimon Peres keeps insisting, why not give them the entire Golan Heights right now? If the Arabs can really be trusted, why should Israel need "security guarantees" from the United States, as advocates of Israeli retreat are recommending?

Despite all the talk about Arab "moderation" that one hears from Prime Minister Rabin and other Labor Party leaders, the fact is that they are not proposing to give the Arabs everything they want.

They may say that the Palestinian Arabs are now "moderate," but at the same time, Rabin says he is opposed to Palestinian statehood, opposed to autonomy turning into independence – because he doesn't trust them to enjoy their independence peacefully. They may say that the Syrians now "want peace," but Rabin says he will not give them the entire Golan Heights, and even the parts he would give up would have to be demilitarized because, ultimately, he doesn't trust Hafez Assad. Rabin and his colleagues may say that "the Arabs are now "moderate," but they want (U.S. "security guarantees" because they don't really believe that the Arabs can be trusted to adhere to peace treaties, and the (the U.S. might, therefore, have to intervene at some point in the future.

Thus, the reality of what concessions Rabin is willing to make clashes directly with his claim that the Arabs are "moderate." His refusal to give into all Arab demands proves that, deep down, he doesn't really believe they are moderate and trustworthy at all.

Nonetheless, Rabin seems determined to stake Israel's future on the illogical gamble that the Arabs might somehow turn out to be moderate. And he wants to sell these high-stakes gamble to the Israeli public with the promise of U.S. "guarantees" that won't be worth any more than the "guarantees" that the (U.S. made to South Vietnam or Taiwan.

What is it that drives Rabin and his Labor Party cronies to risk the safety of their country? What motivates their irresponsible behavior? How can they propose concessions to enemies that they don't really trust? How can they speak of relying on (U.S. guarantees that they know are useless?

The answer may be found in the socialist ideology that has shaped and guided Labor Zionism since its inception. "in the pre-state years, much of the [Labor Zionist] political elite in the *yishuv* regarded the Soviet Union, despite certain obvious failings, as a society to be emulated." notes John Goldberg, international secretary of Young Mapam (the farthest-left wing of Labor Zionism). "This affinity permeated virtually every field of life. Economically, the Histadrut, the major economic expression of the Israeli Labor movement, was an ideological and structural outgrowth of the Marxist notion that political power springs from economic hegemony. Culturally, the new literature, poetry, and song were strongly influenced, if not virtual translations of, Russian and Soviet culture And, not least, the collective enterprises which characterized the *yishuv kibbutz, moshav,* and cooperatives – were, of course, unique interpretations of a socialist society in the making" (**Jerusalem Post,** Nov 1985).

Anita Shapira, the noted Zionist historian, has made the same point (in **Studies in Zionism**, spring 1981): "Beneath the [Labor] movement's democratic surface flowed a current which sprang from the revolutionary trends in Russia... This was evidenced by admiration for the state-building in the Soviet Union, on the one hand, and condonation of the terror there, on the other, by people like [David] Ben-Gurion and [Yitzhak] Tabenkin among the front-rank leaders of Mapal, the largest labor party." Into this political and cultural milieu, Yitzhak Rabin and his fellow Labor Party leaders were born.

They imbibed Marxist ideology with their mother's milk. Ben-Gurion and Tabernkin were their heroes. A socialist "one-world" was their dream.

There is no reason to think that Yitzhak Rabin has changed. He has never repudiated the socialist ideology that guided him throughout his life. The political party he leads still unfurls the red flag on May 1, the international worker's holiday which Labor Zionists still regard as their holiday, too. Barring evidence to the contrary, one must assume that in his heart of hearts, the ultimate dream to which Yitzhak Rabin clings is that of social universalism. In such a future world, ethnic differences will disappear. National barriers will be broken down. Religions, which socialists regard as the "opiate of the masses," will be eliminated, Judaism included —which is something that Rabin and his fellow hardline secularists would not lose many sleepovers.

For Israel to fit into Labor Zionism's social dream, it must abandon its nationalistic, "chauvinistic" ways. Territorial claims rooted in historical and religious rights must be abandoned. The Jewish identity of the state must be phased out. In its foreign policy, Israel must succumb to the will of the international community, appease the demands of the rest of the world so that it can be accepted into the un-Jewish "new world order" that lies just around the corner. The policies of Yitzhak Rabin's government seem to be paving the way for precisely this eventuality. In foreign affairs, Rabin responds to a very complaint by the Arabs or the State Department with a host of new concessions. In domestic affairs, his Absorption Minister, Yair Tzaban (a former Communist Party activist), and the anti-religious zealot Shulamit Aloni are implementing ultra-secularist policies that are stripping Israel of its Jewishness. It seems, tragically, that Yitzhak Rabin is well on his way to implementing the un-Jewish dreams of his Marxist adolescence.

June 4, 1993

Peace Now, Leader Defends Lying About the Holocaust

Two recently-published books (one by Prof. Deborah Lipstadt, the other by an official of the American Jewish Committee) describe the activities of Holocaust-deniers, the crackpots who claim that the murder of six million Jews either did not take place or is a vast exaggeration. However, it may soon be necessary for a third book to be written this one to expose those Jewish radicals who are prepared to distort the Holocaust to further their narrow political agendas.

Case in point: Letty Cottin Pogrebin, leader of Americans for Peace Now and fighter for assorted leftwing causes, who is now claiming that the lies about "Black liberators of the Nazi death camps" are justified if they facilitate "Black—Jewish harmony."

The controversy began with the recent release of the PBS documentary "Liberators," which describes the experiences of the all-black 761st Battalion of the (U.S. Army, which fought in World War II. They fought valiantly, and they deserve to be honored. But the problem with the film is that the filmmakers had a political agenda unrelated to historical facts. They wanted to show that Black-Jewish relations have not just been a one-way street, with Jews financing the NAACP and joining civil rights marches. They wanted to show that Blacks "rescued" Jews from the Holocaust. So the film makes it appear that the 761st "liberated" the death camps of Buchenwald and Dachau.

Jesse Jackson and Al Sharpton loved that. It fit so neatly into their view that Jews "owe" something to Blacks. They arranged for the film to be shown all over the country, with Jackson appearing at the showings to milk them for all they were worth. It was a political goldmine.

Then the lie began to unravel. The Black soldiers who are shown in the film "returning" to Dachau and Buchenwald 50 years later told reporters that, in fact, their "return" was their first visit. Historians confirmed that the 761st was nowhere near Dachau or Buchenwald when they were captured by the

Allied armies. A different Black unit was involved in overrunning an Austrian concentration camp (not a death camp) called Gunskirchen, but that was hardly a "rescue" mission. They were simply fulfilling their orders in driving the German army out of Austria, and in the process came across Gunskirchen by chance.

When confronted by the truth, the co-producer of "Liberators," Ms. Nina Rosenblum, insisted that she had done nothing wrong and denounced her critics as "racists."

Enter Letty Cottin Pogrebin, leader of Americans for Peace Now and crusader for Black rights. Writing in the May-June issue of the radical journal **Tikkun**, Pogrebin contends that the lies "Liberators" are less important than the political goals it might accomplish goals that she shares with the Jesse Jackson crowd.

Yes, the filmmakers were "wrong," Pogrebin concedes, but the main problem is that their tactic was "stupid" because it has distracted public attention from "what I believe was the film's greatest potential: to advance the radical notion of reciprocity in the historical relationship between Blacks and Jews by showing Blacks in the 'helping' role that has most typically been played by Jews."

The facts of the Holocaust are not as important to Pogrebin as the chance to promote her agendas of Jewish guilt. "Hope crossed out by the fact-checkers," she moans, obviously wishing that those "fact-checkers" (a better name would be "truth-tellers") would just mind their business so that she and the Rev. Jackson can proceed without interference. For Pogrebin, all that counts is that the film is anchored in "a premise that I applaud ... the Jews in the film were vulnerable men who had to be rescued by Black angels."

There was no rescue, and there were no angels, there were just soldiers doing their duty and coming across the Jews completely by accident. But Pogrebin doesn't care about that. She is perfectly prepared to let the Holocaust be distorted, twisted, revised – so long as it suits her narrow political goals. "Truth must be defended," Pogrebin declares, "but so must the liberal vision of Black advancement and the struggle for Black-Jewish harmony." For Pogrebin, it is that "liberal vision," which takes precedence over the truth about the Holocaust. Is there really any difference between an extremist who revises the Holocaust to promote anti-Semitism, and an extremist who revises the Holocaust to promote a "liberal vision?"

June 25, 1993

A 'Moderate' Arab Cheers Terrorism

The problem with Arab merchants staging strikes in the Old City of Jerusalem is that "when you have a strike, the streets are empty, and all that does is make life easier for Israeli soldiers on patrol." That's what Mr. Ziad Abu Zayyad told the **New York Times** on June 4.

It's not at all unusual for Arabs in Israel to regard Israeli soldiers as the enemy. Whether they are citizens of Israel or Jordanian citizens living in Judea and Samaria, a substantial number of the Arabs who reside in the Land of Israel see themselves as residents of "occupied Palestine." Israeli soldiers on patrol – in Tel Aviv, in Hebron, or, in the case of Mr. Zayyad, in the Old City of Jerusalem – are the "occupiers" and anything that makes life easier for them is therefore undesirable.

So Ziad Abu Zayyad wants the streets of the Old City to be as crowded as possible, to make it harder for Israeli patrols to do their job. Thus an Arab knifes a Jew in the Old City and then can melt into a nearby crowd; it'll be much harder for the Israelis to catch him. If Arabs stage a rock-throwing attack on Israelis in the area, and soldiers tried to apprehend the rock-throwers, they'll have to fight their way through the crowds – thus giving the attackers time to escape.

What makes Mr. Zayyad's statement significant, however, is that for many years now, he has been touted by Israeli liberals and Western journalists as perhaps the most moderate Palestinian Arab around. In 1986, for example, the **Miami Herald** published a huge feature story portraying Zayyad as "the most ardent Arab advocate of Palestinian-Israeli coexistence," a man who "has been battling for Arab-Israeli understanding since in 1967." As proof of Zayyad's desire to get along with Israelis, the Herald pointed out that he had learned fluent Hebrew (courtesy of a Hebrew University ulpan), speaks to Israeli audiences regularly, and is about to launch the first Hebrew-language Palestinian-Arab newspaper. The newspaper was called "**Gesher**" or "bridge," which the Herald saw as symbolic of Zayyad's desire to build bridges between Arabs and Israelis.

Now then: how does all of this square with Zayaad's remark to the **New York Times** (issue of June What kind of "coexistence," "understanding," and "bridge-building" could Zayyad have in mind if he was to prevent Israeli patrols from capturing Arab terrorists? Aren't "moderate" Arabs opposed to terrorism? Does Zayyad really wants peace with Israel (instead of "Palestine" in place of Israel), why would he be opposed to "making life easier for Israeli soldiers?" Does Zayaad want Arab terrorists to be able to escape after they murder Jews? The answer, clearly, is **yes**, which says plenty about the myth of Arab "moderation" and the reality of Arab extremism.

And there is more. Zayyad happens to be one of the "advisers" who direct the Palestinian Arab delegation to the Arab-Israeli talks. He is thus one of the handfuls of local Arab leaders who have become the official "representatives" of the Palestinian Arabs in the negotiations. The Clinton Administration has insisted that these Arabs are "moderate" to justify negotiating with them. Zayyad's cheerleading for Arab terrorists explodes the myth that he is "moderate," just as recent statements by other leaders of the negotiating remark by Faisal Husseini, leader of the delegation, in the Jordanian newspaper **A Rai** last November 12, that his long-range goal is to "dissolve the Zionist entity in stages.")

Israel should not be negotiating with those who encourage, support, or cheer terrorism any more than Roosevelt should have negotiated with Hitler or Bush should have negotiated with Saddam Hussein. Ziad Abu Zayyad's statement to the **New York Times** necessitates a thorough revamping of Israeli negotiating policy immediately before an Arab terrorist state is forced down Israel's throat through negotiations, in the guise of autonomy.

July 2, 1993

Israel's Security and America's Ever-Changing Mood

"The United States has declared itself ready to provide Israel with guarantees for alternative security on the Golan Heights," Israeli Foreign Minister Shimon Peres boasted to the Knesset Foreign Affairs and Defense Committee on June 8. What Peres did not address, however, is the question of whether or not such U.S. guarantees would be any more reliable than the various guarantees that the U.S. has previously made (to Israel and other countries) and abandoned.

It's no surprise that the Clinton Administration is willing to offer Israel "guarantees" as an incentive to surrender vital strategic territory to the Arabs. Like his predecessors, Clinton will promise Israel anything to convince it to surrender land to Arab dictators. Then, when he campaigns for re-election, Clinton can claim that he brought "peace" to the Middle East.

In exchange, Israel will receive two pieces of paper, one with Hafez Assad's signature, the other with Bill Clinton's. Assad's will, of course, be worthless before the ink has dried. Even now, while negotiating "peace" with Israel, Assad is stocking up on the latest Chinese and North Korean missiles and developing chemical and biological weapons to mount on them. The Syrian government-controlled press and television still speak of the need to "liberate" all of "Palestine." Giving Assad the Golan Heights won't change that; on the contrary, it will merely make his lifelong dream of turning Israel into "southern Syria" all the more possible.

What about Clinton's signature on the U.S. "security guarantees?" What will that be worth? No doubt, the American president will have every good intention when he makes such promises. But good intentions have nothing to do with political realities. Lyndon Johnson had good intentions when he guaranteed South Vietnam's security; that didn't stop Richard Nixon from abandoning Saigon when the war became unpopular. Dwight Eisenhower had good intentions when he guaranteed Taiwan's security; Jimmy Carter had other ideas. Henry Kissinger intended to refrain from recognizing the PLO, as he promised Israel in 1975, but George Shultz did not feel bound by Kissinger's promises.

Presidents leave the office or change their minds. Perceptions of U.S. interests are always shifting. The public's mood may be interventionist one day, isolationist the next.

Indeed, at this very moment, when the Clinton Administration is quietly offering to "guarantee" Israel's security and Shimon Peres is crowing about how Uncle Sam will protect the Jewish State, the American public is growing ever more resentful of foreign entanglements. Issues such as the Iraqi plot to assassinate former President Bush, the Serbian atrocities in Bosnian, and Clinton's whitewashing of Chinese human rights violations "excite almost nobody," Thomas Friedman reported in the **New York Times** on June 13. "Clinton aides barely bother anymore even to prepare the President for foreign policy questions," Friedman noted, "for they know he is much more likely to get asked about the trimmings of Christopher, the barber than the travels of Christopher, the diplomat." The reasons are simple, Friedman notes: "the nation's thin wallet and its ambivalent will."

If that is the case today when Clinton promises Israel every guarantee under the sun, what will happen tomorrow, when Syria is on the warpath, or when Palestinian Arab "freedom fingers" launch terrorist attacks from their "autonomy" zone and Israel turns to the U.S. to "guarantee" its security? Will the U.S. public be willing to risk American lives and invest billions of taxpayer dollars in military expenses – to rescue the Jews? Of course not, which is why Peres's talk U.S. "security guarantees" is not merely foolish but frankly dangerous. The Peres line, which Prime Minister Rabin seems to have approved, threatens to lull the Israeli public (and Diaspora Jewry) into believing the myth that America's worthless guarantees can save Israel from Arab missiles.

What US. Law Says About Surrendering Territory

"There is wisdom among the nations," the Talmud teaches. It means that every once in a while, the Jews can learn a thing or two from their neighbors. The late Zionist leader Ze'ev Jabotinsky used to cite that Talmudic saying to dramatize his argument that Jews should learn how to shoot guns; since everybody outside the *shtetl* knew how to shoot, the Jews had better learn, too, if they wanted to survive.

If one looks at the laws of various countries regarding the subject of surrendering territory, it becomes apparent that the nations do know a thing or two about that, as well.

If an American president wanted to give some part of United States territory to, say, Canada, as part of a peace treaty between Washington and Ottawa, he can't just sign it away. There are several conditions the president has to fulfill first. According to the US. Law, the American government, would have to hold a national referendum; the proposed surrender would have to win a majority of votes in each of the 50 states; even then the law requires that a substantial amount of time would have to pass before the land could be given to the Canadians.

If France wanted to hand over part of its territory, to, say, Spain, a majority of the French citizens living in that territory would have to give their approval. England doesn't even have a law on the books because it hasn't considered the idea of giving up territory since the Middle Ages (the 1300s, to be exact).

These are just a few of the findings of a research study recently undertaken by Israel's prestigious Nativ think tank. The researchers examined the laws in 67 different countries to determine under what conditions they permit the surrender of territory to another sovereign government. Most of them require the holding of a referendum in which a large majority would have to approve the surrender the most common definition of that majority being

66 2/3% Such difficult condition makes it virtually impossible for a government to voluntarily transfer part of its country's land to another sovereign power.

The exception, unfortunately, is Israel.

Only in Israel can a majority of one hand over part of its territory to a different government. (If Israel followed the lead of most other countries, it would require a Knesset majority of 80 votes to surrender territory.) No matter how strategically vital that territory is, no matter how untrustworthy the proposed recipient is, if a majority of the Knesset votes in favor, the land is surrendered. Israel has no constitution; all power resides in the parliament Arab Knesset Members who are more loyal to the PLO than to Israel could provide the crucial votes in a Knesset debate over whether or not to hand over parts of Israel to some Arab dictator.

Now consider all of that in the context of whether or not Israel should give up the Golan Heights. Democracy? Every public opinion poll shows that the overwhelming majority of Israelis don't want to give up any of it. Trustworthiness? Syria already used the Golan as a springboard for three invasions of Israel (in 1948, 1967 and 1973) and regularly shelled Israeli villages during the years in between; Assad now wants Israel to give him the Golan, but he still won't even say that he recognizes Israel's right to exist. Security? The U.S. Joint Chiefs of Staff concluded, in a study after the 1967 war, that Israel needs the entire Golan (and more) to protect itself from Syria. History? The Golan was part of the ancient Jewish kingdoms, Law? Israel extended its law to the Golan in 1981.

As a matter of fact, from a strictly legal point of view, the Golan is probably more a part of the State of Israel than the Israeli cities of Ramle and Lod. Those two cities were not part of the areas allotted to Israel by the 1947 United Nations partition plan, so David Ben-Gurion, as acting prime minister, awarded the title "military governor of Ramle and Led" to the young military commander who captured them, Yitzhak Rabin and Rabin promptly issued a proclamation annexing the cities to Israel. The Golan Heights decision, by contrast, was made by a democratic majority of the Knesset.

Despite all this, Yitzhak Rabin has made it clear that he is preparing in violation of his campaign pledge to "never go down from the Golan Heights" – to surrender all, or virtually all, of the Golan, in exchange for a worthless piece of paper signed by Assad. On the day that he presents his proposal to the Knesset, all Rabin will need is 61 votes (or less, if not all MKs are present), and an integral part of the State of Israel will be torn away and handed to an Arab dictator.

And of course, once the Golan is gone, the Arabs will begin clamoring for the "return" of Ramle and Lod. Why not? If they have a right to the Golan, which a majority of the Knesset voted to keep, they will certainly lay claim to Ramle and Lod, which were kept by the proclamation of one lone military commander.

Ironically, Israel's claim to its land is stronger than that of any of the 67 countries whose laws make it extremely difficult to give up land. Those other countries established their boundaries mostly through unjust conquest. Israel, by contrast, has a birth certificate anchored in the Bible, countless centuries of continual sovereignty, and two thousand years of uninterrupted devotion, in exile to its homeland. Yet one Israel is ready to forsake a vital portion of its homeland on hardly a moment's notice. Does that make sense? Shouldn't some things be sacred – and shouldn't a people's homeland be one of those things?

September 10, 1993

The Short Road from Jericho To Jerusalem

The distance from Jericho to Jerusalem can be measure in miles; it's less than fifteen, but today a more accurate way to measure it is in years or months. As Israel's Labor government prepares to surrender Jericho to the PLO, it is only a matter of years, or more likely, months, until Jerusalem is surrendered as well.

The Arab self-rule plan for Gaza and Jericho, as proposed by the Rabin government, creates the nucleus for a PLO state. But don't take my word for it take Yasser Arafat's. The PLO lender has already declared that he will mow his terrorist headquarters from Tunis to "be "liberated" Jericho. That will put him in easy striking distance, of the other areas to "liberated" beginning with Hebron and Shiloh, continuing with Jerusalem, and concluding finally with Tel Aviv and Haifa. According to the Palestinian Arabs, all of those cities are part of "occupied Palestine." All of them are designed, by the PLO National Covenant, as areas to be "liberated" from the Zionists. Exactly how to liberate them is a matter of strategy, whether bullets or ballots, terrorism or diplomacy, autonomy, or "self-rule." However, they do it, and the result is the same: the birth of "Palestine," and the end of Israel.

Is there any way to stop the slide toward concessions, surrender, and Israeli suicide?

One hopeful sign is the anti-retreat campaign launched by the Habad Lubavitcher movement in Israel. In large newspaper advertisements placed in the Israeli press last week, Habad declared unequivocally that Judaism forbids the surrender of Jewish Land to the PLO. One can only hope and pray that other segments of the Orthodox community will follow suit, and quickly. Swift and determined action are necessary to prevent the Rabin-Peres-Aloni coalition from handing over the heart of the Jewish homeland- to the Arab enemy.

Imagine, for a moment, if the Labor government issued a decree forbidding the lighting of Sabbath candles, or compelling Israeli Jewish to eat pork. The Orthodox world (and most non-Orthodox Jews, as well) would be up in arms. There would be rioting in the streets of Meah Shearim and b'nei B'rak – just as there has been rioting there over past episodes of Sabbath desecration, mistreatment of ancient Jewish cemeteries, and the like. Religious Jews would turn the country upside down. They would shake the Rabin government to its foundation. Shas, the Orthodox party that has been propping up Rabin's coalition, would be forced to withdraw, and no other Orthodox party would dare consider joining. Rabin's majority in the Knesset would dissolve.

If that is how observant Jews would respond to government decrees regarding *Sabbath* candles or pork, how should they respond to a government decree surrendering the Land of Israel to those whose aim is to murder Jews and destroy Israel? If the saving of Jewish lives is the top priority in Jewish law, how should Orthodox Jews respond when an Israeli government endangers Jewish lives by allowing PLO killers to set up a state in central Israel?

Killing Jews is what the PLO is all about. Regardless of whatever "moderate" sounding statements that PLO officials make for the consumption of outsiders, the simple fact remains that the PLO believes that all of Israel is "occupied Palestine," which must be conquered in stages. That's why until last year, it was illegal for Israelis to meet with the PLO. That only changed when Israeli voters were deceived into electing a government filled with individuals who secretly longed to cut a deal with the PLO. Until last year, Shimon Peres would have been arrested for his secret meetings with the PLO (just as Abie Nathan was jailed for doing so), and Yitzhak Rabin would have been arrested as his accomplice, for permitting and approving such meetings.

The fact that Rabin and Peres are ready to make concessions to the PLO is not evidence that the PLO has changed it is merely evidence that Labor and its leftwing allies have been working overtime to condition the Israeli public to the idea that the PLO must eventually be accepted and given a state. Slowly but surely, for Labor's first year in power, they broke down the taboos. First, Arab Knesset members were allowed to meet with the PLO, and no legal action was taken. Then Meretz MKs did it, and Rabin took no action to punish them. Then leftwing Labor MKs like Yael Dayan did it, and again Rabin did nothing. Then the law against meeting with the PLO was formally repealed, with Rabin pretending that he didn't really want it repealed. Of course, he wanted it repealed, and now we know why if it hadn't been repealed, he would be in jail today.

All along, Rabin was playing a clever game. He was using his leftist allies as his stalking bones, making himself look more moderate than they, while at the same time slowly conditioning the Israeli public to the idea that it was not so bad to meet with the PLO. He couldn't reveal his plan to the Israeli public in one fell swoop, for they would have rejected it with disgust. Israelis would be appalled at the risks Rabin is taking with Israel's survival at the wanton manner in which he has violated every one of his 1992 campaign pledges. So Rabin had to move slowly. The PLO had to be sanitized most gradually. Step by step, Rubin altered the status quo even though nothing had changed about the PLO's terrorist nature or tin PLO's goal of destroying Israel. Those who have harmed Jews over the centuries always used a step by step approach, gradually conditioning the Jews so that the deadly dangers they faced would not be obvious until it is too late. That an Israeli leader would do such a thing is as shocking as it is outrageous.

Make no mistake about it: the danger that Israelis face today is deadly. The PLO's new "State of Palestine" in Gaza-Jericho will use every means at in disposal to make the Old City of Jerusalem its capitol. The PLO has declared again and again that Jerusalem must be surrendered. The United States and most of the United Nations support that position. International pressure will intensify. Jewish leftists will join launch a "surrender now" campaign. "Peace is more important than the Western Wall," they will say. Our rabbinical leaders know that the opposite is true. They know that Jewish control of Jerusalem, of the Temple Mount and the Western Wall, is more important than "peace." When Jews throughout the ages prayed, they did not pray for peace with the Arabs; they prayed for Jewish control of Jerusalem. Today, leading rabbis must not merely pray for Jerusalem, but they must speak out, loudly and forcefully, and mobilize the masses for political action to save Jericho and Jerusalem. For if Jericho is lost, Jerusalem will not be far behind.

October 1, 1993

America's Idea of Israeli Security

Israel shouldn't worry about the security risks that come from surrendering territory; President Clinton assured Prime Minister Rabin recently (according to a transcript of their conversion, which appeared in **The New York Times**). America, he said, "will work to minimize those risks."

Now it may not be surprising that Clinton would make such promises. Anxious to be perceived as the president who helped bring peace to the Middle East, Clinton would probably promise the Israelis almost anything in exchange for Israel's surrender to Arab's "peace" terms.

But the fact that Rabin is apparently putting his trust in Clinton's promises suggests that he has an astonishingly short memory. After all, every previous American promise to safeguard Israel's security has turned out to be nothing more than empty words. Sometimes those promises were broken because one president wasn't prepared to fulfill what his predecessor had offered. Sometimes they were broken because America's domestic situation interfered with foreign policy commitments. Sometimes they were broken because of an anti-Israel mood in the White House. But whatever the reason, Israel's bitter experience has always been the same: America's concept of "Israeli security" has never squared with what Israel itself needs to stave off Arab invasions and terrorism.

Will America guarantee Israel's security? In 1948, America's idea of "security for the Jews" was to pressure the Zionist leadership to refrain from establishing the Jewish State. When that didn't work, the U.S. declared an arms embargo against the newborn State of Israel. Harry Truman's famous recognition of Israel didn't do much to stop Arab warplanes from bombing Tel Aviv.

Anybody who remembers the "security guarantee" that America gave Israel after the 1956 war must laugh at the idea that Israel would again trust America's word. When Egypt blockaded the Straits of Tiran and sponsored terrorist attacks against Israel, the Israelis took military action to capture Sinai and the Gaza Strip. The Eisenhower Administration, anxious to appease Nasser, pressured Israel to withdraw and promised in return that it would take action to ensure free Israeli navigation through the Straits. Ben Gurion reluctantly accepted that U.S. promise.

But when Egypt blockaded the Straits again in 1967, Lyndon Johnson was suddenly reluctant to fulfill Elsenhower's Guarantee. While Egypt mobilized troops and prepared to invade, Abba Eban raced from the State Department to the Pentagon to the White House, only to be told that Israel should be "patient" while the U.S. considered what to do. Nasser, of course, wasn't particularly patient. As the guarantee of '56 turned into ashes in the spring of '67, Israel found that it could rely on nobody to protect its security.

Will Bill Clinton guard Israel's security any better than the Nixon-Rogers-Kissinger Administration? In 1970, the U.S. pressured Israel to accept a one-sided ceasefire in the War of Attrition, promising that Egypt would not be able to advance missiles to the Suez Canal. The minute the ceasefire was signed. Egypt moved up the missiles. America's guarantee was nowhere to be found. The State Department was busy "studying" the Israeli complaint. Nixon was busy with the Vietnam War. With the missiles in place at the Suez, Egypt gained a military advantage that it used to deadly effect in 1973, inflicting massive casualties on Israeli troops.

Despite the events of 1970, Kissinger had no compunction about waving American promises in front of Israel on the eve of the Yom Kippur War. Don't strike first, he warned, or you won't get any support from abroad Golda Meir foolishly trusted Kissinger's words. She really expected that since Kissinger gad promised American support in exchange for no preemptive strike, that he would fulfill his promise. Instead, Israel had to wait for ten agonizing days for those U.S. weapons, while the Arabs inflicted blow after blow. That was America's idea of "Israeli security," enough Arab military assaults to soften up the Israelis for future territorial concessions. At the end of the war, America demonstrated its concern for "Israeli security" by forcing Israel to release the Egyptian Third Army, pressuring Israel to make vast territorial concessions in the disengagement talks, and then forcing Israel to surrender key oil fields and mountain passes in the 1975 Sinai Deal.

Three years later, it was Jimmy Carter's turn. He, too, assured the Israelis that he cared deeply about their security. His idea of protecting Israel's security was to force Israel to surrender the entire, strategically vital PLO; and to constantly condemn Israel at the United Nations.

Many Jews think of Ronal Reagan as having been a great friend of Israel, but his idea of Israeli security was rather peculiar, too. He condemned Israel for knocking out the Iraqi nuclear bomb factory; he condemned Israel for annexing the Golan Heights, to protect itself against Syrian invasion; and when Israel struck in self-defense against the PLO in Lebanon in 1982, Reagan's idea of "Israeli security" was to pressure the Israelis to lift their siege of Beirut and let Arafat escape.

When Iraq began firing Scud missiles at Tel Aviv in 1991, James Baker's idea of "Israeli security" was for Israel to sit back and absorb the missile hits. On recent television talk shows and the op-ed pages of the nation's newspapers, Baker was insisting that Israeli surrender to PLO demands will bring a "peace" that will be Israel's best security. Sure it will if the peace and security of the grave are what Israelis desire.

Should Israel now put its vital security requirements in the hands of another American president? Can Israel rely on Bill Clinton to protect it from PLO or Hamas terrorist attacks? Will Clinton come to Israel's rescue if Syria invades? This is a president who repeatedly promised to take military action in Bosnia but has since then repeatedly waffled on the issue. If the Arabs attacked Israel, and Clinton responded with the kind of hemming and hawing that have characterized his Bosnia policy, Israel would be wiped off the map long before the U.S. cavalry arrived – if it ever arrived at all.

Third parties can never safeguard Israeli security, however well-meaning they may be Israel's safety depends on maintaining defensible borders with ample buffer zones: developing first-rate modern weaponry without outside interference (remember how the US sabotaged the Laws fighter plane?); getting tough with Arab terrorists and rioters; having faith in the justice of its cause, and receiving maximum support from diaspora Jewry.

American Jews must launch an all-out information offensive to explain to the American public and Congress the flaws in the idea of American "security guarantees" for Israel. The U.S. must be made to understand that it is bad for America and bad for Israel, to make promises that it may not be able to fulfill. For America, a broken promise is an embarrassment; for Israel, a broken promise can make the difference between life and death.

October 8, 1993

A Word of Thanks, From Arafat To U.S. Jewry

On the day that Yasir Arafat hoists the PLO flag over Jericho and begins preparing his battle to "liberate" the rest of "Palestine," perhaps he will take a moment to thank those who have given him crucial assistance these last few months. If so, the American Jewish community should be on the list of those to whom he should express his gratitude. Here's how he might put it:

"Of all those who have helped the PLO reach this glorious first phase in the liberation of Palestine, I am most grateful to my Jewish friends.

"Over the years, whenever we began to despair of defeating Israel, the Jewish Left consistently boosted our morale. There are too many to list them all, but I must single out a few by name New Jewish Agenda, whose leaders were among the first to meet with PLO officials; the Jewish Peace Lobby, which was formed based on my suggestion and which has lobbied in Washington for the cause of Palestine; and Americans for Peace Now, which has done such a fine job of infiltrating its leaders into the senior circles of the Clinton Administration, where they have influenced American policy to be less pro-Israel.

"The leaders of the major American Jewish organizations deserve my heartfelt thanks as well. They kept quiet when the Rabin Government agreed to concessions that most Israelis think are dangerous. They refrained from reminding the American public about unpleasant episodes from the pat, such as when we killed the U.S. ambassador in Khartoum, or when we hijacked the Achille Lauro and shot Leon Klinghoffer. They refused to protest when Jewish officials in the State Department were making America's Mideast policy a more even-handed way; those officials, such as Daniel Kurtzer, Dennis Ross, Aaron Miller, and Martin Indyk, are still warmly welcomed in the Jewish community. The Jewish leaders must also be thanked for accepting Americans for Peace Now into the Conference of Presidents of Major American Jewish Organizations, thus granting legitimacy to Peace Now's support for a PLO state.

228

"A special word of thanks to those American rabbis who have also refrained from interfering in our march towards the liberation of Palestine. At the signing ceremony in Washington, I was pleased to see many prominent rabbis among the guests. The list is too long to mention all their names, but the history books will record that they were there. Their blessing for the Israel-PLO agreement has helped keep the Jewish community from protesting against the Israeli concessions. I am well aware that most Orthodox Jews oppose PLO self-rule in the territories; that the Chabad Lubavitcher movement has been leading the anti-PLO campaign; and that the leading Orthodox rabbinical authorities in Israel and America wrote an "Open Letter to American Jewry" (published in THE JEWISH PRESS on Sept. 17) condemning Rabin's concessions for endangering Jewish lives. Therefore, I am especially grateful to those rabbis who bravely chose to attend the signing ceremony and thereby signal their support for PLO control of territories.

"I look forward to continuing support active support as well as quiet acquiescence from the American Jewish community as we bring our sacred task of building the state of Palestine, **phase by phase.** In one month, we will need billions of dollars' worth of international aid to develop the infrastructure for our state, and American Jewry will again play a crucial role. If American Jews keep silent, the U.S. will give us $250 million this year, and much more in the years to come. I know that the Jews have enormous influence over the entire world's finances, so I must express gratitude to them for the massive financial aid we will be receiving from Europe and other countries if the Jews were to oppose this, the money would not be forthcoming. This financial aid from America other nations will relieve the PLO of the responsibility of dealing with domestic Issues like Jobs and housing, leaving us free to concentrate on the next phase in our battle to liberate Palestine.

"I am especially surprised and grateful that the American Jewish community has refrained from planning about the methods used by the Israeli police against the anti-PLO demonstrators in Jerusalem a few weeks ago. The Israeli State Comptroller's investigation commission has revealed that the police brutally beaten women, children, and elderly demonstrators, dragged women by the hair into the police paddy wagons, and beat men in the genitals with their billy clubs. Of course, these are precisely the kins of methods we in the Arab world use to deal with troublemakers, but I know that Israel is supposed to have different standards, and I would have expressed that American Jews, with their well-known concern about human rights, would have denounced the Rabin government for what happened. Apparently, American Jewry realizes that these anti-PLO demonstrators must be suppressed so that the sacred cause of Palestinian statehood can go forward. And for that, I am grateful.

"The Jews have shown a remarkable ability to forgive their enemies. Even though they know that John Demjanjuk was a guard in the Sobibor death camp, that has set him free. Even though Syria has waged war against it, they are preparing to give Syria the Golan Heights. And even though I have ordered the murderers of many thousands of Jews during our battle to liberate Palestine, **the Jews are now giving me a state and right in the middle of *their* state**. When we achieve Phase 2 of our strategy of phases and liberate the rest of Palestine, Jews and Arabs will live peacefully and happily in a single, secular, democratic Palestine. That's what our Palestine National Covenant has always promised, and the Jews have not insisted that we change the Covenant at all. For that, too, thank them."

October 22, 1993

Arafat Has Violated the Treaty; All Bets Are Off

Three years ago, the U.S. broke off its relations with the PLO because Yasir Arafat refused to condemn to Arab terrorist attack. Now Arafat is again refusing to condemn such an attack. How will America and Israel respond?

President Bush agreed to negotiate with the PLO in December 1988, in exchange for a statement by Arafat recognizing Israel and renouncing terrorism. Bush and his aides made it clear that they understood Arafat's "renunciation" of terrorism to include a commitment by him to condemn all Arab terrorism that was committed by others and to punish any PLO members who carried out terrorism.

But every time there was a terrorist attack, Arafat was silent. Bush's State Department, anxious to avoid confronting the PLO leader, kept coming up with excuses. If the details of the attack were not clear, State Department officials would say they were "not sure" if the incident was actually terrorism; if it was obvious terrorism, they would say they were "not sure" if the PLO was involved; if a PLO faction was clearly involved, they would say that they expected Arafat to condemn it soon.

Finally, in the spring of 1990, a PLO gang was caught redhanded as it was about to launch an attack on Israeli civilians along the Tel Aviv beachfront. Congress and American Jewish organizations demanded that the Bush Administration cut off its relations with the PLO unless Arafat condemned the attack and expelled the guilty faction from the PLO. Arafat, for his part, refused to either condemn it or expel them. After weeks of hemming and hawing, Bush finally had no choice but to end his 18-month romance with the PLO.

Do the events of the past week differ from those of 1990?

Not at all. On October 9, Israeli naval forces intercepted members of a PLO faction, the Popular Front for the Liberation of Palestine, as they were about to attack Israeli civilians on a northern beach. Arafat has refused to

231

condemn the attackers or to expel the PFLP from the PLO. Arafat's position is a blatant violation of the Israel-PLO agreement, which obligates him to prevent PLO factions from carrying out terrorist attacks. Arafat is also obliged to condemn terrorism. President Clinton explicitly told **The Washington Post** on September 13 that "Mr. Arafat has said that he is not only renouncing violence, but he is going to condemn violence."

If the reason Arafat won't denounce the attack and expel the PFLP is because he privately agrees with what the PFLP did, then that proves he was not sincere when he said that he recognizes Israel and renounces terrorism. If, on the other hand, the reason Arafat is silent is that he is afraid that a denunciation would be unpopular among Palestinian Arabs, then that proves Israel has signed an agreement with someone who only represents a minority faction in his movement. Either way, Israel is left with a worthless "peace" treaty.

Arafat's behavior violates the heart and soul of the Israel-PLO agreement. It makes the agreement null and void. It is more than sufficient reason for the Clinton Administration to break off its relations with the PLO and for the Rabin government to scrap its plan to give the PLO self-rule in Judea, Samaria, and Gaza. But whatever Clinton and Rabin choose to do, Israel's "national camp" (the opposition parties and their constituents) has no choice but t regard the Israel-PLO agreement as fundamentally invalid from this day on. A treaty that the PLO so grossly violates is no treaty at all, and no one who cares about Israel's survival can regard such a treaty as having any legitimacy.

From now on, all bets are off. The problem is no longer how to prevent "self-rule" from tuning into a PLO state, or how to come up with "safeguards" to keep the plan from getting out of control. The plan itself must go. Arafat has, in effect, tearing it up.

December 3, 1993

Israeli Visitors Needed Back Home

Up until recently, no respectable Israeli would ever appear on the same platform as a PLO activist. The reason was simple but powerful: appearing on such a platform would grant legitimacy to those who carried out, or justified, terrorism against Jews. But times have changed, and patriotic Israelis now find themselves facing an entirely new situation, one that requires a new way of thinking about how to deal with those who harm the Jewish State.

The traditional refusal of nationalist Israelis to share platforms with PLO advocates was legitimate, and it is legitimate today. It is morally repugnant to appear on a platform on a stage, on "nightlife," on a radio talk show with those who slaughtered Israeli children in Ma'alot and massacred unarmed athletes in Munich. But now the Rabin government itself has embraced the PLO and has become the leading advocate for PLO control of Judea-Samaria and Gaza. Rabin's flunkies, such as Yossi Beilin, Itamar Rabinovich, and David Clayman, are touring the United States in support of their surrender to the PLO. Officials of the PLO are likewise busy on the lecture- and talk- show circuit. Beth Rabin's emissaries and Arafat's emissaries are being given a platform in synagogues, Federation buildings, Jewish schools, and the like. In a sense, the entire United States has become a platform that is dominated by those who favor PLO statehood (or PLO "self-rule," which is no different). An Israeli nationalist politician or activist who comes to America at all now finds himself in the position of inevitably sharing platform with the PLO advocates and therefore granting them a measure of legitimacy.

What makes the situation all the more intolerable is that the nationalist point of view in never given "equal time" at the meetings at which Israeli leftists or PLO Arabs appear. Discarding basic concepts of democracy and free speech, the leftists and Arabs carefully choreograph their appearances so that dissidents are kept out or kept quiet. Often there is no question-and-answer session at all. Even when there is one, the hosts do their best to exclude any audience members who seem to be critical of the Israel-PLO deal. Those

233

well-meaning Jewish nationalists who attend such meetings, often find themselves shut out entirely. Unfortunately, their very presence grants legitimacy to the PLO proponents, by making it appear as if both sides are present and as if it is legitimate for PLO advocates to be on the podium at all.

It is a disgrace that Jewish institutions should be hosting lectures by those who advocate turning over the heart of *Eretz Yisrael* to Arafat's bloody henchmen. Devout Jews who worked hard all their lives, and contributed to the building of synagogues and schools and Federation buildings, suddenly find that the synagogues and schools and Federation buildings that they helped build are being used as forums to espouse PLO statehood.

Consider, for example, the troubling episode in Philadelphia last month, when students of the local Solomon Schechter Day school were pressured by teachers and the administration to sign a document they did not even understand. Nobody mentioned that Arafat is insisting on being given Jerusalem. Does PLO control over the Western Wall fit comfortably into what the curriculum at the Solomon Schechter School teaches about Jerusalem? Angry parents have protested, but the damage has already been done.

Perhaps it's time for American Jews to stop contributing to institutions that will one day be used as platforms for the PLO, and instead send their money where it will make a difference to the Jewish communities in Judea, Samaria, and Gaza. Those communities are suffering deeply, deprived of all government funds as a result of Rabin's campaign to "dry up" the settlements to make room for PLO homeland.

The Jews of Judea-Samaria are becoming the first victims in a new and terrifying war. Terrifying precisely because so many Jews don't realize that it is just a more sophisticated kind of war, one that is being fought with slogans about "peace" and "peace agreements" that lull the public into a sense of false security. It's a war in which a weak and desperate Labor Party leadership has allied itself with a clever and deceitful PLO leadership to begin the phase-by-phase process of dismantling the Jewish State.

Today the enemies of Israel use slogans about "peace" to deceive the Jewish State and hasten its dismemberment. Not long ago, they used slogans like "relocation" and *Arbeit Macht Frei*" ("Work will make you free") to deceive the Jews to hasten their destruction. The names and the dates have changed; there is a new cast of characters, but for the Jews, the horrible result is just the same.

And that's why those well-intentioned Likud MKs and settlement leaders who have been visiting the U.S. should really be staying in Israel, fighting on the home front. Instead of going from town to town in America, seeking support from American Jews who ultimately have relatively little influence on Israeli policy, they should be going from town to town in Israel, altering the Israeli masses to the dangers they face from Rabin's "peace in our time." When the chamberlain coined the phrase "peace in our time," the British people naively believed him, thinking that Hitler could be bought off with a piece of western Czechoslovakia. Appeasing dictators doesn't work. "Peace in our time" led to World War II and the Holocaust. Today the slogan is "Peace Now," and naïve people think that Arafat can be bought off with "self-rule" in part of Israel. It won't work; history proves that dictators can't be appeased except by the destruction of the Jews.

Certainly, they should keep American Jews informed through articles and letters, phone calls, and faxes. Of course, they should remind American Jews of their obligation to help save Israel from national suicide. And American Jews, especially our rabbinical leadership, must accept that obligation and fight for Israel's needs here, instead of burdening the already-overburdened Israelis with the task of educating Americans about Israel. That will leave our Israeli brethren free to fight the battle for Israel's survival where it needs to be fought first and foremost, in Israel itself.

December 26, 1993

Settlers Abandoned, Arab Dictators Protected

The agreement currently being negotiated between Israel and Jordan obligates Israel to provide a "military umbrella" to "protect Jordan from threats from other countries," according to a report in the Israeli daily, **Ma'ariv**. Since Jordan has never been seriously threatened by any existing country, it appears that King Hussein is thinking ahead -and is correctly assuming that Prime Minister Rabin's plan for PLO "self-rule" will turn into a full-fledged PLO state that might one day seek to swallow up Jordan. How ironic that Jordan should be (justifiably) worried about the PLO self-rule plan. At the same time, Israel's leaders forge ahead with the plan, oblivious to the dangers that even the PLO's fellow-Arabs recognize.

The Jordanian dictator knows the Palestinian Arabs all too well. He remembers how, in 1970, as soon as they thought they had the military advantage, they turned on him and tried to overthrow his regime. Hussein responded by expelling the PLO and its constituents from Jordan. They went to Lebanon, which would have kicked them out if its government had been strong enough to do so. Instead, the PLO gradually took over the country, plunging it into a bloody civil war, which eventually gave birth to the term "Lebanonization." King Hussein knows full well that the PLO will Lebanonize Judea and Samaria, turning it into a chaotic war zone as the many factions vie for power; the PLO versus Hamas, rival PLO factions against one another; Moslems versus Christians, and of course, A eventually, the PLO versus Israel. After they have thoroughly Lebanonized Judea and Samaria, they will turn their attention to Jordan. That's why Hussein wants "protection." He knows what's coming.

There is an extraordinary disparity between the way Rabin treats Jordan and the PLO and the way he treats his fellow-Jews. Consider, Rabin heaps praise on the Jordanians for their alleged "moderation," and is offering them military protection from their enemies. Rabin likewise heaps praise on Yasir Arafat; indeed, he even tried to suppress the news that Arafat's terrorists were responsible for the murder of an Israeli Jew, Chaim Mizrachi. Despite such murderous activity, Rabin is busy trying to help the PLO establish *a de-facto* state in Judea, Samaria, and Gaza. He has been pressuring European leaders to give the PLO funds; he sent word to Congress not to link aid to the PLO to the Arab boycott issue, and he has cut off all funds to Jewish residents of the territories to get them out of the way so that the PLO can rule the area.

Now contrast Rabin's coddling of Jordan and the PLO with his raging hostility against the Jewish settlers. He doesn't speak of giving them a "military umbrella" to protect them; instead, he has ordered the Israeli Army to withdraw from the area and leave major roadways unprotected gradually. He doesn't ask foreign leaders to contribute to Jewish development projects in the territories; his agenda only has room for Arab development projects. He doesn't praise the settlers for their moderation and restraint; he has blasted them as "crybabies" and, in an echo of classic anti-Semitic stereotypes, has accused them of causing trouble by going into Arab marketplaces in search of less expensive food.

That's why it is no surprise to learn that growing numbers of nationalist-minded Israelis are refusing to perform their reserve duty in the Israeli Army. It's a development that has been ignored by the international media, and human rights groups like Amnesty International, which regard extreme-left "refusers" as "prisoners of conscience," are not likely to regard rightwing refusers with similar sympathy. But within Israel, the topic has become big news, as ever-larger numbers of patriotic Israelis are concluding that they cannot, as a matter of conscience, serve in an Army that is abandoning Jewish pioneers and preparing to protect an Arab dictatorship. They have preferred to sit in jail, which is the penalty for refusing to report for army duty rather than become accomplices in the abandonment of their fellow-Jews. Refusing to serve is an agonizing decision, and it is sure to engulf Israeli society in yet another wrenching controversy. It's a controversy that could tear Israel apart but if it does, let's keep in mind that responsibility lies with those who are trying to radically redefine the mission of the Israeli Army, to change it from the Israel Defense Forces to the Jordan or PLO Defense Forces.

December 31, 1993

Israel Faces A New Danger from Russia

The huge success by extreme Russian nationalists has left the Clinton Administration "startled and shaken," according to news reports. What troubles me is why Israel's Labor government is not even more startled and shaken.

America, after all, is powerful enough to handle whatever global turmoil may ensue from the latest upheavals in Russia. Israel, however, is considerably more vulnerable to the shock waves that may be felt around in the world as a result of the Russian troubles.

Vladimir Zhirinovsky, leader of the extreme-nationalist "Liberal democrats," won the largest share of any of the parties competing in the Russian elections. He's not president, but he's now a powerful figure on the Russian political landscape, and he will surely be a frontrunner for the presidency when Boris Yeltsin completes his term of office. And that's bad news. First, because he's a professed Jew-hater. Second, because he is a passionate admirer of Arab dictators.

Defying the international sanctions imposed on Iraq, Zhirinovsky recently visited Saddam Hussein. He still proudly shows visitors to his office a large autographed photo of himself and Saddam together in Baghdad. Zhirinovsky is also reported to be an admirer of Moammar Qaddaffi, the Libyan dictator. If Zhirinovsky takes over, one can expect that Russian arms will begin pouring into Baghdad and Tripoli and Damascus, too.

The Syrians recently received Russian missile parts (which the Clinton Administration tried to cover up, according to **The New York Times**), and that will be just the beginning if an Arabist and Jew-hater like Zhirinovsky is in charge.

Of course, nobody can be sure that Zhirinovsky will rise to the presidency. But that's just the point. Russia is in a state of extreme uncertainty.

Anything can happen. Its nuclear arsenal could end up in anybody's hands. Its arms-export policy can change overnight. Arab tyrants who today can't get Russian arms might suddenly start receiving them tomorrow. Even if Zhirinovsky doesn't take over, another cash-starved Russian leader could decide that Arab petrodollars are more important than Israeli lives. Boris Yeltsin hailed around the world as a democrat, and humanitarian had no compunctions about selling missile parts to the Syrians. Who knows what he'll give them next?

Israel is at the mercy of the ever-changing world political situation. The peaceful "new world order" that was supposed to follow the demise of Communism was an illusion. This is a world racked by nationalist conflicts rising Islamic fanaticism, and eager arms dealers running amok. Israel is sure to be the first victim of the new world chaos. If the plan for PLO self-rule goes forward, Israel will find itself facing a landmass controlled by Moslem dictators stretching from Jericho to Teheran. Into that vast, the nightmarish region will flow, Russian, Chinese, and North Korean weapons and "volunteers." What will Israel be able to do to stop it?

The lesson from the latest events in Russia is painfully clear; at any moment, the global situation can turn upside down. In such a world, is Israel better off protecting itself, or relying on foreign guarantees? Is Israel better off giving up strategic territory in exchange for Arab promises, or holding on to that territory as a buffer against enemy invasion? The answer should be obvious.

January 7, 1994

Clinton Faces the Ghosts of Lockerbie

The ghosts of Lockerbie will be hovering over Geneva when President Clinton meets Syrian dictator Hafez Assad there in January 270 ghosts, to be exact. That's how many innocent Americans were murdered when Pan Am Flight 103 was blown up over Lockerbie, Scotland in 1988, and there's new evidence that the Assad regime had a hand in the massacre.

Officially, Clinton's meeting with Assad is for "facilitating Mideast peace." That sounds pleasant enough; who could be against peace? The bitter truth, however, is that the "peace" which Clinton's State Department has in mind involves America embracing Syria and forcing Israel to make suicidal concessions to the Syrians. The meeting with Assad in Geneva is the first major step in that direction. According to some media reports, Clinton intends to announce in Geneva that he is removing Syria from the State Department's official list of countries that support terrorism. That certainly would pave the way for an improvement in American—Syrian relations. But it would also be a grotesque travesty of justice.

After all, Damascus is still headquarters to a whole variety of international terrorist groups, most of which spend their time murdering Israelis. However, some specialize in attacking Turkish targets, and others have a broader agenda for the international Marxist revolution. The Syrians, of course, refuse to acknowledge that such groups are "terrorists"; they call them "freedom fighters." Will the Clinton Administration now accept that bizarre and morally offensive designation?

The other major problem Clinton faces if he wants to whitewash Syria's sponsorship of terror is the new evidence about Lockerbie. An investigation by the **London Sunday Times** has found that the American attempt to blame Libya for the Lockerbie attack was flawed and that there is strong evidence of a Syrian role, which was overlooked for political reasons.

According to the **Times**, the major portion of the case against Libya rested on the testimony of Edwin Bollier, a Zurich electronics dealer who identified part of the bomb that blew up Pan Am 103 as being from a batch of electronic timers that he sold part to Libya, part to East Germany. The investigators pursued the Libyan connection but ignored the East German link, perhaps, according to the **Times**, because of the close ties between East Germany and the Popular Front for the Liberation of Palestine-General Command. This Syrian-backed terror group was a likely suspect in the bombing. Uncovering a Syrian-Palestinian role would have been politically inconvenient at a time when the Bush Administration was courting Syria to join the alliance against Iraq.

In fact, other evidence that had been accumulated by Western intelligence sources already pointed to the possibility that Iran had hired the PFLP-GC, with Syrian approval, to blow up Pan Am 103 in retaliation for the accidental downing of an Iranian jet by the Americans. But the evidence of a Syrian—Palestinian role was shunted aside in 1990 while President Bush rushed to Damascus to convince Syria to join the West against Saddam Hussein (in the end, the Syrians only contributed a token force, which was under orders not to harm their "Iraqi brothers" during the Gulf War).

The likelihood that a Syrian-backed terrorist group, which is still headquartered in Damascus, is responsible for murdering 270 innocent Americans should have been reason enough for President Clinton to refuse to meet with Hafez Assad. After all, American policy in the Middle East should be rooted in basic American values, such as respect for human life, democracy, and freedom. Syria represents the exact opposite of American values. It suppresses freedom. Its leader rules through violence and intimidation. It has no respect for human life, certainly not for the lives of the 270 Americans aboard Pail Am Flight 108.

An outpouring of public protest could still force the president to cancel his shameful meeting with the Syrian butcher. Is it too much to hope that angry Americans will bombard the White House with telegrams and phone calls?

January 21, 1994

The PLO Covenant: No More Excuses

During the negotiations leading to the Israel-PLO agreement last summer, the Israeli delegates brought up the issue of the Palestine National Covenant. This PLO ideological charter calls for the destruction of Israel, If the PLO were now sincerely ready to live in peace with Israel, surely Yasir Arafat would amend or cancel the Covenant or so the Israeli negotiator assumed.

After all, the key clauses in the Covenant all contradict the principles of the Israel-PLO agreement. Article 15 says that Arabs must "purge the Zionist presence from Palestine." Article 6 says that the only Jews who can remain in Palestine are those who lived there before 1917. Article 9 and 10 say that "armed struggle," i.e., murdering Jews is the way to "liberate Palestine." Article 22 says that Zionism is, by definition, "racist," "fanatical," "aggressive," "expansionist," "colonialist," "fascist," and "Nazi."

During those hectic days before the Israel-PLO mutual "recognition" and the signing of the Israel-PLO accord, the newspapers were filled with soothing statements by Israeli officials reassuring the Jewish public that the Covenant would be changed at the time of the accord. But, then, on the eve of the exchange of recognition letters between Arafat and Yitzhak Rabin, Rabin's aides started saying that the Covenant would be changed "soon." When the actual text of the Israel-PLO agreement was released a few days later, it turned out that Arafat had only made a vague promise to raise the issue of the Covenant at some future meeting of the Palestine National Council. No deadline was mentioned.

Two-thirds of the members of the Palestine National Council are required to change the Covenant. Since the Council is an arm of the PLO, and the PLO is presumably now at peace with Israel. The PLO's chairman is now presumably a peaceful and trustworthy moderate, and there should have been no problem convening the Council and changing or canceling the Covenant. But it hasn't happened.

Instead, both the Rabin government and the Clinton Administration have been totally silent about the Covenant issue. When the question is raised, they say that Arafat "doesn't have a two-thirds majority in the Council yet." That's a frightening claim because it reveals that Israel has an agreement with only one part of the PLO, and no matter how many concessions it makes to Arafat's faction of the PLO, its citizens will still be murdered by other factions of the PLO.

Ultimately, the whole issue of the PLO Covenant challenges the viability of the Israel-PLO accord itself. What kind of peace Israel has with an organization that is still publicly pledged to a Covenant calling for Israel's destruction? It is impossible to believe that the PLO wants peace if it refuses to amend that savage document,

There is no room for political partisanship when it comes to the PLO Covenant problem. Jews from the right, the center, and the left should be equally concerned, and should all forcefully demand that the Clinton administration pressured Arafat to change the Covenant. The PLO is dependent on American political and financial aid; America's aid should be withheld so long as the Covenant remains unchanged. American Jews must launch an all-out educational effort to make the American public and government aware of this critical issue

Americans must understand that **American** interests are endangered by the extremism and violence that the Palestine National Covenant embodies. So long as the Palestine National Covenant remains intact, young Palestinian Arabs will regard it as their ideological guiding-light and will grow up committed to the eventual destruction of Israel. There can be no hope of real moderation or democratization among the Palestinian Arabs so long as they regard the unaltered Covenant as their agenda. For endless decades to come, Palestinian Arabs will be fomenting radical violence, hatred of Israel and America, and destabilization in a region of the world that is crucial to America's strategic interests.

The effort to educate Americans about these realities will soon shift into high gear, thanks to the election of Morton A. Klein as national president of the Zionist Organization of America. Klein is a distinguished and inspiring activist who forcefully challenges and condemns Arafat's lies; under his leadership, the ZOA is sure to play a leading role in helping Americans understand what is really happening in the Middle East today. This important change in the ZOA national leadership could be a turning point in the history of American Zionism and American-Israeli relations.

Too many American Jewish "leaders" are self-appointed bureaucrats who are preoccupied with preserving their positions of power, enjoying the perks of office-holding, and adopting only "safe" positions on the issues of the day. Mort Klein, by contrast, is a democratically elected activist leader who truly represents the sentiments of the Jewish masses, who understands that helping Israel is more important than personal prestige, and who will not be intimidated by the powers that be. A new day is dawning for the pro-Israel community in America.

January 28, 1994

A Ray of Hope at A Time of Gloom

With Judea and Samaria soon to be handed over to the PLO and mounting evidence that the Golan Heights will soon be surrendered as well, there is every reason to feel gloomy about the prospects for Israeli security. But the devoted young Jews who are building the new Jewish neighborhood of Beit Orot, in "east" Jerusalem, offer us a ray of hope at a time it sometimes seems that all hope is lost.

The danger to Israel's survival cannot be denied. Control of the country's heartland is being given to an organization that has spent the last 30 years murdering and maiming Jews all over the world. That's right 30 years, meaning that they began in 1964, three years before there were any settlements in the territories," when the only issue was whether or not Israel Should exist. That's one of those inconvenient facts that the State Department and the Jewish Left would like everybody to forget because it reveals so much about the PLO's real agenda.

But the truth is that the PLO does not hide its agenda. It spelled out its goals, in writing, in 1964, in a document called the Palestine National Covenant. The Covenant declares that Israel must be destroyed. The PLO can pursue various strategies, it can sometimes use diplomacy instead of terrorism, it can gain control of land in stages, but ultimately its final goal remains the same: the destruction of Israel. That goal has not changed, and the proof is that the Covenant has not been changed, even though Arafat promised last September that he would change it. A few minutes after the signing ceremony in Washington, Arafat appeared on Jordanian Television and reassured his Arab viewing audience that the Agreement with Israel was just Phase One in his strategy to destroy Israel in phases. Today, Gaza and Jericho, tomorrow the rest of Judea, Samaria, and Gaza. And in a few years Tel Aviv, Haifa, Beersheba.

The threat to Israel is not only from the east but from the north as well. Some Israeli leaders seem to be willing to surrender the Golan Heights to the

Syrians. In recent months media reports have quoted Israeli officials saying that Assad might not be a pleasant person, but he always keeps his agreements. To make such a claim, of course, you have to forget everything that happened before 1967. History can be so inconvenient. Syria signed an armistice agreement with Israel in 1949. Let's talk about how they "kept" that agreement. Did they keep it by firing shells at kibbutzim throughout the 1950s and 1960s? Did they keep it by forcing a whole generation of Israeli children to grow up in bomb shelters? Did they keep it by sending terrorist squads into the Galilee to murder Jews?

What are we supposed to do about all of this? How can we prevent the surrender of the Land of Israel? How can we save Israel from such dangers? The answer is to be found in Jerusalem's newest neighborhood, Beit Orot. It's beyond the "Green Line," that is, in those parts of Jerusalem that were liberated in 1967, and from which the Arabs would still like to bar Jewish residents. And it is precisely because it is beyond the Green Line that Belt Orot is so important for it is a powerful and vibrant statement of the Jewish determination to make all of Jerusalem a truly Jewish city once again.

When the Jordanians controlled the Old City of Jerusalem, from 1948 until 1967, they did everything they could to wipe out the memory of the Jewish presence. They destroyed 58 synagogues almost as many synagogues as the Nazis destroyed on *Kristallnacht.* They desecrated the Mount of olives cemetery. They took Jewish tombstones and used them to pave roads and to line the latrines in Jordanian army barracks. Their goal was to eliminate the Jewish presence. And today, in Beit Orot, close to that very same Mount of Olives, the Jewish presence is being rebuilt. Beit Orot reverses the horrible desecrations of the Jordanians and tells the world that Jerusalem is ours and will always be ours.

The name "Beit Orot" means "house of lights." How appropriate for it truly provides some light, some rays of hope, just when Israel needs it most.

March 4, 1994

The Real Lessons from Hebron

When a Hezbollah car-bomber massacred 241 American Marines in Lebanon, the world was horrified for a few days. Then the story faded from the headlines, the public lost interest, and before long, the State Department was again pressuring Israel to refrain from hitting Hezbollah bases for fear of "increasing tensions in the Middle East."

When an Arab terrorist bomb massacred 270 Americans aboard Pan Am flight 103, the world was shocked until evidence began to emerge that Syria and a faction of the PLO (the Popular Front for the Liberation of Palestine General Command) were involved. Suddenly it became **politically inconvenient to find out who was guilty**. Those who are devoted to pressuring Israel to make concessions to the PLO and Syria the United Nations, most of the media, and of course, the State Department immediately began drawing attention away from the PLO and Syria and focusing it on more convenient targets like Libya and Iran.

Yet when Arabs murder and maim Jews every day in Israel, and a lone Jewish man, overwhelmed by his grief over Arab terrorism, strikes at the Arabs, the hue and cry from around the world are deafening. Accusing fingers are pointed at all of Israel. The Israeli government is pressured to make concessions to the Arabs to "atone" for a deed it did not commit. There are calls to expel all Jews from Hebron, and from all of Judea and Samaria.

Of course, all violence and killings are bad. In an ideal world, one could simply condemn all such behavior, and that would suffice. But we don't live in an ideal world. We live in a world in which **Israeli Jews are constantly victimized. Thirty-three Israeli Jews have been murdered since the signing of the Israel-PLO accord last September**. Countless others have been injured. Jewish blood is shed every day in the land of Israel, although it does not often make it to the pages of the **New York Times. Jewish holy places are frequently desecrated**. In Hebron's Cave of the Patriarchs on the evening before the killings, a mob of Arabs disrupted the reading of the *Megillah* with shouts of "*Itbach al-Yahud,*" or "Slaughter the Jews."

"Itbach al-Yahud" is a slogan that has special meaning for the Jews of Hebron. **It was the rallying cry of the raging Arab mobs that tortured and slaughtered 59 Jews in Hebron in the summer of 1929**. Not one lone individual pushed over the edge by watching his friends die in his arms, but **huge mobs of frenzied, hate-filled Arabs** - in other words, **virtually the entire Arab community was bent on massacring peaceful Jewish civilians**.

If last week's events in Hebron were to be judged by an American court, the results would not be black and white. The American justice system, quite properly, takes into consideration the factors that drove the perpetrator to commit his deed. Those factors do not absolve the perpetrator of guilt - but they do define the level and quality of guilt. There was a hung jury in the trial of the Mendez brothers because of evidence that they acted out of fear and desperation due to years of abuse. Lorena Bobbitt was declared not guilty because of temporary insanity after the jury found that what drove her to extreme behavior was the violence she had suffered from her husband. Surely a Jewish doctor who constantly treated victims of Arab terrorism, and who literally held in his arms his dying friends, would be found to have experienced as much suffering as the Lyle Mendezes and Lorena Bobbitts of this world.

In the wake of the latest violence, the Israeli government has announced tough new measures to enforce law and order. The problem is that **the wrong people are being targeted**. In the Arab-Israeli conflict, it is the **Arabs who are the aggressors, the Jews who are the victims**. But the new decrees, which seem primarily designed to appease world opinion, **are directed at the victims rather than the aggressors**. Jews who have not killed anybody are being disarmed - while PLO terrorists, now called "Policemen," are being armed. Jews are being thrown into jail without charges, under the euphemism of "administrative detention," while 1,000 Arab terrorists who have engaged in anti-Jewish violence are being let out of jail. Jews who have committed no crime are to be prevented from living in Judea and Samaria - while PLO terrorists who have devoted their lives to attacking Israelis are being given control of Judea and Samaria. And all this comes at a time when the Israeli Army has already been withdrawn from key roads and regions in the territories, depriving the Jewish residents of any meaningful security.

Rabin's crackdown on the Jews in the territories may be intended to establish law and order, but it is likely to achieve just the opposite. Making concessions demonstrates to the Arabs that Israel is weak and that Israelis can be terrorized into making further concessions. Depriving the Jews of basic security makes them sitting ducks for Arab killers. Taking guns out of the hands of the Jews and putting them in the hands of the PLO guarantees that the terrifying cycle of Arab terrorism and Jewish retaliation will only continue.

March 18, 1994

Once Again, They Blame the Jews

Yitzhak Robin's ferocious rhetorical assault on Jewish residents of Judea and Samaria last week was ostensibly aimed at the "extremists" among them. But because the Arabs and their allies make no distinction between "moderate" and "extremist" Jews, Rabin's verbal blasts will ultimately help legitimize future attacks on Israel and the Jewish people.

"You are a foreign implant, a poisonous weed," Rabin declared, in reference to Jewish militants in the territories. "You are not part of the community of Israel. Sane Judaism spits you out." Caught up in the emotion of the moment, the prime minister did not seem to realize the sweeping nature of his own statements. Zionism does not recognize the concept of any Jew being a "foreign implant." The basic Zionist concept of ingathering the exiles means that all Jews are foreign implants or, more accurately, that no Jews are foreign implants because nobody can be regarded as a foreigner in his true homeland.

Therefore, one can only be shocked at the news that Rabin has permitted Knesset Members from his party to introduce legislation that would prevent Jews from "extreme" opinions from immigrating to Israel. Certain Labor Zionist officials tried doing that sort of thing once before; during the Holocaust, they used a policy they called "selectivity" to keep Jabotinsky's followers from reaching the Land of Israel. Will Jews fleeing famine-ravaged Ethiopia or the rising anti-Semitism in Russia now be screened before being given entry permits to Israel? Will those who are considered too nationalistic be turned away?

As for the attitude of Judaism towards the Jews of Judea-Samaria, one would hope that in the future, the prime minister would leave that subject in the hands of those who are authorities on the subject. Certainly, our rabbinic leadership can provide a point of view that is more firmly grounded in traditional Jewish sources than a perspective born of socialism and secularism. Secular politicians should take care before claiming that Judaism endorses their particular view; their past actions, if scrutinized by rabbinic authorities, might not emerge untarnished.

At the heart of Rabin's attack on the Jewish Settlers is the theme he has repeatedly invoked during the first 20 months in office: the Jews are to blame. Each time the settlers have protested his policies, Rabin has unleashed another verbal barrage. He has denounced them as "crybabies" and "not real Israelis." Concerning their demonstrations, he has said that "they can spin like propellers for all I care, it will not change my mind." When a Jewish shopper was murdered while buying eggs from an Arab merchant in Ramallah last October, Rabin criticized the victim for risking his life "to buy cheap eggs in Ramallah." Critics charged that the remark had overtones of the classic attacks on alleged Jewish stinginess.

In life and death, the Jews are blamed. When they are alive, they are blamed as "obstacles to peace"; when they are dead, they are blamed for "provoking" their killers by buying from Arab merchants.

No matter who gets killed, the Jews are blamed. When Arabs kill Jews, the Jews get the blame; when Jews are driven to acts of retaliation and desperation, they get the blame.

How ironic that some Israeli cabinet ministers use language against their fellow-Jews that would evoke horror and outrage if used about any other ethnic group. Israel's Minister of Housing said that it was "the presence of the Jews in Hebron that is causing the problem." Imagine if the US. Secretary of Housing declared that the presence of blacks in some mostly white area was the cause of racial tensions. There would be an uproar, and rightly so. Yet there is no such uproar when such accusations are hurled at Jews. Indeed, the Clinton Administration, which is (appropriately) the first to defend the right of Americans of all colors to live wherever they want, is pressing Israel to limit the right of Jews to live wherever they want in the Land of Israel.

What the critics of the settlers seem to forget is that the Arabs make no distinction between "extremist" settlers and "moderate" settlers. Nor, for that matter, do they distinguish between the settlers and other Israeli citizens.

The Arabs regard **ALL Israelis Yitzhak Rabin included** as occupiers, persecutors, murderers, and thieves. Note how Arab denunciations of the Hebron killings routinely list the killing of 18 Arab rioters on the Temple Mount in 1990 as an earlier "massacre," even though the 18 were obviously killed in self-defence by policemen who were being attacked by murderous mobs. From the **Arab** point of view, the militant settlers, the moderate settlers, **and the doves of Labor and Meretz are all "foreign implants" and "poisonous weeds" who should be "spit out."**

What Rabin has done is **to provide bundles of fresh ammunition** for the Arabs and their many supporters in the media and governments around the world. In the future, their accusations against Israel will be laced with quotes from Israel's prime minister. Rabin's attempt to blame the settlers will ultimately backfire against all of Israel and all Jews, precisely as the attempt to blame Ariel Sharon for Sabra-Shatilla backfired. To this day, the Sabra-Shatilla killings are routinely blamed on Israel as a whole, not on some individual "militant" cabinet minister. The names and the places have changed, but the world's never-ending passion for blaming the Jews goes on and on. How tragic and ironic that the international community is now being helped in its bash-Israel efforts by officials of Israel's minority government, who are giving ammunition to the haters instead of focusing blame where it belongs to the Arabs who have been responsible for a century of aggression against Jews and Zionism.

March 25, 1994

Israel Grovels, Arafat's Heart Hardens

As if they are re-enacting the cruel drama of ancient Egypt, Yitzhak Rubin and his aides have been spending the days before Passover pleading with Yasir Arafat to "let my people live in peace," but with each new Israeli plea or concession, Arafat's heart just hardens further.

Arafat, always the shrewd bargainer, knows that by hardening his heart, by continually demanding more and more, will eventually get everything he wants because he is dealing with an Israeli leadership that is desperate to prove that it wants "peace," and a U.S. leadership that will support PLO demands to get credit for "promoting Mideast peace."

And so, every time he can find a pretext, Arafat unleashes a flood of extremist demands. After the Hebron violence, Arafat had his list ready; release Arab terrorists imprisoned in Israel; arrest Jewish settler activists; disarm all Jewish settlers, expel all Jews from Hebron, pass a UN resolution denouncing Israel. Such would be the price was being paid. Rabin set free 1,000 Arab terrorists and jailed or disarmed dozens of prominent Jewish settlers. The mass expulsion of Jews from Hebron may yet follow. Meanwhile, in Washington, the Clinton Administration appears ready to do its part by supporting (or at least abstaining from) the UN resolution denouncing Israel.

But as the Israelis are beginning to discover, what they will get for the price they are paying may not be so desirable after all. Consider:

- Many aspects of the crackdown on the settlers violate democratic norms. Harsh treatment of the settlers could also provoke a violent reaction, and even drive Israel to the brink of civil war.

- Setting free Arab terrorists guarantees further bloodshed. Israel knows from previous prisoner releases that a percentage of terrorists who are freed always return to their terrorist ways.

- Having Arafat back at the negotiating table will preserve the illusion that the "peace process" is "on track." But that's just a slogan covering up the cold, hard reality, that the "peace process" is the process by which Israel surrenders Judea, Samaria, and Gaza to the PLO in exchange for a piece of paper.

Nor will the Israeli concessions further U.S. interests in the region:

- Israel's weakness has encouraged the meddlesome Russians to stick their noses back into the Middle East cauldron. The Russian Foreign Minister showed up in Israel, uninvited, and clamoring for Israeli concessions to the PLO. U.S. officials were surprised and concerned to see the Russians back on the scene. The last thing the U.S. needs is a revival of old Cold War-era competition between America and Russia for influence in the Middle East.

- Giving Arafat a *de-facto* state means creating another hotbed of anti-American sentiment in the Middle East. **Has the U.S. already forgotten whose side Arafat took during the Gulf War?**

Israel's longing for peace is natural. But just because one side in a conflict wants peace does not mean peace is attainable. The Rabin government's policies have not brought Israel closer to peace. On the contrary, Israeli concessions have merely raised Arab expectations, but those Arab expectations cannot be satisfied, because when they get to issues such as Jerusalem, PLO statehood, and the like, the Israeli public cannot possibly agree to surrender. At that point, Arab frustration and extremism will reach the boiling point, and an explosion will follow. Thus, ironically, the Rabin government will deliver the exact opposite of what it promised the voters in 1992, it would inadvertently bring about war, not peace.

April 8, 1994

A Different Kind Of Exodus

On the eve of Passover, as Jews around the world were preparing to commemorate the exodus of the Jews from ancient Egypt, Yitzhak Rabin was preparing the groundwork to eventually engineer his kind of exodus in Rabin's ghastly version, the Jews are not saved from bondage and brought to the Promised Land, but are instead taken out of their homes in the Promised Land and sacrificed to a modern-day Pharaoh named Arafat.

Reports from Israel suggest that the Rabin government is laying the groundwork for eventually expelling the Jewish community from Hebron. Rabin has said that the Jews in Hebron are a "time bomb." He has emphasized that he opposed letting them reside in the City in the first place, and he has complained that the presence of Jews in Hebron "unfairly" forced the Israeli Army to keep the entire Arab population of the city under curfew.

Is there any reasonable basis for Rabin's remarks? The Jews in Hebron are no more a "time bomb" than were any of the original Jewish towns established in Arab-populated areas of *Eretz Yisrael* by the Zionist pioneers early in this century. Tel Aviv was no doubt something of a "time bomb" when it was established right next door to the mostly Arab city of Jaffa.

As for the curfew in Hebron, it's hard to see what could be unfair about such a measure when it is used at a time when Arabs; in Hebron are most likely to try to kill Jews. It's an appropriate means of preventing aggressors from reaching their victims. Rabin, however, chooses to blame the victims for inconveniencing the aggressors. Those who are familiar with Jewish history need not be reminded of the many occasions on which enemies of the Jews likewise claimed that it was a "handful of Jews" who were raining the rest of the world by allegedly controlling the world economy, stirring up Communism, or what-have-you.

Hebron, however, is only the tip of the iceberg. For some time, Rubin and his aides hate been trying to prepare Israeli (and Diaspora) public opinion for the abandonment of all the Jewish residents of Judea, Samaria, and Gaza. They've delegitimized the settlers as "crybabies" and "not real Israelis." Shimon Peres has said that the Gaza Jewish community of Netzarim and the Jews living near Jericho, maybe "expendable" since they are in the way of the projected PLO self-rule zones. Rabin himself has said that the establishment of many of the settlements in the territories was a "mistake."

What remains to be seen is how long it will take Rabin to move from the stage of rhetoric to the stage of action. What is clear is that some of Rabin's actions will be determined following the level of public reaction. At each stage, Rabin and his aides pause to gauge the public's response. They test the waters because they know that their fragile government, leaning heavily on the votes of pro-PLO Arab parties, cannot withstand fierce public opposition. Rabin and Peres are nervously watching the polls, which these days show that less than 40% of Israelis support the Israel-PLQ agreement. Rabin and Peres are also watching American Jewry, well aware that large numbers of U.S. Jews have serious misgivings about handing over Judea, Samaria, and Gaza to Arafat and Hamas. The question is if Rabin sends the Israeli Army to evict Jews from their homes, in Hebron or elsewhere, will American Jews Protest or will they sit back quietly, as they had done at ether times in recent history when Jews were expelled from their homes?

And so it is a Passover of watching and waiting. In ancient times, too, there was watching and waiting. Pharaoh watched and waited to see if the Jews' demands were serious if the plagues would really strike, as Moses promised. They did strike, and Moses led the Jewish people from Egypt to the Promised Land. Today, the roles are reversed: Arafat watches and waits to see if Rabin will surrender to all of his demands to see if Rabin will lead the Jews out of their homes in the Promised Land.

D-Day and The Jews

Americans and Europeans alike commemorated the 50th anniversary of D-Day with a vast array of ceremonies, tributes, and celebrations. Television documentaries recreated the Normandy landing and the liberation of France from Nazi occupation. Politicians made grandiose speeches recalling the events of 1944. Newspapers published special supplements adorned with large photos of the cemeteries where the soldiers who fell on D-Day were buried, row after row of crosses marking their final resting place. For those who understand the full scope of what happened during World War II, those creases were a grim reminder of what was missing from all the D-Day events: a recognition of the unique role assigned to the Jews during those dark years.

The popular perception of World War II is of a war between countries, between the Allies America, England and Russia, and the Axis Germany, Italy, and Japan. But historians know better. They know, first and foremost, that Hitler was fighting a war against the Jews, and it was precise because his main target was the Jews that the German military was obsessively preoccupied and distracted. This caused the downfall of the German military, allowing the Allies to overcome the Germans.

World War II was not at all a conventional war. For Hitler, the war was a racial and ideological struggle, a war to establish "Aryan" superiority by annihilating the Jews worldwide. If he was interested in conquering territories or other countries, it was only so that he could get at the Jews living there. That explains the very different way in which the Nazis treated those that they conquered; Hitler had no intention of destroying England, or France, or Scandinavia. He merely intended to occupy them. No use of the Jews. When it came to the Jews, the Nazis had no thoughts of mere occupation or subjugation. Hitler would settle for nothing less than mass murder. For the Jews, there we no way out they could not emigrate; they could not assimilate; they could not even convert to Christianity; nothing would satisfy Hitler except their death.

That is why Hitler's war against the Jews took precedence over his war with the Allies. Any time that there was a choice between focusing on the murder of the Jews or focusing on fighting the Allied armies, Hitler gave priority to killing Jews. The German military high command wanted to delay the invasion of the Soviet Union until late 1941, but Hitler insisted on going ahead with it in June of that year because he knew that the USSR was home to millions of Jews, and he could not wait any longer to slaughter them.

The German generals needed railroad cars to transport soldiers and weapons to the front; Hitler insisted on using the railroads to transport Jews to the death camps. Enormous amounts of German manpower, resources, and energy were diverted from the war effort, and they were concentrated on the Jews ghettoizing them, rounding them up for deportation, deceiving them about their fate, and finally murdering them. The Nazis could have need virtually all of the Jews as slave laborers, which would have been a significant asset to the military production industry but instead, they only used a small minority for slave labor and sent the rest to the gas chambers immediately, because they were in such a hurry to kill the Jews.

Again and again, throughout the Holocaust, the Nazis focused their attention on the Jews and made unwise decisions from a military point of view to hasten the genocide process. The Jews became the unwitting sacrifice on the altar of Allied Victory; it was the role played by the Jews that left the Germans militarily vulnerable at crucial points, making it possible for the Allies to defeat the Nazis in less than four years. Without the Jews to distract Hitler, the Germans would have been much stronger, the war would have lasted much longer, and there is no telling what the outcome might have been.

While the American forces were landing in Normandy in the spring of 1944, the Germans were busy deporting Hungary's Jews to Auschwitz. Instead of concentrating on holding off the Allied attack in France, Hitler still primarily interested in how to kill as many Jews as possible. If the Germans had focused on the war in France rather than on the war against the Jews, things might have gone very differently.

But as always seems to happen, the Jews' sacrifices go unrecognized. The D-Day commemorations ignore the role of the Jews. The Holocaust is relegated to the footnotes of World War II history, instead of being understood for its pivotal role in the entire conflict. The cemeteries of France hold row after row of graves marked with crosses, but there is no burial place for the Six Million; their ashes were scattered across the skies of Europe long ago.

Jewish leaders should have insisted that the D-Day anniversary events include appropriate recognition of the role played by the Jews. But some Jewish leaders seem to have become so accustomed to the Jews being victims, being trivialized or being ignored, that they find it difficult to imagine things being any different. And so, as the D-Day commemorations proceeded, the Jewish world remained silent while the truth of what happened during World War II and the Holocaust was shunted aside.

July 1, 1994

AIPAC Joins ZOA'S Fight Against PLO Violations

For the past half-year, the Zionist Organization of America has been waging a valiant but lonely battle to expose the PLO's many violations of the Israel PLO agreement. Valiant because the ZOA has accomplished so much with so few resources. Lonely because other major Jewish organizations were afraid to touch the issue. The ZOA was the target of more than a few barbs from leftists who claimed that criticism of Yasir Arafat was "anti-peace." Fortunately, the ZOA ignored such illogical arguments (how could it be "anti-peace" to insist that Arafat be peaceful?) and continued its efforts to publicize the PLO's violations.

The ZOA's judgment was fully vindicated recently, when the American-Israeli Public Affairs Committee (AIPAC), the Israeli lobby, announced for the first time that it, too, will denounce PLO violations and will urge that U.S. aid to the PLO be made conditional on the PLO living up to the promises that it has made.

It's only a pity that it took AIPAC 80 long to realize that the ZOA had it right all along. Arafat's violations have been obvious from the day the Israel-PLO deal was signed back in September. On the very afternoon of the signing ceremony, Arafat appeared on Jordanian television and assured his Arab audience that the Israel-PLO agreement was just "Phase One" in the PLO's old "Strategy of Phases" for destroying Israel. It was Arafat's first violation of the agreement, but there were many more to come.

In the months since the signing, Arafat's Fatah gang continued to carry out terrorist attacks. Arafat didn't stop them, didn't punish them, didn't even condemn then even though the Israel-PLO accords obligate him to do so. Other PLO groups, like the Democratic Front for the Liberation of Palestine, also continued to murder Israelis. Arafat didn't stop, punish, or condemn them, even though the accords require him to do so.

There have been other violations, too. Arafat said he would make speeches to Arab audiences, urging them to reject violence. He didn't do it. In fact, he continued making statements praising the *intifada* and calling for a *jihad* against Israel. Arafat said he would change the PLO Covenant, which calls for the annihilation of Israel. But he didn't do that, either.

AIPAC, of course, knew all this. The violations have been plain to see. Yet, for some reason, AIPAC's leaders chose to close their eyes and pretend that nothing was happening. Perhaps this was the result of pressure from left-wing Israeli officials. Perhaps it was because AIPAC president Steve Grossman himself is known to be decidedly left of center (in 1980, be signed one of those infamous leftwing newspaper ads denouncing the Israeli government for not making more concessions to the Arabs). Whatever the reason, AIPAC's behavior was unsettling to many in the pro-Israel community, and the new AIPAC decision to join ZOA in fighting PLO violations is welcome news indeed.

One can only hope this AIPAC reversal will mark the beginning of the return of the AIPAC of old. The AIPAC of yesteryear told the truth about the Arabs in its annual guide, **Myths, and Facts.** There, one could find a detailed description of the PLO's whole "Strategy of Phases." There, one could read about the history of Arab belligerency towards Israel, about the duplicity of Arab "peace rhetoric," and about the futility of Israeli surrender to Arab territorial demands. In those days, AIPAC said, loudly and clearly, that the Arabs, not Israel, are to blame for the Arab-Israeli conflict. Back then, AIPAC made it clear that Arab opposition to Israel's existence, not settlements or territories, was the real issue at stake.

AIPAC's wise decision to join the ZOA effort against PLO violations leaves some questions to be answered: Has AIPAC had a sincere change of heart or is this a tactical move that is being made for internal reasons? Will AIPAC fight PLO violations forcefully, or will it pull its punches? Is AIPAC going to use its substantial political weight to promote legislation that will really cut off U.S. funding to the PLO, or is this just posturing for the media? In the weeks to come, we should learn the answers to those important questions.

August 8, 1994

King Hussein's Big Lie About Terrorism

To nobody's surprise, one of the first questions raised at the Rabin-Clinton-Hussein press conference in Washington concerned the recent terrorist attacks against Jewish and Israeli targets in Argentina, Panama, and England. Rabin and Clinton responded with their standard lines about how the terrorists are "enemies of peace." The response of King Hussein, however, was extraordinary.

"I have always been against terrorism," the Jordanian announced.

Such a claim might impress American journalists who know nothing about Jordan's real record on terrorism, and who don't want to know about it because it would shatter their comfortable illusion about Jordanian "moderation."

But just a few feet away stood Yitzhak Rabin, who earlier this year publicly denounced King Hussein for permitting Hamas and Muslim Brotherhood terrorists to make their headquarters in Jordan. Rabin specifically blamed the Jordanian-based terrorists for recent murderous assaults upon Israelis. He demanded that Hussein expel the terrorists. Hussein's response: silence.

If Hussein has "always been against terrorism," how is it that he allowed Hamas and Muslim Brotherhood terrorists to operate from Jordan?

And if Hussein has "always been against terrorism," how are we supposed to understand Jordan's response to previous terrorist attacks against Israel? For example, when Arab terrorists opened fire on a crowd of shoppers in downtown Jerusalem in April 1984, wounding 50 of them, the Jordanian government newspaper **Ad-Dustur** called the attack "a great and daring fedayasn operation ... an inevitable and expected reply in light of all actions of Judaization, annexation, confiscation, and aggression." A few weeks later, **Ad-Dustur** denounced American foreign policy as "the root of international

262

terrorism." (And in September of that year, Ad-Dustur called for a worldwide economic boycott of the United States.)

More recently, in 1991, another Jordanian government organ, the **Al-Rai** newspaper declared that the bombing of Pan Am 103 over Lockerbie Scotland (in which 270 Americans were killed) was no worse than what it claimed was the U.S. policy of "burying Iraqi troops alive, and the continued starving of the civilian population of Iraq." The Jordanian newspaper said that if the bombers of Pan Am 103 are caught and put on trial, the U.S. officials responsible for America's role in the Gulf War should likewise be put on trial. It also called for the arrest of the U.S. pilots who accidentally shot down an Iranian jet.

That's why King Hussein can claim he "has always been against terrorism" because he like other Arab leaders, and has his peculiar view of what constitutes terrorism. In King Hussein's eyes, the actions of Hamas and the Muslim Brotherhood are not terrorism. Murdering Jewish civilians in downtown Jerusalem is not terrorism. Blowing up a Pan Am flight full of American citizens is not terrorism. But when Israel acts in self-defense, or a U.S. pilots shoot down another aircraft by accident, or the U.S. takes legitimate action to repel Iraqi aggression that, according to King Hussein, is "terrorism."

No matter how many treaties King Hussein signs, no matter how many smooth press conferences he holds in Washington, no matter how moderate-sounding the statements he makes to Western journalists, there remains a gap between Arab thinking and Western thinking that cannot be bridged. King Hussein will sign whatever piece of paper it takes to get U.S. aid and U.S. weapons. But Muslim terrorists will continue to find a haven in Jordan because there they are not viewed as terrorists. The murder of Jews will continue to attract cheers in the Jordanian-controlled press because such murders are not considered terrorism. The Arabs have their own definition of "terrorism," just as they have their definition of "peace," and those who think that those definitions are similar to American definitions are simply engaged in wishful thinking.

August 12, 1994

Yitzach Rabin and The Politics of Fear

Prime Minister Yitzhak Rabin and his aides have made many controversial statements in recent months, but none can compare to Rabin's extraordinary declaration recently that Israel must surrender the Golan Heights because otherwise, there will be a war with Syria. Rabin's statement is a recipe for unilateral Israeli surrender to every conceivable Arab demand.

"Syria has ground-to-ground missiles of quality and quantity that make what we suffered from Iraq during the Gulf War look like child's play... if we do not make peace, there will be war with Syria in three or five years," Rabin declared. By "making peace," Rabin was referring to the idea of signing a treaty that would give Syria control of all, or virtually all, of the Golan Heights, Israel's most crucial buffer zone.

To realize just how absurd Rabin's statement was, try putting his words into the mouths of other foreign leaders who are also confronted by hostile dictators, and see how they sound. For example, imagine if an American president announced that "Cuba has advanced missiles, so we must cede southern Florida to Castro; otherwise, there will be war with Cuba in three to five years." Or what if the president of South Korea told his people, "North Korea has advanced missiles, so we must surrender our most strategic border zone; otherwise, there will be war with the North in three to five years."

If the presence of sophisticated weapons in the hands of Israel's Arab enemies is sufficient reason to surrender to Arab demands, there will be no end to the demands and no end to the surrender. Today the Syrians are demanding the Golan. In the future, they will reassert some of the other demands they have made in the past, including an end to *aliyah*, self-rule for the Israeli Arabs in the Galilee, and the demilitarization of Israel. At each stage, those who endorse Rabin's politics of fear will say: "If we don't make peace by agreeing to Syria's demand, the Syrians will use their missiles against us."

And not just Syria. The PLO will soon have missiles, and Iran and Libya are now developing nuclear weapons. If they demand Islamic control of Jerusalem, should Israel surrender to that demand, to avert a war?

What is at stake, really, is the entire basis of Israeli national self-defense. Israel **cannot** survive as a sovereign state if its military and political decisions are calculated according to whether or not the Arabs have this or that weapon. Of course, the Syrians have missiles, and of course, the other Arab states do, too. That's why Israel develops, or purchases, the weapons it needs to counter them. Israel is not some weak little Third World country that must tremble in fear every time some Arab despot rattles his sword. Israel is a country filled with brilliant military strategists, brave soldiers, and scientific geniuses who have always been able to take the steps necessary to ensure that Israel can survive and prosper, regardless of Arab demands and regardless of Arab arsenals. When Arab regimes took threatening action, Israel didn't surrender to their demands; it took appropriate counter-action. When the Iraqis started developing nuclear weapons, the Israelis bombed the Iraqi nuclear factory. When Syrian fighter-jets tried to interfere with Israel's strike into Lebanon in 1982, the Israelis have developed a formidable nuclear arsenal.

Which raises an interesting question. Why is it that no Arab leader ever tells his people, "Israel has advanced missiles and nuclear weapons, so we had better make peace with the Israelis; otherwise, there will be a war...?" Because the Arabs understand that in the Middle East, it is strength, not surrender, that is the key to survival. Why doesn't Yitzhak Rabin understand that?

265

August 19, 1994

U.S. Weapons for Jordan - A Dangerous Idea

King Hussein of Jordan is about to get the best deal since the island of Manhattan was purchased from the Indians for a handful of trinkets. The Jordanian monarch is going to receive a huge arsenal of sophisticated American weapons, a hundred miles or more of Israeli territory, and Jordan's $900-million debt to the U.S. is going to be forgiven all in exchange for his signature on a meaningless piece of paper that his successor can, and probably will discard.

Amidst all the media hype and manufactured euphoria over the impending meeting between Hussein and Israel's Prime Minister Rabin, one glaring fact has been overlooked: there has been peace along the Israeli-Jordanian border for 27 years. It is not the kind of peace that is ratified in a treaty, because in the Middle East, where dictators rule, a treaty has no practical value. The peace between Israel and Jordan is the only kind of real peace that can be achieved in the Mideast peace enforced by fear. Jordan attacked Israel in 1967 because Hussein did not fear Israel's military power. He lost badly, and he learned his lesson. The next time the Arabs invaded Israel, in 1973, Jordan took part only along the Syrian frontier. The Jordanian- Israeli border remained quiet. And when the 1973 war ended, with the Israeli Army close enough to capture Damascus and Cairo, Hussein learned another lesson that Amman could be next. That's why he hasn't and attacked Israel since then, and that's why he would, in all likelihood, never attack Israel again, treaty or no treaty.

In short, Israel has nothing significant to gain from signing a treaty.

What will Jordan gain?

First, Jordan will apparently acquire a piece of Israeli territory. Hussein is demanding that Israel surrender over 150 square miles of land along the southern part of the Israeli-Jordanian borderland that is within Israel's pre-1967 border. Media reports suggest that Rabin is ready to give in to Jordan's demand.

266

Second, Jordan's $900 million debt to the United States will be forgiven. After Jordan sided with Iraq during the Gulf War, the U.S. cut off financial aid to the Jordanians. Now they will get $900 million, with more to come in the future. For a small, poor country like Jordan, that's quite a sum.

Third, and most important from Israel's point of view, Jordan will get sophisticated offensive weapons from the United States. Why you may ask, does Jordan need such weapons if it is making peace? That's a good question, but nobody's asking it. Instead, we'll hear vague warnings about how Jordan needs the weapons to fend off other Arab regimes such as Syria and Iraq. Of course, we are told that Syria is also now "moderate," and Iraq is still devastated from the Gulf War. But logic will be tossed aside as the weapon shipments start to flow from Washington to Amman.

The weapons issue is crucial. It is widely known that Hussein is dying of cancer. Since his regime is a dictatorship, there is no way of knowing who will replace him. And since the Moslem fundamentalist Hamas movement is strong in Jordan, there is good reason to fear that it will take over when the king dies. We've seen this all before in Iran. America poured weapons Into Iran when the Shah ruled, but when Khomeini took over, all of those deadly arms were suddenly in the hands of America-hating Moslem fanatics.

Such a disaster can be headed off if pro-Israel groups in the U.S. mount a full-scale lobbying effort against the provision of U.S. arms to Jordan. But if American Jews are silent, they will bear much of the moral responsibility if a future Jordanian regime aims its sophisticated American missiles at Jerusalem and Tel Aviv.

September 2, 1994

An Israeli General's View Of The Golan Heights

Emerging from a meeting with the U.S. joint chiefs of Staff recently, General Ehud Barak, chief of staff of the Israeli Army, declared that Israel "should remain on the Golan Heights, even in peace."

Barak is a military man, and as such, was offering a common-sense military perspective on the Golan Heights. He knows that when Syrian occupied the Golan during 1948-1967, it used the area to bombard Israeli villages below. He knows that it is Israel's presence on the commanding terrain of the Golan, just down the road from Damascus, that keeps Syria from attacking. He knows that even if the Syrians sign a peace treaty, they can't be trusted to honor it.

As a matter of fact, Yitzhak Rabin used to say the same thing. During the 1991 Knesset campaign, Rabin said that even in peace, Israel should not surrender the Golan. But Rabin, the politician, has replaced Rabin, the military man, and for months he has been trying to prepare the Israeli public for a phased surrender of the entire Golan.

Those like General Barak, who want Israel to choose military safety over political convenience, are finding that Rabin has little interest in their views. Indeed, a second statement that Barak made after his recent meeting with the U.S. Joint/Chiefs suggests that he is no longer privy to all of Rabin's plans. Barak told reporters that Rabin had not asked the U.S. to deploy troops on the Golan Heights if the territory is surrendered to Syria. During his last visit to Washington, in January 1993, Barak had made a similar statement. "Israel has never asked for American troops to protect us, and we never will," he declared. Yet during the 19 months between Barak's two visits and his two denials about U.S. troops on the Golan, American and Israeli officials have repeatedly confirmed that the Rabin government **has** asked for U.S. troops to be stationed on the Golan and that the Clinton administration is prepared to provide them.

Then-Defense Secretary Les Aspin told the Senate Armed Services Committee on April 1, 1993, that a plan for U.S. troops on the Golan was under consideration. Secretary of State Christopher has said the same thing on several occasions. Rep. Lee Hamilton has revealed that a survey is already underway to determine the exact sites on the Golan where GIs would be stationed. Assistant Secretary of State Robert Pellatreau told the House Foreign Affairs Committee on June 14, 1994, that a foreign presence on the Golan "is envisaged... and I think there is a large expectation that the United States would be part of that international presence."

On the Israeli side, Foreign Minister Peres has said that the idea has been discussed; Deputy Foreign Minister Yossi Beilin has argued that American troops would be "peacekeeping monitors" rather than "a fighting force": and Police Minister Moshe Shahal has revealed that the U.S. and Israel are considering a plan for stationing GIs on the Golan for 15 years. In a July 1, 1994 interview with the **Bottom Globe**, Prime Minister Rabin himself denounced the opponents of deploying GIs on the Golan, arguing angrily that the U.S. troops would be comparable to the U.S. forces in the Sinai. Why would Rabin go out of his way to make such a case, if the idea of putting Americans on the Golan was not under discussion?

Rabin's actions speak louder than Barak's words. Last month a coalition of pro-Israel groups led by American For a Safe Israel (AFSI), the Christians' Israel Public Action Campaign (CIPAC), and Frank Gaffney's Center for Security Policy asked Congress to pass a bill instructing the Pentagon to undertake a study of the risks of putting GIs on the Golan. The Rabin government and AIPAC pressured members of Congress to oppose the bill. Rabin is understandably worried that if the American public understood the risks that American troops would face (such as terrorist attacks by the Hezbollah gangsters in southern Lebanon), there would be substantial opposition to the proposal. That would take away Rabin's fig leaf, and leave him to explain to the Israeli public how he can put Israel's security in the hands of Syrian dictator Hafez Assad. Despite the valiant efforts of Senators Malcolm Wallop and Strom Thurmond, the bill was defeated.

Fortunately for the American public, it turns out that the Rand Corporation, a recipient of federal funds, has already done a study about the risks of stationing U.S. troops in various trouble spots, including the Golan. Despite the best efforts of the State Department, word of the Rand report leaked out, and AFSI, CIPAC, and the Center for Security Policy pressed for Senate action. The Senate, led by Senators Nichols and D'Amate on the Republican side, and Senator Inouye on the Democratic side, voted unanimously on August 10 to order the Rand Corporation to hand over the report by October 13.

The U.S. Congress has displayed an appropriate sense of responsibility toward the American public. Americans have a right to know the risks of a Golan deployment so that they can decide whether or not they want their sons turned into shooting targets for Hezbollah.

September 30, 1994

Mitterand And Peres: Birds of A Feather?

After years of deceiving the public about his past, French President Francois Mitterand has been revealed as a collaborator with the pro-Nazi Vichy regime in France during the Holocaust. Friends of Israel will note a second, interesting angle to the story; one of Mitterand's closest friends among international statesmen is Israeli Foreign Minister Shimon Peres, who has been engaged to deceive the public about his political activities for the past year.

The Mitterand revelations appear in a new biography by the French writer, Pierre Pean, entitled a French Youth. That title suits Mitterand just fine since he has responded to the revelations by claiming that he joined the pro-Nazi forces because he was a misguided youth who didn't realize that the Vichy regime was deporting Jews from occupied France to the Nazi death camps. Mitterand now claims that he "never flirted with the extreme right," but Pean's book covers clearly that he was active in the extreme-right "National Volunteers" group in pre-war France.

When the pro-Nazi Vichy forces occupied part of France during the war, Mitterand Joined them. He was a government archivist for Vichy, worked for other Vichy agencies, and was an ardent admirer of the Vichy leader, Marshal Petain (the book cover even features a previously unknown photo of Mitterand meeting Petain). Mitterand's claim that he did not know that the Vichy government was departing the Jews seems absurd when one considers that he was a Vichy government official and a passionate admirer of Petain. The book also reveals that to this day. Mitterand maintains close friendships with his old Vichy pals. Including Rene Bousquet, a Vichy police chief who was arrested for organizing the deportations of French Jews to Auschwitz.

Perhaps it is no surprise that during his years as a French political leader, Mitterand has always been strongly pro-PLO, pressuring Israel to make cessions and urging the creation of a PLO state in Israel's backyard. After all,

Arafat's "final solution" and the Vichy government s final solution were not very different.

And perhaps it is no surprise that Shimon Peres and Mitterand became such good friends, since Peres, too, is an International leader with a record of deception and a soft spot for the PLO. After campaigning for office in 1992 on a Labor Party platform that opposed talks with the PLO, Peres became foreign minister of Israel and promptly devoted his time to arranging secret talks with the PLO.

Like Mitterand, who did not care about the illegality and immorality of what Petain was doing, Peres was not bothered by the illegality and immorality of dealing with the PLO. Like Mitterand, who hid his activities to preserve his political career, Peres hid his dealings with the PLO so that he could present the Israeli public with a "peace" agreement that would advance his political career.

Peres may yet receive a Nobel Prize for his efforts. Many statesmen had received prizes and honors even when they engaged In reprehensible behavior. (Note the recent knighting of Kurt Waldheim by the Pope.) But eventually, his past may catch up with him, as it has caught up with his old friend Francois Mitterand. And history may not judge Peres any more kindly than it will judge Nazi collaborators like Mitterand.

November 4, 1994

If Clinton Was Going to Havana, Rather Than Damascus, What Would the Reaction Be?

President Clinton's announcement that he intended to visit Syria should have sparked an outpouring of angry protest from the American Jewish community. Instead, most American Jewish "leaders" have been silent. Afraid of "rocking the boat," they prefer to stand idly by while bloodthirsty Syria has its image whitewashed, and Israel gets squeezed for one-sided concessions on the Golan Heights.

Imagine the reaction if Clinton announced he intended to visit Castro's Cuba. The Cuban-American community would be up in arms. There would be massive protests. Castro, after all, is a brutal dictator, and Cuban Americans would be justifiably furious at the thought of an American president appeasing the Communist tyrant who has enslaved their former homeland.

And imagine the reaction if, during the years of South African apartheid, an American president had announced a visit to Pretoria. African-Americans would be horrified. They would besiege the White House angrily - and justifiably - resenting the idea of an American president granting legitimacy to a racist tyranny.

American Jews should be equally outraged by the Clinton visit to Damascus. The American Jewish community is much larger than the Cuban-American community and much more politically influential than the African American community. Surely American Jews could offer as many reasons not to appease Syria as Cuban-American or African-Americans would have offered for their causes. Here are a few that immediately come to mind:

- Syria is continuing to stockpile huge amounts of sophisticated new weapons, including advanced Scud missiles armed with chemical warheads; Syria behaves as if it is preparing for war, not peace.

273

• Syria is still sponsoring international terrorism. A variety of Arabs. European and Asian terrorist groups have offices in Damascus and training camps in the Syrian-occupied parts of Lebanon. In fact, Syria is still on the official State Department list of terror-sponsors.

• Syria is the primary patron of the Hezbollah gangs that regularly terrorize northern Israel. Hezbollah fires its rockets at Israeli villages from Syrian-occupied southern Lebanon. Iranian weapons can reach Hezbollah only with the permission of the Syrian army. The Hezbollah suicide bomber, who killed 241 U.S. Marines in 1983, came from Syrian territory.

• Senior Syrian officials are still deeply involved in the international narcotics trade. Congressional committees have gathered ample evidence on Syria's drug activities. The opium fields of Syrian-occupied Lebanon are a source of income for Syrian middlemen, who are not troubled by the fact that the drugs they market are helping to destroy America's inner cities.

• Vicious anti-Israel and anti-Jewish hate still appears regularly in the Syrian government-controlled media. Syrian newspapers openly cheer Arab terrorist attacks against Israel.

• Syria is harboring Alois Brunner, the most notorious Nazi war criminal alive today. While the American government is co-sponsoring the new Holocaust Memorial Museum in Washington, the Syrian government is thumbing its nose at the Holocaust by giving shelter to Brunner.

• Syria spits on American values. Syria is ruled by a fascist dictator. There is no freedom of the press, no freedom of religion, no freedom of assembly. Everything about Syria is the exact opposite of what Americans believe and cherish.

For these reasons and so many others, American Jews must speak out. The time has come for American Jews to say to President Clinton about Syria, as Elie Wiesel said to President Reagan about Bitburg: "No, Mr. President, that is not a place for you." Wiesel has, above all, a keen sense of history. So should the rest of us. History will deal harshly with American Jewry if it is silent at this crucial moment. Today our history books appropriately condemn American Jewish leaders for their silence during the Holocaust. One tremble at the thought of what future history books will record if Jewish leaders stand idly by while an American president whitewashes an Arab dictator who dreams of doing with chemical-tipped Scud missiles what Hitler did with gas chambers.

November 9, 1994

A Letter from A Quaker To an Orthodox Rabbi Brother

Dear Rabbi _____, BROTHER'

I have been watching the unfolding events in the Middle East with considerable interest, as I know you have. But I wonder if even a clergyman such as yourself has grasped the startling theological implications of what is happening.

It seems to me that the position adopted by most Jews, observant and non-observant alike, concerning Israel today has redefined Jewishness in, a radical and - from my point of view - delightful way. **What I am saying to you is that World Jewry's support for the policy of giving the PLO control over parts of Israel represents a de-nationalizing of Judaism which is making Judaism a religion that now hardly differs at all from liberal Christianity, such as the Friends (Quakers), to which I belong.** As a Quaker, I am overjoyed by this development, and I feel compelled to try to help you understand it, too.

I am aware, of course, that not all Jews are happy about what the Israeli government is doing. Yet it seems clear that the vast majority of Jews today fall into two categories: those who support the Rabin government and those who refrain from fighting it, even if they are not happy about it. In other words, the majority of world Jewry is going along with the Rabin policies.

You know that we Quakers have long advocated that Israel surrender the territories to the PLO. As pacifists, we are convinced that one must appease one's enemy and tum the other cheek to violent attackers, and for many years we have been counseling Israel to do just that. It gives me great pleasure to see that Israel finally has a prime minister who has taken our advice.

By giving up control of those territories, and by declaring its readiness to negotiate the future of Jerusalem as well, the Israeli government has taken a giant step in breaking down the barriers that separated Jews and Judaism from

276

the rest of the world. Let's face it, Rabbi_____, Brother. Now that peace is dawning in the Middle East, there is no reason for Judaism to retain its national element. Nationalism only leads to persecution and suffering, and Jewish nationalism was no different. A government that recognizes that land has little or no value is a government that has gone a long way towards declaring that nationalism has little or no value.

Hopefully, Israel will soon realize what the next stage must bring. For if Rabin and most of world Jewry understand that peace is more important than Hebron and more important than eastern Jerusalem, soon they will realize that peace is more important than Tel Aviv,

Haifa and Beersheba. On that day, all of the residents of the Holy Land can join hands in a single, secular, democratic state of Palestine.

We Quakers recognize your sincere belief in the All-Mighty and respect the Jewish rituals that go along with that belief. Those few rituals need not divide Jews from non-Jews. The main barriers were nationalism, borders, and land, and now that you are renouncing such things, we can, at last, welcome the Jews into the family of nations.

There will be no logical reason left for Jews to remain exclusive to only marry among themselves. It should be obvious that the main religious and social activities of the Jewish community will hardly differ from those of we Quakrs and other Christians helping the poor, the sick, the orphans, and so on.

Let our children mingle and marry each other, let what we have in common overwhelm the minor differences that still divide us. Let the dramatic changes that have taken place in the Middle East harbinger the dramatic changes in Jewish-Christian relations of which we Quakers have always dreamed. For the sake of peace, you have given up the land that you once held dear. Now, for the sake of brotherhood and universalism, isn't it time for you to give up whatever else divides you from us?

Sincerely, Your Quaker Friend.

November 16, 1994

The Crime Bill: A Lesson for Israel

The Clinton anti-crime bill bears a powerful message for Israel. The Rabin government can learn some valuable lessons by paying attention to how the United States deals with its own killers.

The anti-crime bill puts 100,000 additional policemen on the streets of America. It mandates the death penalty for some 50 crimes that were previously punished with lesser penalties. It also includes the "three strikes and you're out" provision, which metes out life imprisonment for somebody who is convicted of three separate violent crimes.

If ever there was a country that needed to implement a similar crackdown on killers, it's Israel. Every single day, violent Arabs hurl deadly rocks and firebombs at innocent Israeli motorists. And virtually every single week, Arab terrorists murder an Israeli, whether in Gaza or near Tel Aviv. The two young Jewish construction workers whose throats were slit by Arab terrorists on August 26 were the latest in a long series of victims of Arab violence.

The Israelis should take a leaf from Clinton's book. They should be putting additional police and soldiers in trouble spots. They should be implementing the death penalty for terrorist murders. They should have a "three strikes, and you're out" law.

Yet Prime Minister Rabin is doing exactly the opposite.

Rabin has been withdrawing Israeli soldiers and border police from areas in Judea, Samaria, and Gaza, where Arabs have been attacking Jews. Rabin has refused to consider the death penalty (although, ironically, the PLO self-rule government is reportedly· considering having a death penalty of its own). Instead of keeping terrorists in prison, Rabin has been releasing them by the thousands, as a concession to the PLO.

The last time a Prime Minister from the Labor Party made such a concession, Israel got the *intifada* as a result. Prime Minister Shimon Peres' release of over 1,000 terrorists in the 1985 prisoner exchange with the Popular Front for the Liberation of Palestine gave the PLO the men and women who became the leaders of the intifada rioting. The terrorists who are being released by Rabin and· Peres now are not likely to become artists and accountants. They will soon return to doing what they know best, murdering and maiming Israelis. While President Clinton is trying to put violent American criminals behind bars, Rabin and Peres are putting violent Arab criminals back on Israel's streets.

And those streets are not safe, to begin with. Israeli children who live in towns in Judea and Samaria cannot travel to school except in buses with buffet-proof armored plating. Nobody who lives in those areas can drive to work, or a shopping center, except in cars with shatter-proof windshields, or they risk being inundated with shards of glass when the Arab rocks start flying. Rabin's policy of withdrawing more and *more* troops from the territories means that the roads are safer for Arab terrorists, who can *move* freely about and strike at their victims without fear of being captured.

As Israel's security deteriorates, as widows and orphans tum to Mr. Rabin, pleading with him to do something, how does the prime minister respond? He tells them that in -Judea, Samaria, and Gaza, peace will bring security - even though everyone can see that his "peace" has brought less security. And he tells them that in the Golan Heights, the presence of foreign (probably American) troops will bring security. Zionism's most basic principle, independence, and self-reliance are being exchanged for PLO promises and foreign troops. How sad and how frightening.

December 2, 1994

U.S. Generals Warn Against Risks of Putting Troops on The Golan Heights

In recent months, the Clinton Administration has repeatedly rejected calls by pro-Israel activists and loading members of Congress for a Pentagon study of the risks of stationing American troops on the Golan Heights. Dissatisfied with the administration's stand, a group of prominent former U.S. Army generals have taken matters into their own hands and authorized, a compelling analysis of the pros and cons of deploying American GIs on the Golan.

The study, published by the Washington, D.C. based Center for Security Policy, is called "U.S. Forces on the Golan Heights: All Assessment of Benefits and Costs." One glance at the credentials of the authors makes it clear that they know what they're writing about. They include, among others, Lieutenant General (Ret.) John Pustay, former president of the National Defense University; General (Ret.) Bernard Schriever, Commander of the U.S. Air Force Systems Command from 1959-1966; and Admiral (Ret.) Elmo R. Zumwalt, Jr., Chief of Naval Operations from 1970-1974.

The generals' study begins with a helpful summary of the strategic value of the Golan Heights, particularly in this age of missiles. "Even thou missiles can fly over the highest terrain feature, including the Golan Heights, they do not negate the strategic significant territorial depth," the generals note. Without the Golan, the Syrians could only fire long-range missiles that aren't accurate and could not pinpoint crucial military targets. With the Golan, however, the Syrians could fire short-range missiles that are precise and could knockout specific targets of military importance to Israel.

The study then proceeds to an in-depth exclamation of the many risks involved in all the possible situations that a U.S. force might be expected to undertake on the Golan.

280

For example, could a U.S. force be useful in monitoring Syrian activity on the Golan to provide Israel with an early warning about suspending attack? Not really. The Israelis could not rely on the intelligence-gathering of a third party that would be anxious to remain "neutral."

What about the argument that the mere purpose of Americans would serve as a political deterrence so the Syrians would be reluctant to ever attacks and harm Americans? The generals point out that Syria knows "that its aggression will antagonize the United forces **whether or not U.S. troops are stationed on the Golan**. At most, such troops could serve as the main factor in Syria's calculations."

Could the U.S. troops serve as a military defense to block a Syrian attack? Hardly. The force under consideration involves 800 to 1,000 lightly-armed soldiers. They would be in no position to stop a Syrian attack.

How about serving as a "tripwire" that can trigger automatic U.S. military intervention in the event of Syrian invasion? That would assume that the U.S. could and would intervene. The generals contend that "it is not likely given current constraints on U.S. military capabilities, especially in the field of sea-and-air-lift that the United States are making the necessary intervention in a timely frame. Months were required to get U.S. forces in place, ready for action in the recent Persian Gulf conflict. Golda Meir once remarked, when asked about giving territory in exchange for a "guarantee" of U.S. intervention, "By the time you get here, we won't be here."

The Center for Security Policy study also sees the impact that a U.S. deployment would have on Israel's ability to launch a pre-emptive strike against the threat to U.S. troops from Arab terrorist going the region; the effect of a U.S. deployment on Arab-Israel relations; and the advantages and disadvantages of having a multilateral, rather than purely Arab force on the Golan. There is also an interesting revision about the flawed analogy between the U.S. now in the Sinai and the proposed U.S. force in Golan.

This study is, without doubt, one of the important documents about Israel to be published in recent memory, and no friend of Israel should be unknown to it. Copies may be obtained by calling the Center for Security Policy at 202-466-0515.

December 30, 1994

Zionism Under Attack from Within

The Zionism-is-racism resolution may have been stricken from the books, but Zionism is still under attack - this time from within.

Left-wing Israeli historians, who call themselves "revisionist historians," have taken upon themselves the task of revising Zionist history to suit their political agenda. They point an accusing finger at Israel and Zionism, claiming that Israel expelled the Arabs in 1948, that Israel started the various Arab Israeli wars, and that Israel has deliberately squandered numerous opportunities for peace with the Arabs.

Consumed with guilt and perhaps even self-hatred, their unstated goal is to erode the Jewish people's pride in its heroes - such as the founders of Israel and the Israeli Army - and to glorify enemies of the Jews.

The second category of accusers of Zionism consists of those left-wing Israeli politicians who · seek to replace Zionism with· other "isms," such as:

- Regionalism the idea that Israel should integrate itself into the region around it as if that region has anything to offer in the way of culture or morality of values;

- Economism, the idea that the most important thing is for Israel to become the "Hong Kong of the Middle East," as if the goal of Zionism is to make money as if concepts such as a Jewish homeland or Zionist pioneering are irrelevant;

- One-worldism, the illusion that old hostilities are really ending, that age of international brotherhood began to dawn on the day of the White House Handshake.

There are the same Israeli politicians who describe Jewish settlements as "thorns" that "must be uprooted," or who say that "for the sake of national security," Jews must be evicted from their homes a concept, by the way, which was articulated with violent force by another regime, earlier in this century. One wonders if Shulamit Aloni was aware of the frightening historical irony she was invoking when she said on Israel Radio, on November 11 (1994), that "for the sake of security, the settlements should be removed." And what was Yossi Sarid thinking, when he recently declared that 50 to 60 Jewish towns in Judea and Samaria should be immediately dismantled for the sake of Israel's security?

In the Yad Vashem Archives, in Jerusalem, there is a letter dated July 19, 1942. It's an order for the immediate expulsion of all remaining Jews from central Poland, signed by the chief of the SS, Hein Rich Himmler. "These measures," *it* says, "are demanded following the necessary ethnic separation of races and peoples in the framework of the new order of Europe, also in the interest of the security and cleanliness of the German Reich..."

These are Zionism's challengers today: those who seek to defame Zionism by rewriting its post, and those who seek to replace Zionism by steering its future down the empty, un-Jewish path of regionalism and one-worldism, and mass expulsions of the Jews in the name of "Security."

February 24, 1995

Russian Jews In Israel: A New Political Force

In recent weeks, there has been considerable talk about Russian Jews in Israel establishing their political party to compete in next year's Knesset election. Ethnic protest parties are nothing new in Israel, but the Russian Jewish community in Israel has more reason than most ethnic groups to be disillusioned with Israel's governing parties.

Ethnic-based parties have been tried before in Israel; some have succeeded, and others have failed. The Tami Party, which sought the votes of Moroccan Jews, won two seats in the 1981 elections but soon faded away. On the other hand, the Shas Party, which is supported by religious Sephardim, has won from four to six seats in each of the last three elections and has played an occasionally significant role in Israeli political life.

A Russian party has the potential to be larger and more successful than previous ethnic parties. Because of the huge influx of Russian Jewish immigrants in recent years, such a party could conceivably win ten or more Knesset seats. With that many seats, it could emerge as the third-largest party and function as the "kingmaker" in determining the makeup of the next governing coalition.

But will significant numbers of Russian Jewish immigrants vote for such a party? In the 1992 elections, most Russian Jews voted for the Labor Party. Opinion polls found that while most of the Russians were more "hawkish" on security issues than Labor, they voted fi Labor because of what they perceived as a bread-and-butter issue: the loan guarantees. Labor's election propaganda successfully conveyed the idea that if Labor won, Israel would receive the $10-billion in U.S. loan guarantees, which would provide jobs and houses for Russian immigrants. The Bush Administration, which was anxious to get rid of the Likud government, helped out by dropping loud hints that Labor would qualify for the loan guarantees.

The new Labor government did indeed get the loan guarantees - but it didn't use them for the immigrants. Instead, billions of shekels were spent bailing out Histadrut-owned factories that were failing and rescuing *kibbutzim* that were deeply in debt because of socialist mismanagement.

When the average Russian immigrant is asked the question, "Are you better off today than you were to 1992, before Rabin was elected?" the answer is inevitably "no."

There is another important factor that Russian Jews should keep in mind when they go to the polls next year. When they look back at the historical record, to see which Israeli parties contributed to the struggle for Soviet Jewish freedom, they will discover that the Israeli Left - the Labor Party and its left-wing allies - were consistently uninterested in the plight of Soviet Jewry. Some Labor Zionists were reluctant to criticize the Soviet regime because their youthful affection for Marxism blinded them. Others on the Israeli left were simply so enthralled by the idea of having Israel-Soviet relations, that they didn't want the Soviet Jewish problem getting in the way.

When Russian Jewish voters step into the voting booths in 1996, they will be thinking about how to Labor Party treated them in decades past, and how it has been treating them now. The consequences are likely to have a dramatic impact on the future of Israel.

March 3, 1995

An Arab Dies In Jenin

A Palestinian Arab by the name of Zaki Udeh, traveling in his car near the city of Jenin (in northern Samaria) on February 17, was killed when Arab terrorists raked his auto with gunfire.

At first glance, one might consider Udeh just another in a very long line of Arabs who have been executed by Arab terrorist death squads in Judea, Samaria, and Gaza. There have been so many such killings since the *intifada* began in 1989 - well over 1,000 that it would be all too easy to forget his name and forget his death.

Many of the victims were killed because they were accused of being "collaborators," meaning that they had some dealings with Israelis on one level or another. But quite a few of the victims had nothing to do with any Israelis and were murdered because they were suspected of "immorality" (which, according to the Islamic definition, covers a wide variety of offenses).

Zaki Udeh, it so happens, was suspected of having some unspecified connection to Israelis. That fact leads us to the first important lesson to be learned from his murder.

Think about it. If the Palestinian Arabs have really become "moderate," if they really want to live in peace with Israel, why should they murder a fellow Arab for having cooperated with Israelis? Why should it bother them that Zaki Udeh had some Israeli connection? If we have entered a new era of peaceful coexistence, then Udeh was just peaceful - which should not bother anybody?

The Udeh murder is a reminder that among the Palestinian Arabs, hatred of Israel remains strong. Israel is still regarded as the enemy, and Arabs who have some connection to Israelis are regarded as traitors who are aiding the enemy. There is no new mood of peace, love, coexistence, and forgiveness. There is the same burning hostility that there always was. The "peace agreement" is perceived by the Arabs as a clever tactic for wresting Judea, Samaria, and Gaza away from the Jews.

The site of the Udeh murder is also significant. He died near Jenin the same week that the Rabin government was offering to let the PLO extend its self-rule to Jenin. In the latest round of Israel-PLO negotiations, Rabin practically begged Yasir Arafat to take over Jenin. Arafat, ever the shrewd bargainer, refused so that in a few weeks or months when he does take it over, the world will see it as some kind of concession.

At that point, when the Israeli forces withdraw from the Jenin region, there will be many more Zaki Udehs. Every Arab who ever had anything to do with Israelis will be the target of terrorists. And Jews who live in the Jenin area will likewise be left to fend for themselves against the various Hamas and Fatah (PLO) gangs that roam the region.

An Arab died in Jenin Feb. 17. His death was a vivid reminder that Palestinian Arab extremism is alive and well. And it was a warning of what will come if the Rabin government continues to hand over the heartland of Israel to the PLO.

April 7, 1995

Senator Kyl And the Future of Jerusalem

Why is the PLO so determined to make Jerusalem its capital? After all, Jerusalem is not even mentioned in the Koran. When Muslims ruled the area during the Middle Ages, they never made Jerusalem any kind of regional capital. When the Arabs (that is, the Jordanians) occupied Jerusalem during 1948-1967, no Arab leader bothered to visit the city. King Hussein could have declared eastern Jerusalem to be his capital, but instead, he kept Amman as his capital, and, in fact, he let the Old City of Jerusalem deteriorate into a slum without basic municipal services. So why do the Arabs now suddenly seem so passionate about Jerusalem?

Because the Jews are ruling it - and that's something Arabs can't accept. Jewish control of Jerusalem symbolizes Jewish sovereignty and strength. It's a powerful physical reminder of the rebirth of Jewish nationalism, and the triumph of Israel over is enemies. Arab nationalism and Muslim theology demand that the Jews live as third-class citizens, under the heel of Arab Muslim overlords. The Arabs have set their gunsights on Jerusalem because they understand that Jerusalem is the heart of the Jewish State. By tearing the Old City of Jerusalem away from Israel, the PLO will be striking a mortal blow at the entire concept of Jewish sovereignty.

The Arabs understand the deeper meaning of the struggle over Jerusalem. It's not just a fight over this or that neighborhood in a very real sense; the fate of the entire State of Israel is at stake. That's why Yasir Arafat repeatedly calls for a *jihad* to conquer Jerusalem from the Jews. That's why the PLO has set up 10 "government ministries" in the city, as part of its plan to establish a *de-facto* "capital of Palestine" right under Israel's nose.

What can American Jews do to protect Jerusalem?

Congress will soon consider two separate, and very different bills, concerning the embassy question. The first, which is being proposed by Senators Daniel Moynihan and Alfonse D'Amato of New York, requires that the

U.S. embassy be moved to Jerusalem by 1999. Senators Moynihan and D'Amato are stalwart friends of Israel, and the American Jewish community is certainly grateful for their well-intentioned bill concerning Jerusalem. The problem, however, is that 1999 is too far off and things could change between then and now.

What if the political climate in the United States shifts between now and 1999, and Congress no longer regards it as wise to move the embassy? What if the balance of power in Congress changes, and the majority supports the administration's position (which is against moving the embassy)? What if the Rabin government, under international pressure, makes concessions on Jerusalem (so that moving the embassy would become irrelevant)?

That's why the other congressional initiative, by Senator Jon Kyl (of Arizona), is so important. The Kyl bill will prevent government funds from being used to operate the U.S. embassy in Israel, **as of October 1, 1995,** unless the embassy is located in Jerusalem.

The Moynihan-D'Amato bill is well-intentioned, but it has no teeth, which is why the Clinton Administration is not opposing it.

The Kyl bill means a business, which is why the Clinton Administration is vigorously fighting against it.

For the Kyl bill to pass, in the face of stiff opposition from the Administration, American Jews will have to launch an all-out effort on its behalf by calling, writing, and faxing Members of Congress to urge them to support Kyl's measure. This will have to be a grassroots effort because Jewish establishment groups like AIPAC and the Conference of Presidents of Major American Jewish Organizations are refusing to endorse the Kyl bill. (Remember how AIPAC refused to oppose the administration when it intentionally wouldn't veto the UN resolution calling Jerusalem "occupied territory"....?) Too many so-called Jewish "leaders" prefer to cozy up to those in power, rather than take part in the battle for Jerusalem.

There is no room for timidity or compromising when the future of Jerusalem is at stake. Moving the embassy to Jerusalem would declare to the entire world that America supports Jerusalem as Israel's capital. This would be a vital boost for Israel's morale and would strengthen Israel's ability to resist pressure to redivide the city.

Now is the time for American Jewry to join hands with Senator Kyl to help save Jerusalem from Arafat and the PLO.

April 28, 1994

Where Are the Tears for Americans Killed by Syrian-Sponsored Terrorists?

The very week that the Clinton Administration was vowing to severely punish the terrorists who bombed the Federal building in Oklahoma City, **The New York Times** reported that the Administration was responding with kid-gloves treatment to Saudi Arabia's sabotage of a U.S. effort to capture a terrorist who murdered hundreds of Americans in Lebanon in 1983.

The news broke on Friday, April 21, and it couldn't have been more ironic. While rescue teams were still desperately searching for survivors amid the rubble in Oklahoma City. **The Times** was revealing that Saudi Arabia had deliberately blocked an attempt by the Federal Bureau of Investigation to capture lmad Mughniyah. He's the Muslim terrorist leader who was responsible for the kidnapping of Americans in Lebanon during the 1980s, the Syrian-sponsored bombing of the U.S. Marines headquarters in Lebanon in 1983 (killing 241 Americans) and the 1985 hijacking of an airliner, during which the hijackers murdered an American serviceman, Robert Stethem.

The FBI had discovered that Mughniyah was on a flight from Sudan to Beirut in early April, with a stopover in Riyadh, Saudi Arabia. They informed Prince Bandar, the Saudi Arabian ambassador in Washington, of their plans. The Saudis responded by canceling the flight's stopover so that Mughniyah could escape.

How did the Clinton Administration react to the Saudi rescue of a terrorist with the blood of hundreds of Americans on his hands? The White House kept the Incident secret for more than two weeks until **The Times** got hold of the information and published it. Evidently, the Administration didn't want to embarrass its oil-rich Saudi friends. Questioned by reporters, Clinton officials "gave Saudi Arabia the benefit of the doubt," **The Times** noted. Secretary of State Warren Christopher offered the excuse that the operation had taken place within a "fairly short time frame," as if the Saudis didn't have enough time to think it over. Christopher acknowledged that "we did not get the kind of cooperation that we hoped we might have." But he refrained from any meaningful criticism of the Saudis.

The Clinton Administration covered up the Saudis' vile behavior even though this episode was only the latest ma series of Saudi slaps in America's face:

- The U.S. has asked to station a brigade's worth of military equipment in Saudi Arabia to save time and money in the event of Iraqi aggression in the future. The Saudis said no.

- When Secretary of State Christopher visited Saudi King Fahd in March, Fahd kept him waiting for seven hours.

- Saudi Arabia has violated the U.S. led sanctions against Libya.

- The Saudis have rejected the Clinton Administration's request to stop financing the Hamas terrorists who have been massacring Israelis.

That's right, this is the same Saudi Arabia for whom the United States sacrificed hundreds of soldiers during the Gulf War, to protect it from being overrun by Iraq.

The Clinton Administration's failure to get tough with the Saudis over blocking the arrest of the terrorist leader Maghniyah is only the latest in a long series of weak responses to terrorists and their supporters. The Administration keeps trying to cozy up to Syria (by pressuring Israel to give up the Golan Heights), even though Syria is one of the major international sponsors of terrorism The Administration refuses to put financial pressure on the PLO (by withholding aid) to seriously crackdown on Hamas and Islamic Jihad. The Administration pressured Israel to permit the early return of the 415 Hamas terror leaders that it deported in December 1992. The Administration has called the victims of the Oklahoma City bombing "victims of terrorism," while referring to Israeli victims of Arab terrorism as "victims of the peace process."

That kind of double standard will no doubt seem confusing to logical people; one wonders what terrorists, to whom logic means nothing, will read into it.

What kind of message does that send to would-be terrorists, whether they are Muslim fanatics in the Mideast or ultra-right-wing fanatics in the Midwest? How shall we understand the tears the Administrations sheds over victims of American terrorists in Oklahoma City if it won't take action against Syria for sponsoring and assisting terrorists who murdered Americans in Lebanon? For all of President Clinton's tough words about meting out "swift, severe, and certain" punishment to terrorists, will the terrorists believe that he really means what he says? Actions speak louder than words, and when it comes to taking real action against terrorism and its supporters, this Administration's record is disappointing indeed.

May 12, 1995

Going from Retaliation to Rewards for Terrorism

The word "Entebbe" has come to mean a great deal more than an airport in Uganda, even more than the Israeli rescue of hostages there in 1976. "Entebbe" summarizes the approach to terrorism that used to be Israel's policy: don't bargain with terrorists, don't make deals with them, just track them clown wherever they may be, and use whatever force is necessary to crush them. Israel's smashing victory over the PLO hijackers in Entebbe in 1976 sent an iron-fisted message around the world: no rewards for terrorism.

There was an important corollary to the Entebbe approach: forceful retaliation against terrorists. Once a particular terrorist attack was repelled, and the hostages were freed, there had to be swift and merciless retaliation. The terrorists had to know that they would pay a high price for their evil deeds.

Thus, when the "*fedayeen*" terrorists of the 1950s, the forerunners of the PLO attacked Israelis, a special Israeli Army Counter-terror unit, led by Ariel Sharon, launched tough and effective raids on villager; in Jordan and the Gaza Strip that harbored terrorists. When the PLO slaughtered Israeli athletes at the Munich Olympics in 1972, Prime Minister Golda Meir sent out special hit teams to assassinate senior PLO terrorists around the world. When the PLO massacred 37 Israeli bus passengers on the Tel Aviv Highway in 1978, the Israeli Army undertook "Operation Litani," to crush terrorist encampments in southern Lebanon, and when the PLO rebuilt its forces there, Israel responded to PLO terror in 1982 with "Operation Peace for Galilee."

But along the way, something happened. Western governments, anxious to preserve their access to **Arab oil**, began pressuring Israel to stop retaliating. Criticism by the International media and the Jewish Left wore down the Israeli government's morale and determination. And in 1992, lured by the illusory promise of getting U.S. loan guarantees, Israeli voters elected a government that has chosen to reward terrorists rather than retaliate against them.

Instead of being punished for its 30 years; .of slaughtering Israelis (and several Americana); the PLO was handsomely rewarded: recognition by Israel; the release of thousands of imprisoned terrorists and rioters; phase-by-phase control over Judea, Samaria and Gaza; billions of dollars in international aid (including a promise of $500-million from the U.S.); hints that it will be given control of some part of Jerusalem; a promise to permit the return of hundreds of thousands of Arab "refugees"; and more.

And the rewarding of the terrorists continues. Every time there is a Hamas or Islamic Jihad attack, the Rabin government, with encouragement and pressure from the Clinton Administration, announces that it will continue and even speed up the "peace process." that is, the process of giving control of the territories to the PLO. The terrorists are being told that their murders will result in even faster Israeli concessions. Thus, the terrorist attacks perfectly suit the PLO'S strategy. As the PLO's "Justice Minister," Freih Abu Medein recently declared the Hamas attacks "complement" the PLO's diplomatic efforts.

Syria, too, is enjoying rewards for its terrorism. Even though Syria is, according to the US State Department, a sponsor of international terrorism; even though Syria arms and controls the Hezbollah terrorists who regularly attack Israel from southern Lebanon; and even though Syria harbors at least ten terrorist groups in Damascus and others in Syrian-controlled Lebanon - despite all this, the Clinton Administration and the Rabin government have been actively courting the Syrian regime. President Clinton has twice rewarded Syrian dictator Hafez Assad by meeting him publicly in Damascus. Rubin and his aides are constantly heaping compliments on the supposedly "moderate" Syrian regime. The Syrians have not taken a single step to reduce their support of terrorists, and why should they, when they are so handsomely rewarded?

Rewarding the PLO, Hamas and Syria send a dangerous message to terrorists in every country: that there are political and financial reward: to be gained from massacring innocent people. In these difficult tunes, when potential terrorists are carefully watching to see how the Free World responds to terrorist attacks, it is vital that they not believe that they will be rewarded for their violence.

June 30, 1995

Our Men in Jerusalem

There are many and varying rumors about an Israeli-Syrian agreement being reached in the· near future, but what all of the rumors have in common is that they involve an agreement based on the Rabin government capitulating to Syria's terms. Years ago, a book was published, entitled **Our Man in Damascus,** about an Israeli who successfully infiltrated senior Syrian government circles and obtained crucial information for Israel. Will there one day be a book published under the title "Our Men in Jerusalem," about how certain individuals in the Israeli government did their utmost to hasten Israel's surrender to Syria's demands?

It may never be known precisely who played the key role in manipulating Israel's policies to the advantage of Damascus. Was its Cabinet Minister Shulamit Aloni, with her declarations that the Golan Heights belong to Syria under international law (a total lie)? Was it Deputy Foreign Minister Yossi Beilin, who, despite his junior title, has been the real architect of the Rabin government's foreign policy? Was it Foreign Minister Shimon Peres, who, according to media reports, has constantly been going behind the prime minister's back to make additional, unauthorized concessions to the Arabs? Or, in the end, was it really Prime Minister Yitzhak Rabin himself, pretending to be "reluctant" and "hawkish" while initiating, engineering, and approving all the concessions that are being made?

We may never know for sure. But one thing is clear: the Assad regime is watching the results and enjoying them immensely:

* To get elected, Rabin vowed never to give up the Golan Heights. Now he has made it clear that he has no intention of keeping his word.

* Rabin government officials used to say that they would give up *some* of the Golan, but not all of it. Now they have said that they will give it all up.

*At one point, Rabin's aides were telling reporters that Rabin was insisting on a reduction in the size of the Syrian army as part of an agreement with Damascus. A few weeks later, the media was reporting that Rabin had dropped that demand because it was hindering "progress" in the negotiations.

* From the beginning, Rabin's negotiators insisted that Syria would have to pull its forces back from a certain amount of territory beyond the Golan Heights (since even a demilitarized Golan, in Syrian hands, is not wide enough to ensure Israel's safety). Syria promptly demanded that Israel do likewise in the Galilee, an obviously absurd demand. When Syria dropped that demand, Rabin's aides declared it was a "major Syrian concession." In fact, it was no concession at all, but now there is reason to fear that Rabin is dropping his demand for a Syrian pullback and will portray it as a reciprocal gesture to match the "Syrian concession."

One by one, the Rabin government has dropped every one of its demands and capitulated to all of Syria's terms. There is really almost nothing left to negotiate about except the schedule for the Israeli surrender, which would explain why an agreement could be likely in the near future. When the time comes for the signing ceremony, and Rabin and his colleagues gather around to finalize this "peace in our time," their Syrian counterparts will be smiling broadly at the people whom only they know as "our men in Jerusalem."

July 7, 1995

Democracy or Lack of It the American Jewish Community

If there is one issue that unites the overwhelming majority of American Jews, it is Jerusalem the need for Israel to keep all of Jerusalem, and the need for the U.S. to recognize Jerusalem as Israel's capital by moving its embassy from Tel Aviv to Jerusalem. Yet many major Jewish organizations are ignoring what the Jewish public wants, and are refusing to support the Dole-Kyl-lnouye legislation to move the embassy.

On June 15, the Conference of Presidents of Major American Jewish Organizations met to discuss the Dole-Kyl-lnouye bill. Representatives from pro-Israel organizations spoke up in favor of the bill. Representatives of fringe-left groups, like Americans for Peace Now, spoke up against it.

At that point in the meeting, if there was any democracy in the Conference of Presidents, a vote would have been taken on whether or not to endorse the Dole-Kyl-lnouye bill. But there isn't any democracy in the Conference. Its staff members presented their own "compromise" statement and insisted that the assembled Jewish leaders vote on the statement. Request for a direct "yes or no" vote on Dole-Kyl-lnouye was rejected.

The "compromise" statement is not a compromise at all, but rather a capitulation to the State Department's demand that American Jewry refrains from helping the Dole-Kyl-Inouye bill. The conference's statement praises the "objective" of the bill moving the embassy but does not endorse the bill itself, which actually mandates a specific timetable for beginning construction on a Jerusalem embassy building in 1996.

At the Jewish Telegraphic Agency reported, the Conference of President's statement meant, in effect, that the Conference has "withheld its endorsement of Dole's measure. "Malcolm Hoenlein, executive vice chairman of the Conference, said (according to the JTA) that the statement "only endorsed the objective of the legislation, but not the bill explicitly." That's not a too subtle way of saying that the statement did not endorse the bill at all. You can't just support the "objective" of a bill; Senators and Representatives are going to vote on the bill itself, not just on its "objective."

Hoenlein and company are trying to have their cake and eat it, too. They know that grassroots Jews support moving the embassy, so they want to be able to claim that they endorsed the "objective" of Dole's bill. But they also want to keep the State Department happy, so they can say that they did not explicitly endorse the Dole bill. Nobody on Capitol Hill is going to be fooled by this kind of double-talk. They will read the Conference's position as a non-endorsement of Dole. That's the bottom line.

But that's not what most American Jaws want Most Jews to understand that U.S. recognition of Jerusalem now would help fortify Israel against the pressures that will mount during the forthcoming Israel-PLO negotiations about Jerusalem. Most Jews also realize that while the current Congress in very friendly to Israel, there is no way of knowing if the next Congress will take such a sympathetic position on Jerusalem. This really may be our last chance to move the embassy.

Congress is being misled. American Jews want the embassy to move as soon as possible. But a handful of Conference of President's staff members are telling Congress that American Jews don't really want It moved so quickly. These individuals, who were not elected and had no democratic mandate to speak on behalf of American Jewry, have managed to position themselves so that they can control the message that is being sent from the organized Jewish community to Congress regarding the Dole bill (and other Israel-related issues).

July 28, 1995

De-Judaizing Israel: Has the Process Begun?

Since the Rabin government took office in 1992, its spokesmen and cabinet ministers have become best known for making two types of statements: declarations about the need to give up territory, and remarks deriding aspects of traditional Judaism. Is it just coincidental that these two topics seem to be the passion of the Labor government, or does it indicate that what motivates and inspires this government is the drive to alter the character of Israel in these two areas permanently?

It is clear from Shimon Peres's book, **The New Middle East**, that his vision of the future Israel is a state which is much smaller geographically - and which is altogether different Jewishly. Peres dreams of a new world in which all boundaries between people are torn down. He begins with the military, political and economic boundaries. But what must inevitably follow are ethnic cultural and religious boundaries. His deputy foreign minister, Yossi Beilin, some had said that Beilin is the powerhouse and Peres his deputy summed it up quite bluntly when he told a New York audience last year that he would have no counter-argument to present if his daughter wanted to marry a non-Jew. Beilin was honest. He and his colleagues, having long ago abandoned Judaism and embraced ultra-secular Socialist Zionism, are in no position to argue against the one-worldism, including marriage between different peoples that the ideologies of secularism and Socialism promote.

It is precisely because they have no feeling of Jewish attachment to the Land of Israel that Rabin, Peres, Beilin, and the rest are so ready to surrender large sections of the country in exchange for treaties. The religion that teaches the holiness of the Land of Israel means nothing to them. The sacred books that speak of sacred, Jewish land mean nothing to them. Why not trade Jewish land for some material advantage, just as they traded Judaism for the material pleasures of an ultra-secular lifestyle?

Rabin, Peres, and Beilin are entirely comfortable with Arab Muslim powers ruling the most sacred areas of the Jewish homeland, from Shiloh to Hebron. The first phase of their "peace process" gave the Arabs both Gaza and Jericho; the next phase will give them much more. Under Rabin, the Arabs have been granted the final say in the (imposition of Israeli territory. Why did Rabin cancel the Jerusalem land expropriations? Because of Arab protests. Why Is Rabin blocking legislation that would require a majority of 70 Knesset Members to give away the Golan Heights? Because if only 61 votes are required. Arab Knesset Members will have the deciding votes. Why will Robin's referendum on surrendering the Golan require only 51% of the votes to pass? Because that way, Israeli Arabs will be able to tip the balance in favor of surrender.

Rabin and his colleagues are also ready to have large numbers of Arab Muslims settle in Israel and the territories. Negotiations are already underway to permit the entry of hundreds of thousands of Arab "refugees" to Judea and Samaria. Many of them will subsequently migrate, legally or illegally, into the rest of Israel. A July 10 feature story in the **Miami Herald** described how thousands of Arabs from the territories arrange fictional marriages to Israeli Arab women to gain residency rights inside Israel.

In Jerusalem, the forces of Christianity and Islam will combine to take over what is rightfully Jewish with the permission of the Rabin government. The Muslims, who already have *de facto* control over Judaism's holiest site, the Temple Mount, will gain formal control of the Mount and other areas. Other sections of the city are apparently slated to be ruled by the Vatican, according to a telegram, bearing Pere's signature, which was leaked to the media earlier this year.

With large proportions of Israel being Islamicized or Christianized, with Muslim "refugees" flooding in form around the Middle East, with Judaism being mocked by representatives of Israel's government, one may legitimately ask: when Rabin is done, what will be left of Israel that can be called Jewish?

History will not reflect well on those who bartered away the Jewish homeland and eroded Israel's Jewish character. One wonders how it will reflect on those, especially rabbinical authorities, who stood idly by while this process took place. What will the history books of the future have to say about Rabbi Ovadia Yosef, the spiritual mentor of the Shas Party, which is keeping the Rabin government in power...? Future generations will look back and wonder how Rabbi Yosef could instruct his party to prop up a government that handed over the Land of Israel to the PLO and the Vatican and presided over the de-Judaizing of the Jewish homeland.

August 18, 1995

Jewish Weakness Invites Persecution

One can cite countless factors that helped pave the way for the Holocaust to occur, but surely the most basic is this: the Jews lacked a state, and therefore they were ripe to be victimized. If there had been a Jewish state in the 1930s and 1940s, European Jews could have escaped Hitler by going to the Land of Israel. Instead, the British refused to permit the creation of a Jewish State and refused to permit Jewish immigration to the Holy Land. Since no other country would take in Jewish refugees, it meant that Europe's Jews wore doomed to whatever fate Hitler chose. Ho chose genocide.

The point is not to speculate about "What if...?" but rather to learn some lessons from that experience to apply to today's crises. Mass persecution of the Jews could retake place, in our times, if the State of Israel no longer existed, or if it was weakened to the point of being unable to defend itself, to rescue immigrants from far-flung corners of the globe, and to absorb the newcomers. Could a weak and demoralized Israeli Army have rescued tens of thousands of Jews from Ethiopia? Could a feeble Israel have absorbed one million Jews from Russia? Would persecute Jews even want to come to live in a militarily crippled and economically unviable Jewish State? They might well reason that they would be better off staying where they are, rather than settling, in a country where the government's weakness is allowing the continuing knifings, suicide-bombings, and the like.

Nobody should assume that the present lull in violent Diaspora anti-Semitism means that Israel doesn't have to worry about rescuing or absorbing new immigrants. Just because Western anti-Semitism is, today, more **under** the surface than above it, does not mean that it will not rear its ugly head again, in the near future, in response to particular local, national, or international crises. Too many Diaspora Jews have grown comfortable and feel safe in their lands of residence, shunting Israel aside in the naive assumption that they don't need it. They forget how quickly the black clouds of anti-Semitism can gather.

And they neglect to consider that however comfortable they are today, there is no way of knowing what the future of the Diaspora may hold for their children and grandchildren. Governments come and go, leaders come and go, but anti-Semitism is always there, bubbling just below the surface, getting ready to explode. When the awful fury of violent anti-Jewish hate is again unleashed upon a Diaspora Jewish community, will Israel be ready to aid them? Or will it be so weakened by its unilateral concessions to the Arabs, and so demoralized by its abandonment of Jewish concepts that it will be unable to assist?

Lacking leaders of stature and principle, the Jewish masses must themselves study the lessons of Jewish history so that the catastrophes of the past will not be repeated. They must look to the centuries of statelessness persecution forced conversions, pogroms, and gas chambers, and understand the urgent imperative to strengthen Israel in every way possible to ensure a safe Jewish haven for this generation and future generations of Jews. The more heinous anti-Semitism has become, it has now reached the point of dozens being murdered in the bombing of Jewish community centers, as in Buenos Aires, the more necessary are the safeguards which, as the experience of centuries has shown, are essential for Jewish survival.

September 1, 1995

Left-Wing Kibbutzniks, Too, Are Occupying 'Arab' Land

"Who needs them?" So asked Yitzhak Rabin in his latest outburst against the Jews living in Judea and Samaria. The settlers are provoking the Arabs and undermining peace, Rabin claims.

But before Mr. Rabin hurls more bitter invective at the Jews of Judea-Samaria, he ought to keep in mind that religions-nationalist Israelis are not the only ones whose presence aggravates the Arabs. Members of a left-wing Hashomer Hatzair settlement, Kibbutz Sasa, recently celebrated their 45th anniversary 45 years on land once known as "Sa'sa," an Arab village that used to stand on the land where the kibbutz was established.

While other Israeli leftists wallow in guilt over Israel's alleged "mistreatment" of the Arabs and point accusing fingers at the "extremist settlers" "who are "taking over Arab land," the leftists of Kibbutz Sasa live with the knowledge that their history hardly differs at all from that of the Jewish nationalists who have settled in Judea and Samaria.

In fact, the right-wing Jews of today are, if anything, far kinder to the local Arabs than the Hashomer Hatzair leftists of 1949. When the kibbutz Sasa founders arrived in the Upper Galilee in January 1949, they were like their right-wing counterparts of today - playing a vital security role by settling in a strategically-sensitive border area. But unlike the Gush Emunim pioneers, who in almost every case have built their homes on land that has been deserted for centuries, the Hashomer Hatzair group set tip Kibbutz Susa right in the heart of the Arab village that had been abandoned just days earlier. Leaves of tobacco, the villagers' main crop, were still drying from the ceilings of the Arab homes that the left-wing settlers took over.

Shortly after the settlers arrived, the Ben-Gurion government sent army explosives experts to blow up most of the homes in the village, something which the Likud government never did, except in isolated cases, when homes were used by **identified terrorists.**

307

On one occasion, the kibbutzniks were visited by several rabbinical scholars from Safed, who pointed out that a Jewish town had existed on the site back in Talmudic times, long before the Arabs occupied the area. The ardently secular kibbutzniks ordinarily would not care too much what some rabbis had to say, but the rabbis' remarks concerning the Jewish claim to the territory carried considerable significance since they had a bearing on the very right of the Hashomer Hatzair members to their homes in Sasa.

Interestingly, the Kibbutz Sasa settlers - unlike many of their friends and colleagues on the Israeli left never seem to have been particularly troubled about their past.

The saga of Kibbutz Sasa, on its 45th anniversary, bears lessons for all of Israel. Whether Jewish settlers are left-wing or right-wing, whether the land is within the pre-1967 border or beyond it, whether there are Arabs in the way or not, the sacred principles of classic pioneering Zionism must override all else. The Jewish homeland, **all of it** must be developed, settled, and made to bloom, Jewish refugees from around the globe must be ingathered. Israel's young must be imbued with **Jewish pride** and **strength.** Through unity and devotion, from Kibbutz Sasa to Kiryat Arba, Israel must remain whole, and its faith must remain unshaken.

"Who needs them?" Mr. Rabin asked. Who needs the residents of Kibbutz Sasa and the residents of Hebron or Shiloh? **We** need them, the **entire** Jewish people need them, to protect and develop the Land of Israel for this generation, and for generations to come.

And who else needs them? The **United States** needs them. Last week, an American aircraft carrier, *Theodore Roosevelt,* was dispatched to the Middle East in what was described as a "show of solidarity" with the government of Jordan, for having given asylum to Saddam Hussein's two sons-in-law. The U.S. ship showed its solidarity by docking in an **Israeli port**; Israel is the only country in the Middle East that is sufficiently friendly and has sufficient facilities for a U.S. aircraft carrier to dock. With a substantial Jewish population settled in Judea-Samaria, those territories will remain firmly in Israel's control, giving Israel the strategic depth and military strength that enables Israel to function as a useful ally to the United States. But if the settlers are abandoned or forced out, and the territories turned over to PLO control, Israel will be shrunken and weakened. It will be in no position to serve America's strategic interests in the region.

September 8, 1995

P.O.W. Controversy? Israel Has Nothing to Feel Guilty About

The allegation that a few Israeli soldiers may have killed a small number of captured Arab soldiers has been used by the media, the Jewish left and the Arabs, a stick with which to beat Israel and make it feel guilty. But Israel has nothing to feel guilty about.

The first question is the reliability of the accusers. Three of the Israeli "experts" who have been quoted prominently in the American media, Benny Morris, Uri Avneri, and Meir Pa'il, are not exactly neutral, objective scholars. In fact, they specialize in smearing Israel's name.

Morris has written two books, one about the 1948 war and one about Arab-Israeli clashes in the 1950s, which try to blame Israel for the conflict pretty much what one would expect from somebody who went to prison for refusing to do his Anny reserve duty beyond the 1967 border (**Jerusalem Post,** September 18, 1988). Avneri is a veteran ultra-leftist, longtime publisher of the pro-PLO magazine **Haolam Hazeh,** author of a book called Israel **Without Zionists,** and most recently, organizer of a campaign calling for the Old City of Jerusalem to be made "the capital of the State of (Arab) Palestine." Pa'il, a veteran extremist, entered politics "after he was dropped from the Tel Aviv University faculty" (according to the **Jerusalem Post,** Dec. 30, 1973, he then became the leader of the radical Democratic Communist Party.

Even if there were isolated cases in which a few **Arab** P.O.W.s were killed, one might legitimately ask: which country has clean hands and can, therefore, accuse Israel? The United States, with its My Lai massacre? The European countries, which so eagerly collaborated with Hitler? Japan, with its savage treatment of the Chinese during the 1930s?

The most laughable of the countries that are pointing fingers at Israel are, of course, the Arabs. Egypt is "demanding an explanation." The other Arabs are yelling, too. But the torture and murder of Israeli prisoners was routine behavior among Egyptian and Syrian soldiers during their wars against Israel.

310

While Israel, at the very worst, had a few aberrant instances of individuals killing P.O.W.s, Egyptian and Syrian soldiers were encouraged by their governments to brutalize "the Zionist enemy," and they did so frequently, and with gusto.

Hirsh Goodman had written in the **Jerusalem Report** (July 13, 1995) about how, when he was soldier, "I used to pray first and foremost not to get killed and then not to fall into Syrian captivity. And if I had been given a choice between being a Syrian POW or losing a leg, I would gladly have chosen the latter." Goodman recalled what his unit found upon recapturing Mount Hermon from the Syrians during the 1973 war:

"Lying with their hands tied behind their backs were the bodies of perhaps 12, I don't remember the number clearly, Israeli soldiers, who had been bled to death in the snow after being castrated ... while they were still alive. They were the guards, bottle-washers, and service people considered worthless intelligence value by the Syrians. The others were flown back to Syria for interrogation, and the horror stories they told on their return still resonate in my mind."

Should the Israeli nation now wallow in guilt because a few of its soldiers, on their own, gave the Arabs a very small taste of their own medicine? It is difficult to believe that the majority of grassroots Israelis would want or expect their Army to be bound by mythical "rules of ethical warfare" that don't exist in the real world and which the Arabs laugh at.

September 29, 1995

Jerusalem Bus Bombers Find A Haven In Jericho

Abel-Majid Dudein and Rushdi Khatib are having a good laugh.

Dudein and Khatib masterminded the recent Jerusalem bus bombing massacre, which left five Jews dead and another ten wounded, some maimed for life. After the bomb went off, they needed a place to hide from the Israeli security forces. So they went to the PLO-controlled City of Jerusalem.

In theory, Jericho should have been the last place to which fugitive terrorists would flee. After all, one of the most crucial aspects of the Oslo accords was its **extradition** clause. The accords obligate the PLO authorities to honor every request that Israel makes for the extradition of terrorists. Terrorists are supposed to fear that if they go to Jericho (or Gaza), they will be handed over to the Israelis.

But that's only in theory. The reality is quite the opposite.

The reality is that every time Israel has requested extradition, the PLO has either ignored it or rejected it. Israel asked for the extradition of the Abu-Sita cousins, who murdered Israeli farmer Uri Megidish in March 1993; the PLO rejected it because the extradition agreement does not apply to killings that took place before the Oslo accords were signed. This is wrong, of course; the extradition agreement has no time limits attached to it, but the PLO thumbed, it's now at Israel, and Israel did nothing.

When Israel requested the extradition of Iad Bushti and Yusuf Malhi, they were asking for two suspects in a double-murder that took place in August 1994, nearly a year after the accords were signed. This time the PLO claimed that there were technical errors in the extradition request. **Another lie.**

Then there was Israel's request for the PLO to hand over three PLO policemen who murdered an Israeli border policeman, Jacques Attias, in July 1994. The PLO simply ignored the request.

312

And so it has gone. No wonder the Jerusalem bus-bomb planners, Dudein and Khatib, chose Jericho. They knew that in the PLO's hands, they would be safe. To protect Dudein and Khatib, the PLO took advantage of a phrase in the extradition treaty. According to the PLO, if a terrorist is already in prison when the extradition request is made, the extradition must wait until he finishes serving his sentence. So, moments before the Israeli extradition forms arrived, Dudein and Khatib were "put on trial" for "harming the security of the Palestinian National Authority." The "trial" lasted three minutes. They were given jail sentences, and when the Israeli request arrived, the PLO replied that the two were already in jail. (They may indeed be in jail, for a short time, until the media spotlight has shifted away although according to Israeli media reports, they are not even in prison at all).

That the PLO has made a mockery of the extradition agreement is obvious. But why should anyone have expected anything different? Arafat has made a mockery of every one of its commitments in the Oslo accords. Every time he has committed a violation, the Rabin government has been silent. If Rabin is not going to enforce the agreement, then Arafat has no incentive to abide by it. And thus, the deadly process continues, with Israel surrendering land and freeing terrorists, while the PLO turns Gaza and Jericho into havens for terrorists and prepares to do likewise with the rest of Judea and Samaria.

October 6, 1995

What the Taba Accord Means for Jerusalem

On Wednesday evening, Jews everywhere will conclude the Yom Kippur service with the declaration, "Next year in Jerusalem!" But when they wake up on Thursday morning, they will find that the Rabin government is already taking the first steps in the de facto surrender of Jerusalem, as the implementation of the Taba Accords moves forward.

By giving Jerusalem Arabs the right to take part in the elections to the Palestinian Council, the Taba agreement launches the process of giving the PLO official control over Jerusalem's Arab community. On an unofficial level, of course, this process was already underway. The Rabin government has already quietly permitted the PLO to illegally maintain quasi-government institutions in East Jerusalem, including Orient House and ten other agencies of the Palestinian Authority. The PLO/PA also has de facto control of the educational system for Jerusalem's Arabs.

But the participation of Jerusalem Arabs in the Palestinian Council elections is a dramatic step forward in this process. It formally and officially codifies PLO authority over a portion of Jerusalem's residents. The original Israeli position that Jerusalem Arabs could vote in the elections but not run as candidates were abandoned in Rabin's rush to sign an agreement before Rosh Hashana. The fig leaf is that they can stand for election "only if he or she has an additional valid address in the West Bank or the Gaza Strip." Arranging for a Jerusalem candidate to have a fictitious address outside Jerusalem won't be any trouble for the PLO election-managers.

The other major danger to Jerusalem from Taba is that the agreement enables armed PLO men to begin taking over areas that are literally on the edge of Israel's capital. There is no 'safety zone' to protect Jerusalem's perimeters. The borders of the PLO "entity," which the PLO and its allies will soon be calling a state, go right up to Jerusalem's doorstep. In fact, Arab villages such as Abu Dis and El-Azariya, which are partly within Jerusalem and partly outside of it, will soon have PLO policemen patrolling their streets. Don't expect them to stop when they get to the part of town that is within Jerusalem.

All of this means that the PLO will present some formidable arguments to Rabin's weary and demoralized negotiators when Jerusalem is put on the table during next year's "final status" talks. They will cite statements by Rabin's coalition partners, the leaders of the Meretz Party, favoring PLO control over East Jerusalem. They will note that Rabin never took any serious steps to prevent the activities of Orient House and the numerous PA offices in Jerusalem. They will stress that the educational system is already in PLO hands. They will point out that in the Taba agreement, Rabin already recognized that the jurisdiction of the Palestinian 'entity' extends to Jerusalem's Arabs. "Giving us official control over half of Jerusalem is just a formality," Arafat will say. How will Rabin respond?

With these dangers lurking in the months to come, the tragic reality is that the "Next year in Jerusalem" declaration at the end of this Yom Kippur will most likely mean "Next year, the PLO in Jerusalem."

October 20, 1995

Paving the Way for A Russian Return to The Middle East

One of the crucial strategic advantages that Israel provided the United States over the years was preventing the Soviet Union from taking over the Middle East. The Soviets may be gone, but the Russians are still there, and thanks to the Clinton administration's Middle East policy, Israel will soon no longer be in a position to stop the Russians from coming.

Israel's value as a buffer against the Soviets was dramatically illustrated in the Israeli victory over the Soviet-backed Arab states in the 1967 War. Israel shielded the U.S. and the rest of the Western free world from the strategic danger that would have arisen if the Kremlin-directed Arab allies ruled the entire Mideast.

In 1970, the U.S. asked Israel to shield Jordan from the threat of a Soviet-backed Syrian invasion. Israel complied; it sent troops to its border with Syria as a warning, and Syria and the Soviets-backed off. During the Yom Kippur War, it was General Sharon's bold move to surround the Egyptian Third Army and cross the Suez Canal, and the forceful Israeli counter-strike across the Golan Heights, that put Israel on the road to Cairo and Damascus and prevented an Arab-Soviet triumph. Once again, in the Lebanon War, Israel defeated the Kremlin's proxies, blasting the Syrian Air Force and chasing the PLO from Beirut.

For more than four decades, Israel's military courage and prowess kept the Soviets from overrunning the Middle East and kept strategic oil supplies out of Moscow's hands. But this unparalleled accomplishment is now in the process of being undone, thanks to the Clinton administration's desperate desire to register a "foreign policy success" at any price.

Although the Soviet empire has collapsed, the Russian regime that remains has not forsaken its traditional imperialist goals. The idea of expanding Russian influence southward, into the oil-rich Middle East, is alive and beating in the hearts of Russian leaders. Even those Russian officials who

316

are less interested in Russian expansion are warm to the possibility of making money by selling deadly weapons to Arab customers. Thus, Russian arms, in gigantic quantities, have been making their way to Iran and Syria, and it will not be long before the PLO's police force-turned-army begins receiving its share.

A militarily strong Israel, with defensible borders and encouragement from the United States, would be able to fend off the new Russian threat. But instead, Israel today is growing ever weaker and more dependent on others. Its strategic buffer zones in Judea, Samaria, and Gaza are being turned into a fledgling PLO state. Its hold on the Golan Heights is in danger. Its security *is* to be left in the hands of unreliable Golan "peacekeepers" and paper promises from Arafat and Assad.

The Clinton administration has been actively encouraging Israel to surrender its territory, apparently in the belief that "peace" declarations will increase poll ratings and attract votes in 1996. It won't work. Weakening Israel will strengthen Russian influence in Iran, Syria, and Gaza, endangering America's interests in the process. What began with promises of "peace" will end in war, a war that Israel and America may not be able *to* win.

November 3, 1995

A Tale of Two Prime Minsters

In a vigorous speech to parliament, the prime minister staunchly defended the controversial peace agreement he had attained. He insisted that "the alternative would have been simultaneous war" with his country's neighboring enemies. The prime minister expressed resentment at the idea that he and (his foreign minister) might abandon vital principles or sacrifice any important interest for the sake of the peace treaty.

The prime minister showed no signs of regret for the concessions he had made during the 18 months of negotiations. "If I had to live those 18 months over again, I would not change it by one jot," he said, and the press reported that "cheers" erupted "from his supporters" in parliament at that point. "Even if it were to fail, I should still say it was right to attempt it because the only alternative was war," the premier declared defiantly. "I would not take that awful responsibility upon my shoulders unless it was forced upon me by the madness of others."

Media reports described the prime minister as "irritated" by the statements of opposition members of parliament who had loudly criticized his policies. Ob servers "wondered what had shaken (the premier) out of his usual poise," a leading newspaper noted. Especially curious was the prime minister's declaration that "whatever views may be expressed in parliament, I am convinced that the general public desires us to continue our efforts toward peace."

The prime minister in question was Neville Chamberlain. On my desk sits a frayed, yellowing newspaper clipping from the **Boston Hearld** of December 20, 1938, reporting Chamberlain's speech to parliament in defense of his Munich Pact with Adolf Hitler. I was ten years old at the time, and to this day, I still vividly remember the profound sadness that enveloped our home in the wake of the Munich signing. There was an atmosphere of mourning -

318

mourning for the tragedy that we knew would inevitably follow, since belligerent dictators can never be truly appeased.

If in reading Chamberlain's statements (quoted above), you had thought that Yitzhak Rabin made them, you are probably not alone.

Rabin, too, has defended his controversial peace agreement (with the PLO) because "the alternative would have been simultaneous war" with his country's neighboring enemies even though many leading Israeli military analysts have argued that the Arabs will make *war* when they are ready, peace treaty or no peace treaty.

Rabin, too, enjoys "cheers from his supporters," but his concessions to the Arabs are opposed by nearly half the parliament and, according to the polls, a large majority of the Israeli public. But Rabin chooses to ignore the polls and insists that "the general public desires us to continue our efforts," even without evidence that the public backs him.

Rabin, too, has been "shaken out of his usual poise," displaying "irritation" and "expressing resentment" - hurling epithets such as "racists," "crybabies" and "Ayatollahs" - when anybody raises the idea that he "might abandon vital principles or sacrifice any important interest" for the sake of reaching agreements with the PLO.

Within a year after the Munich signing, Hitler invaded Poland, World War II broke out, and it was painfully clear to everyone that Chamberlain had indeed "abandoned vital principles" and "sacrificed important interests." Of course, it had not been his intention to do so; but prime ministers can make mistakes. Under political pressure at home and abroad, or in the hope of being remembered in the history books or simply out of sheer desperation, prime ministers can take steps in the name of "peace" that will actually lead to war.

December 8, 1995

Israel Is Becoming Part of The Mideast In More Ways Than One

One of the central themes in Shimon Peres' recent book, The **New Middle East,** is that Israel should become an integral part of the Middle East. Comfortable with the traditional Jewish idea that Jews are destined to be "a nation that dwells alone" *(*in the words of **Numbers** 23), Peres and his colleagues argue that Israel should take aggressive steps to assimilate into its Middle Eastern environment.

Not many Arabs are particularly eager to embrace their Israeli neighbors. Government-controlled newspapers in Egypt, Jordan, and Syria have been warning that Israel is trying to "penetrate and take over the Arab world," and to extend Israeli economic domination" over the Arab masses. Ironically, however, despite Arab resistance, Israel under the Labor Party is already becoming more and more like its Arab neighbors.

The Arab regimes, for example, refuse to tolerate opposition political forces. When dissidents try to speak out, Arab leaders arrest them on trumped-charges, smear them in the media and send provocateurs to infiltrate and discredit them. Is the Israeli Labor government mimicking the Arabs in this regard? Israeli nationalist dissidents are being detained without charges and denied access to lawyers. Rabbis are being hauled in for police interrogation based on rumors and gossip.

Most shocking, media reports indicate that the General Security Services (the Shin Bet), under Labor, has engaged in behavior that would arouse the envy of their Arab counterparts. Avishai Raviv, head of the militant "Eyal" group, has been exposed as a government agent who was hired by the Shin Bet to infiltrate rightwing militant circles to get them to take actions that would embarrass mainstream critics of the government. It was Raviv who initiated-and distributed the posters showing Yitzhak Rabin in a Nazi uniform. It was Raviv who staged the phony "swearing-in ceremony" for teenage Eyal members who, it turns out, were paid to take part. It was Raviv who called the media to say Eyal had murdered an Arab in Halhoul when, in fact, other Arabs had done it.

When the Arab regimes are losing popular support, they try to prop themselves up by staging rallies that citizens are "encouraged" to attend, with not-so-subtle warnings about repercussions against those who refuse to participate. According to the New York *Jewish Week* (Nov. 24), the Labor government's Consul-General in New York, Colette Aviatal, is the creator and driving force behind the plan for a Madison Square Garden rally by American Jews to endorse the policies of the Israeli government. Those who have concerns about taking part in such a partisan rally have been warned that they will be smeared and treated like pariahs if they refuse to fall in line.

Arab leaders rule without regard for public opinion. What is one to make of the Israeli Labor Party leadership that ran on a platform of no talks with the PLO, no PLO state, and no surrender of the Golan Heights, and then did, or plans to do exactly the opposite? What is one to think of Labor leaders who say that they have the right to carry out whatever policy they choose, regardless of public opinion, so long as they have a one-vote majority in the Knesset, even if that one vote was obtained through political favors and back-scratching?

Israel is in the Middle East by accident, not by design. Israel didn't choose to have the Arabs as neighbors, and the Arab world is hardly a kind and gentle region into which Israel should assimilate. Surely in areas such as democracy and free speech, the Arab regimes have no qualities worth imitating. Israel's Labor government should look elsewhere for role models.

December 22, 1995

Are the Arabs Mishpocha?

There are, sadly, many obstacles to the building of the "tent of peace," from Syria's development of chemical and biological weapons to Yasir Arafat's *jihad* appeals. But while we all anxiously await the day when Peres's dream will be fulfilled, it is worth pondering the background to his statement that Arabs and Jews are both "the sons and daughters of Abraham."

It is, of course, widely assumed that Arabs and Jews are "cousins." The assumption is based on the fact that Jews are descendants of Isaac, the son of Abraham and Sarah, and the belief that today's Arabs are descended from Ishmael, the son of Abraham and his Egyptian maidservant, Hagar. The notion that Arabs and Jews are *mishpochas* via Abraham is so widespread that there is even an organization called the "Abraham Fund," which claims to promote "Arab-Jewish coexistence" based on the idea that Arabs and Jews are relatives all the way back to Biblical times.

Yet the history books tell a different story. The authoritative **Encyclopedia Judaica** notes that there are scattered references to "Ishmaelites" in various Biblical texts. At this time, they seem to have been a group of nomads residing along the borders of *Eretz Yisrael,* But references to the original Ishmaelites end "around the middle of the 10th century BCE," and they vanish from the historical map in the same way that many ancient peoples (such as the seven Canaanite nations) were gradually eliminated through wars, intermarriage with other tribes, and other factors. During the ensuing centuries, some nomadic tribes in the region were on occasion referred to as "the sons of Ishmael," but the differences between them and the original Ishmaelites were SO significant that there is no doubt, in the words of the **Encyclopedia Judaica,** that "they are not connected with the unified framework of the [original] Ishmaelite tribes." All of this took place more than 1,000 years before the advent of Muhammad, founder of Islam, and the father of today's Arabs.

Muhammad, who lived in the 7th century CE, took many episodes from the Torah, rewrote them, and included them in the Koran. For example, the Koran includes a version of the story of Abraham preparing to sacrifice his son, although, in the Koran's account, the son is not identified as Isaac. Muslims insist that the son in the sacrifice story was really Ishmael. They further tie their lineage to Ishmael through the episode in which Hagar and Ishmael were expelled from Abraham's home and went to "dwell in the wilderness" **(Genesis 21)**. According to Muslims that "wilderness" was really the Saudi Arabian city of Mecca, Islam's holiest city, although it was more than 700 miles from the borders of ancient Canaan. Muhammad declared Ishmael to be a "prophet," and announced that he himself was a descendant of Ishmael. The pagan hordes of the Arabian peninsula, upon whom Muhammad and his friends imposed Islam, were suddenly declared to be the real descendants of Ishmael somehow, new lineage was included m the conversion package - and it was said that the Divine promise of "to your seed I will give the land of Canaan..." really applies to Ishmael, not Isaac - that is, to the Arabs, not the Jews.

If we Jews accepted the Koran as being the literal truth, then we would accept Muhammad's claim of a "revelation that he is descended from Ishmael. We would accept the assertion that the Arabs, as a whole, are descended from Ishmael. And we would accept the Muslim assertion that the promise of the land was made to Ishmael, not Isaac.

Israeli policy should be shaped according to Israel's genuine security needs and Judaism's teachings about the significance and centrality of the Land of Israel. Decisions should not be based on historically inaccurate slogans about cousins and sons of Abraham." We Jews are indeed the sons of Abraham - **but the Arabs are not part of our mishpocha.**

March 17, 1995

Peace Now's Crusade Against the Settlements

Peace Now's a new proposal for the immediate dismantling of 27 Jewish communities in Judea and Samaria is the opening shot in what promises to be a long and difficult struggle that will shape the future of the Jewish State. Are those who support Jewish rights ready to meet the challenge?

Whatever one thinks of the merits of the Peace Now platform, one thing must be acknowledged: Peace Now and its comrades are deeply devoted to their cause and work overtime to translate their proposals into political reality. If Jewish nationalists were as determined as the Israeli Left, they probably would have won this fight long ago.

The "national camp," after all, has had the support for the majority of Israelis for nearly two decades now. The majority of Jewish voters have cast their ballots of the nationalist or religious parties in every election since 1977. (Even when Rabin won, in 1992, the right had received the majority of votes - but many of those nationalist votes were disqualified because they were wasted on small parties that did not receive the 1% minimum necessary to gain a Knesset seat.) Perhaps that's part of the problem. Perhaps having majority support helped breed complacency. Perhaps the leftists work harder precisely because they know they are so badly outnumbered.

There are other factors, of course. Israeli Leftists tend to have fewer children and fewer family responsibilities, leaving them more time to take part in political activity. A religious-nationalist family with six children, or a Right-wing family of eight in an impoverished Sephardic development town, just doesn't have the time to do much, beyond making ends meet.

The Israeli Left also has the advantage of sympathetic international media coverage. **Peace Now's call for the destruction of 27 settlements** made headlines around the world. A long letter from veteran Israeli Leftist Uri Avnery was featured in the March 1 **New York Times.** Israeli Left-wing

324

spokesmen and their Diaspora supporters are frequent guests on major talk shows in Europe and the United States.

What all of this means is that American Jews who care about Israel's future must rise to the occasion to combat Peace Now's crusade against the settlements.

American Jewry's "silent majority," who support the right of Jews to live in Judea and Samaria, the heartland of Israel - must shed their silence and speak out, loudly and clearly, in favor of Jewish Rights.

Those Jewish leaders who sympathize with the settlers but have been afraid to endorse what they think is an unpopular cause, have to muster the co age to speak the truth. Justice is not a popularity contest.

Rabbinical leaders, in particular, find themselves confronted with burning questions. What is the responsibility of American Jewry during this time of crisis? Is it sufficient for American Jews to merely cheer from the sidelines and recite bland expressions of sympathy for the settlers? Should we just sit back and wait, as man did during the Holocaust, quietly hoping that thin will improve? Or should we be marching in protest, affirm the eternal right of the Jewish people to the Land of Israel?

Young Jews, in particular, have a right to ask more than a few questions: Everything that Jews have been taught for 2,000 years about the sanctity of the Land of Israel, is now being tossed aside. How will Jewish national pride survive? What kind of Zionism can be maintained if Jewish communities are dismantled, and the Land of Israel is dismembered? What kind of Jewish identity can future generations hope to have? Without meaningful answers to questions like these, our youth will be lost, and without our youth, the Jewish future will be bleak indeed.

February 23, 1996

The Rise or Pat Buchanan; What Does It Mean for Jews And Israel?

Pat Buchanan's surprise victory in the Louisiana caucuses may well turn out to be no more than a passing curiosity in this year's presidential race. But at the same time, it offers· several important lessons for American Jewry and Israel.

It is, of course, alarming that significant numbers of Louisianans would vote for a candidate who has made bigoted comments about minority groups who has accused Jews of dragging America into the Gulf War who has exhibited a near-obsession with defending accused Nazi war criminals, and who has been bashing Israel for more than a decade.

Not many voters chose Buchanan because of those positions, but what is frightening is that they voted for him **despite** his record. They were willing to overlook his bigotry and extremism because of his anti-immigration, "America first" themes resonate among the frustrated and discontented masses. Inflation, unemployment, and racial tensions feed frustration and drive voters toward extremist candidates. And Buchanan is managing to capitalize on such sentiment at a time when America is prosperous and when social and economic problems are not especially acute. Imagine how many people might vote for a Buchanan, or someone like him, if inflation or unemployment skyrocketed!

It's a reminder of how fragile American Jewry's status really is. We could be one Stock Market crash away from a serious threat to the well-being of the American Jewish community. The economic collapse has led to anti-Jewish scapegoating in many countries throughout history; no country is immune from such developments. If the day comes that substantial numbers of American Jews must begin to think seriously about living in Israel, will Israel be ready to take them in? Or will it be a weakened, demoralized nation cramped within indefensible borders and facing a massive influx of Arab "refugees"?

The second important lesson from the Buchanan phenomenon has to do with his extreme isolationism. Buchanan argues that U.S. troops should not be sent overseas in virtually any circumstances. That position has the support of many, many ordinary Americans. Polls have shown that the majority of Americans are opposed to sending troops to Bosnia. A Luntz poll taken last year found that most Americans are opposed to sending U.S. soldiers to the Golan Heights. The American public is justifiably concerned about sending GIs into danger zones where hostile forces are likely to kidnap soldiers or murder them. Just last week, the first American soldier was killed in Bosnia, and it is hard to believe he will be the last casualty. The demands for a U.S. withdrawal from Bosnia will surely be heard soon.

Now imagine this scenario. The Israeli Labor government asks for American troops to be stationed on the Golan. American Jewish groups sheepishly go along with the proposal, and they even lobby Congress to support. Hezbollah or other terrorists based in nearby southern Lebanon attack the Americans. Average Americans, the people who didn't want the soldiers sent overseas in the first place the people who, in many cases, vote for Pat Buchanan will be furious. At Israel. And at American Jewry.

These are disturbing questions that deserve serious consideration now before more votes are cast for Pat Buchanan, and before any GIs are sent home from the Golan Heights in pine boxes.

March 22, 1996

Israeli Anti-Terror Action, Not Clinton's "Anti-Terror" Devices, Is the Answer to Hamas

Israel is attacked ... The U.S. presses Israel not to retaliate ... The President offers self-defense equipment to "protect" the Jewish State, as a substitute for Israeli retaliatory action.

Sounds familiar? That description could apply to what has been happening in Israel in recent weeks, or it could apply to what happened du.mg the Gulf War. The Gulf crisis is important to recall because of the lessons it offers concerning the current crisis.

When Iraqi Scud missiles began pounding Israel at the beginning of the war missiles that were cheered on by crowds of Palestinian Arabs, together with Saddam's main Arab ally, Yasir Arafat, the Bush Administration immediately began pressuring not to retaliate. Bush and Baker were afraid that Israeli self-defense would anger America's Arab "allies," Egypt, Syria, and Saudi Arabia. Since it would be preposterous to tell Israel just to sit back and absorb the missile hits, Bush announced that he was sending Israel some Patriot anti-missile batteries. At the time, there were a few voices that wondered why Bush had never given Israel the Patriots before. But those questions were drowned out in all the applause for Bush for "rescuing" Israel.

As it happened, of course, Israel was not "rescued." The missiles kept hitting; the Patriots were too little too late. Post-war studies confirmed that the Patriots had an extremely low rate of success. Professors Theodore A. Postal and George Lewis of the prestigious Massachusetts Institute of Technology (M.I.T.), who are missile experts, completed a detailed study last year, which concluded that the Patriots used to "defend" Israel "may have had no direct hits at all." A study by the Israeli Air Force reached a similar conclusion. (In an interesting side note, the manufacturer of the Patriot, the Raytheon Corporation, enlisted another M.I.T. professor to attack Postol. A special faculty committee was established to hear the dispute between Postol and his critic, and it recently ruled that Postol's findings of the Patriot were correct.)

Today, as in the Gulf War, Arabs are attacking Israel, and the U.S. administration is quietly urging the Israelis are not too tough in their anti-terrorist measures; the State Department is worried that strong Israeli retaliation will upset the PLO or other Arabs.

Just like in the Gulf War, the U.S. wants Israel to refrain from defending itself and rely on American equipment instead. As a substitute for Israeli retaliation, President Clinton has announced that he is "rushing" seven anti-terrorist bomb-sensing machines to Israel. One may ask, as in the Gulf War, if such machines are so effective, why didn't Clinton send them to Israel earlier? Why wait until 58 Israelis have been killed in a single week?

To make matters worse, the Clinton Administration is now demanding that Israel share secret intelligence information with the PLO because the PLO needs the data to fight against Hamas. But if the PLO isn't even using its resources to fight Hamas, why should Israel risk handing over secret information? The PLO still hasn't shut down Hamas training camps, taken away their weapons, or arrested their top leaders. If Israel gives Arafat top-secret Israel intelligence data, who can ensure that the data won't be handed over to Hamas?

The analogy between the Gulf War and the current situation also extends to the issue of U.S. financial aid. One of the ways Bush convinced Israel to refrain from self-defense was by promising the Israelis loan guarantees. The Israelis, desperate for funds to absorb the huge influx of Soviet Jewish immigrants, fell into the Bush-Baker trap. Bush and Baker suddenly added a new condition: no more Jews could go to live in Judea, Samaria, Gaza, or the Old City of Jerusalem. Bush and Baker then cleverly used the loan guarantees controversy to influence the 1992 Israeli elections so that Labor would win.

Clinton's State Department, which is almost identical to the Bush-Baker State Department likewise has a plan to influence the Israeli elections on behalf of the Labor Party. It includes the anti-bomb sensors, the summit in

Egypt, and broad hints that Israel will be richly rewarded with additional U.S. aid if it surrenders the Golan Heights.

Israel's citizens deserve better! They have a right to democratic elections without foreign interference. And they have a right to expect their government to use every means at its disposal to thoroughly eliminate the terrorists, regardless of whether or not the PLO might be offended. The only answer is for Israeli troops to go into PLO-occupied areas and wipe out the terrorists, root, and branch. It worked when Ben-Gurion did it in Gaza and northern Sinai in the 1956 war. It worked when Ariel Sharon's troops did it in Gaza in 1970-1971. It would have worked in southern Lebanon in 1982 if political pressure had not tied the Army's hands. And it can work today. Sensors and summits are NO substitute for the Israeli Army.

May 3, 1996

Soothing Words, Then and Now

While the Jews are huddled, weak, and weary, their foes uttered soothing words. The Jews desperately wanted to be reassured, and the haters knew just how to reassure them.

Instead of speaking frankly about the slaughter and destruction to come, they promised that once the Jews had been "resettled," peace would ensue. Their promises were vague and often contradictory," but the Jews heard what they wanted to hear, and the haters gave them just enough so that the Jews could convince themselves that soon all would be well.

A few desperate Jewish voices tried to expose the truth, but they were shouted down as extremists and trouble-makers.

To their people, of course, the haters spoke the truth about their intentions regarding the Jews. They urged their followers to "strike a blow for the fatherland." They instructed them to prepare for a massive war that would protect their race against "the dangers of the Jewish menace."

The international community looked on, nodding in silent and sometimes not-so-silent approval. They knew that the Jews would soon suffer, but they had no intention of lifting a finger to intervene. In some nations, some still hated Jews for religious reasons; in others, some hated Jews for other reasons, but most were simply governed by politicians who found it expedient to let the Jews meet a grim fate.

And the media helped facilitate the charade. When there was news of Jewish suffering, editors doubted its accuracy and put it on the back pages - if they printed it at all.

This could be an account of the early days of the Holocaust. Or it could describe the events of the past week.

As the PLO's Palestine National Council convened in Gaza, weary Israeli Jews, and their timid Diaspora supporters, waited anxiously to be "reassured" by Yasir Arafat that he no longer wants to destroy them. Arafat knew just how to play the game.

First, there were the usual demands, which were hardly mentioned by the media at all: Israel must surrender "the lands of Palestine," Jerusalem must be made "the capital of Palestine," and all Jews in Judea, Samaria, Gaza and the Old City of Jerusalem must be "resettled" and then maybe, just maybe, peace would follow. Fifty-five years ago, another enemy of the Jews promised that all would be well after the Jews were "resettled in the East."

Then came the debate about the PLO National Covenant. They kept it behind closed doors, no journalists allowed, so nobody could know exactly what transpired. Even after the vote, no official text of the decision was issued. But they leaked out just enough so that the Jews "could convince themselves that soon all would be well. They had decided that the articles in the Covenant that contradict other PLO agreements would be canceled, someday, by a PLO legal committee that was appointed to look into the matter. Which articles would be canceled, and when? Nobody said nobody knew.

So the Covenant remains in force, with its words of hatred and violence as vicious as always: "There is a fundamental contradiction between Zionism and colonialism on one side, and the Palestinian Arab people on the other" (Article 8) ... "The liberation of Palestine is a · national duty to repulse the Zionist, imperialist invasion from the great Arab homeland and to purge the Zionist presence from Palestine" (Article 15) ... "The establishment of Israel is fundamentally null and void, whatever time has elapsed" (Article 19) ... "Judaism is not a nationality with an independent existence, and the Jews are not one people with an independent personality; they are rather citizens of the states to which they belong'' (Article 20) ... "Zionism is a racist and fanatical movement in its formation; aggressive, expansionist and colonialist in its aims; and fascist and Nazi in its means" (Article 22) ... "

A few Jewish voices have tried to expose the truth, but they have been drowned out by the cheers the cheers of foreign governments who don't care whether the Jews live or die, the cheers of Jewish liberals who want to believe that the Arabs no longer hate them, the cheers of Israeli politicians whose electoral hopes depend on Arafat's soothing words.

But to their people, Arafat and the PLO are far blunter about their intentions regarding the Jews. The PLO news agency WAFA, reporting on the Covenant vote, did not claim that the Covenant had been changed. The pro-PLO Arab newspapers in Jerusalem reported that a legal committee was looking into possible changes one day, off in the future. The Arab masses understand that Arafat is playing a clever game that will enable the PLO to gain even more Jewish land and hasten the day when their *jihad* to annihilate Israel will be victorious.

The Nazis' soothing words helped keep the Jews in line on their way to the gas chambers. Will Arafat's soothing words keep the Jews in line on their way to the dismantling of Israel?

HA MATZAV (The Situation) - By Cherna Moskowitz

Is Another War in the Middle East Inevitable?

The cause of war in the Middle East has never been basically a problem of territories, but rather an attempt by the Arabs to destroy the Jewish state. The simple proof of that statement lies in the fact that there was no peace in 1967 at 1967 borders. Nor was their peace in 1948 when the Arabs had much more territory than the 1967 borders, which they now claim will bring peace.

Why return to a situation that was proven a failure for over 19 years during which there was a continuous state of war, regular fedayeen attacks, and blockade? (And this after armisties and cease-fire agreements had been concluded in 1948 and 1956.) Senator Jackson termed "short-sighted and illusory" the notion that the key to a stable 'Middle East peace lies in territorial adjustments. "In fact," he said, "a more vulnerable Israel will mean a more vulnerable peace and, ultimately, a more vulnerable American position in the Middle East."

Guarantees? Walls could be papered with the best drawn up judicial documents, guaranteed by the world's most powerful nations, that have proved totally useless. There are no guarantees to guarantee a guarantee.

As outlined by Knesset Member Menachem Begin, former Commander of the Irgun, the most effective means of avoiding war is:

May 1973. Reliable information came to Israel that the Egyptians were planning to attack. Israel mobilized, and no attack took place.

Nov. 1974. Intelligence disclosed that Syria had mobilized 12,000-14,000 men. The reserves were called up, and no attack took place.

Between those dates, Oct. 1973, information suggesting an attack was evaluated, and no alert was called. There was war. War is never inevitable. It is the error of man that results in war.

334

Throughout history, peace between warring nations has been achieved by the parties of the conflict meet, working out their problems, and signing peace treaties before armies retired from battle lines. Israel must not be an exception to the rules governing all nations.

Too long have Jews been subject to special rulings, laws, and levies. Enough! The same rules should apply to Israel as to other nations. The method of attaining peace that has proved successful for others should be used for the Middle East also. Nations of strength who have themselves lived by these rules should make it clear that direct negotiations between the parties are expected.

The only path to real peace is (1) An honest truce - no more killing. (Arab bombs are exploding in Israel almost every day. There is now a one-sided truce, with Israel alone abiding by it.) (2) There must be direct negotiations between Israel and her neighbors. (3) Arabs in Israel must have cultural autonomy and the free option of citizenship and equal rights. (4) Arab refugees under Israel jurisdiction must be allowed the privileges under (3) and supplied jobs, housing, and education. (5) Arab refugees living· under Arab jurisdiction should be supplied with citizenship, jobs, housing, and education by those countries.

All logic and precedent cry out for this humane and simple solution. Next year's oil income to Arab states is estimated at 120 billion, while only 60 million is needed for the refugees. The Arabs have 20 countries in which to integrate them. This is justice. This is the way to bring peace to the Middle East finally.

If that is not done, war can only effectively be avoided by a strong, alert Israel, supported by the United States as a committed friend. Jewish Americans clearly have to insist that the policy of direct negotiation and a strong commitment to Israel take precedence.

Next: Why the U.S. needs Israel.

HA MATZAV (The Situation) - By Cherna Moskowitz

WHY THE U.S. NEEDS ISRAEL?

by Paul J. Hull, M.D. and Marvin Wolff *Guest Columnists*

Dr. Paul Hull is a practicing physician in Long Beach with a degree in Russian language and history from Yale.

Marvin Wolff is a graduate of the U.S. Merchant Marine Academy. He works [or the City of Long Beach Queen Mary Division. He has been a student of Israeli affairs for many years.

Why doesn't the average American citizen know what his country owes to Israel? Had it not been for Israel's defeat of Soviet-backed Nasser in 1967, the Middle Eastern energy sources would today be under Russian control.

Russia's objective today is the same as it was in 1967: to seize the sources of energy which mean life or death to Western economies. And, although the U.S. does not yet have as great a need of Arab oil as do her allies (W. Europe and Japan), America has absolutely no interest in seeing the Russians controlling the direction of its flow.

Meanwhile, the oil-rich sheiks cannot foresee their doom if communism overtakes the area: they are playing the Russian game. They create, by their own oil blackmail, conditions in the West which Stalin only dreamed of bringing about: confusion and bitterness among NATO members, a rift between Japan and the U.S., political crises for Western governments, the threat of severe economic recession throughout the capitalistic world, and a wave of anti-Semitism among those too naive to see the real issues and the real villains.

All that stands in the way of the Soviet's realizing her expansionist dream completely, taking over the oil-rich Middle. East and a large part of resource-rich Africa is a country of 3 million people who refuses to disappear.

Therefore, the destruction of Israel would be a giant Russian step towards overtaking America as a world power.

The strategic posture of the United States concerning the Middle East has become increasingly important over time.

As country after country in North Africa, Southern Europe and the Eastern end of the Mediterranean, has either become allied with the Communist bloc or become "neutral," the position of the United States has become more critical.

The Mediterranean exposes the Southern flank of the NATO countries, with whom we are allied, to penetration by unfriendly forces al numerous points of vulnerability. The regular on-again-off-again entente cordiale between the Communist bloc and the Arab bloc has exposed the Eastern end to the continuing establishment of a Soviet military foothold. The present bases and those who will be developed in the future are a three-pronged threat to the soft underbelly of Europe, the emerging actions to the South, and the oil-rich countries to the East.

The Soviet Union will be using the Suez Canal for the transport of commercial and military shipping, enabling it to operate in two hemispheres with ease. The "showing of the flag" by Soviet warships will be a commonplace sight in all areas. The influence of these ever-present forces upon undecided or emerging countries cannot be overestimated.

The Suez gateway will be a principal route for the transport of both crude and refined oil products by the Communist bloc and its allies.

The Israel government has traditionally been a partner to the United States military efforts in many ways. Not only does it provide friendly ports for U.S. warships, but it has proven a worthy military partner in the test, analysis, and development of highly sophisticated weapons systems.

Secretary of State Kissinger has said that under no circumstances whatsoever can American weapons be defeated by Russian weapons. (Vietnam doesn't really count as a weapons defeat since toward the end of the war the communists had almost as many US weapons as did the South Vietnamese!) After Vietnam, the U.S. cannot afford another example before the world of abandoning an ally to its fate.

The strategic value of Israel on the Mediterranean shores is great. The potential value of the port of Elath on the Gulf of Aqaba with regard to the surveillance and possible interdiction of forces hostile lo U.S. interest is of equal importance. Before too long, the United States may find itself in the position of having to take firm military actions in the Eastern Mediterranean. Israel will prove to be a valuable ally due to its unique geographical and military assets, as well as its positive popular and governmental attitudes towards the United States.

In the January 1975 issue of the United States Naval Institute Proceedings, Admiral Meads Johnson, U.S.N., stated in strong terms that the role of Israel in protecting the southern flank of Europe was extremely important.

His words were brief and to the point, but the message is clear. The United States should do all in its power to strengthen the ties between the two countries for our mutual military advantage.

HA MATZAV (The Situation) - By Cherna Moskowitz

A recent article on the front page of the "Jerusalem Post" brought a little bit of history back to me.

Eliahu Hakim and Eliahu Beit-Tzuri, members of the Stem Group who were hanged, in Egypt in 1945 for killing Lord Moyne, (then British Minister of the Middle East) were buried on Mount Herzl with full military honors.

Their bodies were returned to Israel by the Egyptians on June 25 in return for twenty convicted security prisoners in line with the recent Egyptian practice of using Jewish bodies for barter.

These two boys, aged 17 and 22 years old, assassinated Lord Moyne under orders of - now Likud Knesset member - Yitzhak Shamir. Lord Moyne was killed to protest the British closure of Eretz Israel to Jewish refugees amid the Holocaust when it meant death to hundreds of · thousands who were searching for a possible haven.

Lord Moyne had spoken to Joel Brand, who carried an incredible offer from Adolf Eichman to negotiate the release of one million Jews from the death camps (5,000 at first, then 12,000 a day) for ten thousand trucks, tea, coffee, soap, and other goods. Lord Moyne reportedly told Joel Brand, "My dear fellow, whatever would I do with a million Jews?" And so, they died, and on November 6, 1944, Lord Moyne also died.

In Palestine, reaction to Lord Moyne's assassination was curious. *Haaretz* lamented, "Since Zionism began, no more grievous blow has been struck at our cause." The Jewish Agency expressed horror "at this revolting crime." (They were referring to the death of Lord Moyne, not to the murder and torture in Europe of millions of Jews than in progress.) Dr. Chaim Weizmann said that the shock had been "far more severe and numbing than the death of my son."

The destinies of Eliahu Hakim and Eliahu Beit-Tzuri had been shaped by a lifetime of Arab Programs and British rule. When they were eleven and sixteen, they mourned for Ben Yosef, the first Jew to be hanged by the British in Palestine for an aborted act of revenge against some Arabs who had hacked five Jews to death.

As they were growing up in Palestine, they witnessed the result of the infamous White Paper." When the Jewish Agency asked Britain for immediate admission to Israel of 30,000 children, they were refused. The "S.S. Tigerhill" packed with 1400 refugees from Poland was fired upon by a British patrol boat. Several people were killed, and the ship was sent back to oblivion. It and other ships bearing German and Polish Jews were not permitted to land a virtual death sentence.

On one ship, the "Patria," the refugees, 250 men, women, and children, in despair, destroyed themselves in the Haifa Harbor. Some 1,700 refugees arrived aboard typhoid ridden carrier, the "Atlantic." When deportation was ordered, British soldiers dragged the refugees onto the ship by force and beating them with batons.

Another ship, the "Salvatore," was denied entry and sank with 231 people aboard. The "Struma" sank with 746 passengers after being sent back to sea. The daily papers in Palestine carried news divided between ambushes and attacks on settlements by the Arabs and a running account of the horrors unfolding in Europe.

In Israel, last month, Hakim's brother told of fierce arguments he had with Eliahu over his membership in the Stern Group. "Now," he said, "I believe that this act and others of Eliahu and his friends helped to get the British out of the country."

Before he was hung, Beit-Tzuri said, "Some people live short lives in which nothing significant occurs. That is a tragedy. But to live a short life that includes a deed for one's homeland-that is a triumph."

Eliahu Hakim and Eliahy Beit-Tzuri. Blessed is their memory.

Ms. Moskowitz is currently traveling in Israel with her husband, Dr. Moskowitz, where she hopes to gather more material for her column. She will be participating in several activities for the advancement of Israel.

HA MATZAV (The Situation) - By Cherna Moskowitz

This column was written from notes provided by Eliahu Amiqam, parliamentary correspondent of Yediyeth Aharoneth, Israeli's second most popular newspaper. Eliahu Amiqam has been an observer of the Israeli scene since before the formation of the state. He was an announcer of the underground radio and the very first pilot of the Irgun. He is listed in "Who's Who of the Jewish World."

The Israeli Government is unique in its structure. The existing administration is the oldest in the world, having self-perpetuated itself for forty-one years. Holding second place is Franco of Spain with five fewer years of control.

Some ask for a National Unity Government, which would bring all major parties into the administration. They point to the example of Britain in World War II when the Conservatives joined Labor and were headed by Churchill. This is not relevant to Israel because Britain is a democracy in which the two political parties which united both qualified in the same measure as two equal forces.

No one can call the opposition to the Labor Party in Israel of comparable strength. Opposition in a Democratic regime is not a status, but a temporary situation, unlike the forty-one-year position of the Israeli Opposition (now called Likud). Every citizen of democracy knows that change of administration is a condition without which there is no democracy. Change is usually an expected means of maintaining balance and controlling the power of those in high places. By this means, the people use votes to show displeasure, desire for reforms, and their wishes for a change in policy. The strong will of the people is evident even between elections, i.e., the resignation of Nixon over moral issues.

In Israel, the Labor Government marches on regardless of disaster and corruption. Had the Yom Kippur catastrophe occurred in Japan, the whole cabinet would have been taken out and shot. In all other democracies, surely, there would have been a reckoning at the polls. In Israel, however, the Labor party was again voted into power.

Why is this so? The distance between democracy as we know it and democracy as practiced in Israel is great. Cult and ceremony are the reasons for Knesset elections. The elections are destined for one thing to give witness that Israel doesn't have any other leadership. A possible change of administration is regarded as a calamity.

The Labor Government self-perpetuates itself by maintaining control most despots would envy. Of all wages paid in Israel, 61 % are paid by the government or Histadrut. Histadrut is Israel's only labor union. Wielding enormous power and influence, it owns and controls many industries such as Israel's largest construction company, Solel Boneh. Jobs, job advancement (even in the armed forces), and "proteksia" all depend on party affiliation. The national administration has control over the land, sources of water, military command, and the basic means of production. Television, radio and the tremendous sources of money from abroad are directed by it solely. The Israeli government owns and controls 260 economic companies, some of the largest, most successful financial enterprises in Israel. (The Ministry of Commerce and Industry recently placed full-page advertisements, using taxpayers money, in a Jerusalem newspaper calling attention to price reductions in some retail stores.)

Election monies are distributed to various parties in proportion to the seats they have already won in the Knesset. Naturally, kibbutzim sponsored by the Labor Government vote for the Labor Party. Arabs from Arab villages also vote for the Labor Party upon promises of favors such as electricity or new roads and are brought to the polls in government trucks. The many acts of corruption in the government now being revealed are just the tip of the iceberg. Those under indictment threaten to open "Pandora's Box" with their revelations. There is no doubt that power for such a long period corrupts.

The present administration of Israel is older than the State by fifteen years. It has proved that it doesn't even need a state to rule. Its absolute position for such a long period has made it feel that its removal would be an expropriation, and it will fight to keep its property. It must, by nature, reject any possibility of national unity. They may, however, include some members from another party who are willing to give up their independence for a seat in the government.

Meanwhile, the average citizen has surrendered to the inevitable - He votes for the Labor party, but he retaliates in his own way.

Contempt for the law in Israel is manifest everywhere from the homicidal form of driving on the highways to contractors blithely ignoring building codes. Cheating on tax returns is expected.

The Opposition can never change the situation because it is unable to take the property of the possessors. Instead of trying to replace the administration, they want to join it.

In Israel, voters select the party instead of the man. Thus, individual politicians do not need to review their past performance before the public. Long years of service to their party is more apt to get them on the 'list than the attributes of leadership. Only election reforms will give this small country the government it needs and deserves.

HA MATZAV (The Situation) - By Cherna Moskowitz

In September, I was privileged to meet Admiral Elmo R. Zumwalt and hear him speak. Admiral Zumwalt, the youngest man ever promoted to flag rank, was, until his retirement, Chief of Naval Operations in the United States Navy. He will soon run for Congress in his home state, Virginia, and is head of Americans for Energy Independence, a non-profit group seeking energy self-sufficiency for the United States. Admiral Zumwalt, a man impressive in both physical presence and intellect, had these things to say:

During the Cuban missile crises thirteen years ago, the United States had the strategic advantage by 4 - 11 to 10 - 1 forcing the Russians to back down because they had no alternative. Gromyko said they would never again be caught in that position. Their solution has been threefold (1) Detante (2) A Strategic construction program still going on unabated and (3) Second largest maritime construction.

In May 1962, we had 16,018 missiles to Russia's 1,054, a 300% advantage in megatonnage, and throw weight. President Kennedy asked Russia to limit missiles and said the United States would also. Where the United States had the advantage, Russia was delighted to accommodate us.

While Congress continues to cut parity, the Soviet Union has outspent us by 20% since 1971. They now have a 4-1 advantage in megatonnage and throw weight. The United States is at the smallest fraction of national military budget since 1950--5.6% gross national product. The Soviet Union has a 12% gross national product for its military spending. We have dropped men under arms; the Soviet Union's men under arms have grown. Soviet flags do not fly over their new bases in the Indian Ocean, but we are not misled. "They will soon have a 4-1 to 10-1 superiority in that area. Unlike Russia, the United States is a world island and must use the seas, a military disadvantage. 93% of the supplies to our armed forces and our allies must go by sea. There are 1,000 to one chance against a conventional war with Russia, but, in that eventuality, we would lose the war.

In 1970, the Soviet Union programed Syria to invade Jordan. Jordan fought better than expected, the United States Sixth Fleet was reinforced, and Israel showed clearly that it was prepared to move. Syria was then told to withdraw, after which Russia concentrated on training Syria and Egypt. In 1973, the Russian orchestrated attack by Syria and Egypt met with greater success. When Israel, supplied by the United States, turned the tide and encircled the Egyptian Third Army, Russia (still hailing the merits of detente) demanded the United States pressured Israel to release the Third Army under the threat that Russia would immediately send in their army to do it otherwise. Again, the United States and Russia were up against each other, and this time, we backed down. While the United States had no nearby bases that host countries were prepared to let them use, Russia had four different areas from which to attack: Egypt, Syria, Crimea, and Yugoslavia. In 13 years, our roles have been reversed.

The Soviet Union is exultant because of their victory in this encounter and also because high oil prices have intensified poverty areas in the world and are causing them to turn to communism. In European capitals, there is much talk about the "shift" in the weight of forces, and the consensus is, "We can count. We will have to start looking at Moscow".

Unless United States policy is turned around, we will find ourselves making a series of accommodations to the Soviet Union, such as we did at the Helsinki Summit. It is important to make full usage; of the weapons at our disposal: (1) America's food excesses (2) Stop military technology sharing with the Russians and (3) Cease trade with them until they perform as a partner.

After listening to Admiral Zumwalt's remarks, I find incomprehensible United States arms sales of $4,200 million to Iran, Saudi Arabia, and Kuwait. Since 1973 the Arab countries have ordered approximately eighteen billion dollars' worth of weapons, most of which have been delivered. Four Arab states have formed a Joint Authority in Cairo to establish an arms industry beginning with 1.04 billion in the capital. Libya, a country of 1,500,000 people, mostly peasants or nomads, has concluded an arms deal in excess of two billion dollars. Is there a question in anyone's mind as to the planned usage of the gigantic arsenal surrounding Israel?

As the Soviet Union strengthens her position in the Mediterranean and the Red Sea and concentrates with single-minded purpose to dominate the Middle East, Russia's dream since Catherine the Great, is it possible that this arsenal will ultimately, along with the oil weapon, be at the disposal of the Soviet Union?

Admiral Zumwalt has written a book, yet unnamed, which deserves reading when it is released.

HA MATZAV (The Situation) - By Cherna Moskowitz

The Golan Heights

Even before the ink was dry on the Sinai Agreement, all eyes began to focus on the Golan. While Dr. Kissinger was still on route home on September 3, the Jerusalem Post reported, "Hopes or dreams of an indefinite period of non-activity were quickly and rudely shattered by President Ford's energetic assurances to President Sadat that he would not brock stagnation or deadlock in Middle East peace moves." Although Jerusalem maintains there is an "unwritten understanding," there is neither hint or mention from the U.S. that it will not press for a substantial pullback.

During the recent talks in Washington, President Ford and Egyptian President Sadat agreed, with unprecedented chutzpah, that another Israeli withdrawal on the Syrian front should be the next step.

Therefore, it is a foregone conclusion, baring the unlikelihood of Assad's refusal to accept land, that Israel will next reward Syria's 1973 aggression. The only unknown is: 'How much?

Columnist Jack Anderson reported that Kissinger stated last year that Israel was risking war with Syria because of "six lousy kilometers." In September 1975, Kissinger, during a briefing to journalists, referred to a three-kilometer Israeli withdrawal as a basis for an Israeli-Syrian interim accord.

The Golan Heights greatly differs from Sinai, which has vast unpopulated areas. Those who have visited the heights know that land· once used by Syria for fortified attacks against Israeli kibbutzim now provides homes and farmland for eight kibbutzim, seven cooperative villages, and two regional centers.

Once under Syrian jurisdiction, the Druse, who live on the heights, prefer Israeli jurisdiction and have been promised that their villages will not be returned to Syrian rule. Prime Minister Rabin has said that changes would be "cosmetic," a few hundred yards. Unfortunately, there is a credibility gap since his March 1975, statement or no withdrawal in the Sinai without a promise of non-belligerency from Egypt for ten years was so drastically altered in August.

Because of this credibility gap, several new sites have been chosen for kibbutzim on the heights by Bnai' Akiva on land rumored as negotiable for return. Two more are expected to start amidst the Druse villages. An attempt to relocate the Golan settlers would meet with much greater demonstrations, and reactions than the Sinai Agreement provoked.

The Israeli paper "Maariv" quoted sources in Jerusalem as believing Syria intends to seek an eight to fifteen-kilometer withdrawal by brad. The Syrians want control of the central sector of the hills around Kuncitra and hold on Mount Hermon. Assad wants the removal of at least one Israeli settlement to create a precedent.

Syria, meanwhile, is attempting to heat the situation by flyovers into Israel's airspace, limited shooting, and a recent terrorist attack. A Fatah terrorist captured on the Golan said his squad's mission was "to activate the front and create tension." When asked why they carried an ax:

A. To cut off heads.

Q. Whose heads?

A. Inhabitants.

Q. For what reason?

A. To take them with us to Syria.

Q. Why?

A. Two reasons. To prove that we had reached a settlement, and to spread terror among the settlers.

Obviously, this is not a problem to be easily solved. The battle for the Golan Heights will not be fought on the heights but will ultimately be won or lost in political maneuvering. Therefore, each one of us can help in this struggle by writing Ford, Kissinger, and our Congressmen and taking an active part in the education of family, friends, and neighbors.

HA MATZAV (The Situation) - By Cherna Moskowitz

News is being made in the Middle East by some very strange bedfellows King Hussein of Jordan and Syrian President Hafez Assad, Although only five years have passed since Jordan was attacked by Syria and was saved by movements of the Sixth Fleet and threatened intervention by Israel, Jordan has now established a military union with Syria and set up a joint command based in Amman.

Big brother Syria has promised to obtain from Russia weapons which Jordan cannot get from the U.S., and Jordan will protect Syria's southern flank. Their common goal is "with will and determination we shall restore all occupied land whatever the length of time." According to Assad, the aim is not only military unity but an overall merger. Syria and Jordan hope Iraq will join their military union.

For Hussein, this is somewhat like walking into the lion's den since Syria has always considered that which is now Israel and Jordan as part of "Greater-Syria."

Besides the traditional reasons for Syria to renew war on Israel, there are two new ones: Russia may react to America's recent diplomatic success in the Arab world by using their leverage on Syria to reassert the Russian role. Since the PLO's recent disagreements with Egypt, Syria, along with Libya, has become the frontline support for the PLO and their violent hostility against Israel. President Assad has said there would be no talks for disengagement of forces unless it is linked to the start of talks with the Palestinians.

Syria's semi-official newspaper "Al-Thawra" recently said that Israeli forces in the north have been put on alert and that Israel is planning "large scale aggression." Both untrue allegations are reminiscent of previous statements made by Syria to cover its own aggression. Two violations of Israel's airspace by Syria were reported to the U.N. in October. Despite these things, Syria knows it is unable to win a war with Israel at this time and will most certainly renew its mandate of the U.N. forces, based on the Golan, which is due to expire at the end of November.

Syria has lost approximately 200 planes in the Yom Kippur War. They have been replaced with 300 aircraft from Russia, of which at least 50 are late model MIG 23s (faster than the F--l Phantoms) and several Sukhol 208s.

Syria has received 1100 tanks, many of them T-62s, hundreds of personnel carriers with a range of 40 miles, as well as SCUDS and a dozen ground-to-air missile batteries and several missile-carrying naval craft.

Syria has ordered from Russia an unspecified number of tanks, artillery pieces, surface-surface missiles, surface-to-air missiles, helicopters, and 130 MIG fighters and 45 MIG 23s, according to the International Institute for Strategic Studies' report, "Military Balance 1975-76." And, along with Egypt, Iraq, and Jordan, Syria can raise an estimated million men for their armies, against Israel's 400.000.

Assad's October visit to Moscow led to a new arms deal, according to the Kuwait newspaper, "Ar-Rai Al-Aam." Meanwhile, Syria is also seeking financial aid and possibly a squadron of planes from Saudi Arabia to replace the squadron withdrawn by Egypt in protest of Syria's criticism of the Sinai settlement.

The political picture is old news. Dr. Kissinger tells us that war threatens in the Middle East unless Israel is ready for further accommodations with Syria, and President Ford said that the U.S. would not tolerate a stalemate in the area.

Arms deliveries promised by the U.S. to Israel in early October still have not been delivered. Although Kissinger has reportedly told Israel's Ambassador Dinitz that the deliveries were overdue because of low American stockpiles, some political observers in Washington claim that Kissinger is holding Israel on a "tight leash" to control the next round of negotiations better. The only thing that is still missing is another "reassessment."

HA MATZAV (The Situation) - By Cherna Moskowitz

THE OLD "NEW" ANTI-SEMITISM

Gentiles have been repeating for centuries that Jews are powerful and are trying to control the world. Gentiles usually made this kind of statement just before a pogrom in which they massacred the "powerful" Jews. One might ask, "If Jews are powerful, why is it that Jews are the victims of all tyranny from quotas to slaughter and cannot control as much as their own destinies and life and death?" What would people choose for themselves dispersion, death, torture, and ridicule through the ages? Obviously, Gentiles controlled our destiny and continue to do so. Today we speak of what the U.N. will let Israel do what Russia and the U.S. will make Israel do what the Arabs will allow Israel to do. Does anyone say Israel will do exactly as she feels she must be strong, provide her citizens with a secure, peaceful existence and protect her homeland, a policy all other nations rightfully demand?

You don't have to be anti-Semitic to be anti-Israel, but it seems to help. The Kremlin's virulent anti-Israel campaign (especially since 1967) has been linked in its propaganda with the projection of an image of a world Jewish conspiracy masterminded by Zionists and Jewish capitalists. A 1972 pamphlet issued by the Soviet Embassy in Paris directed against Israel's "ambitions" was challenged in a French court and shown to be a word for word reprint of an anti-Semitic work published in 1906 by the "Black Hundreds" in Czarist Russia. This Soviet projection has penetrated the Western world through the Radical Left, which in its opposition to Israel, has also attacked the supporters of Israel - primarily the Jews. Although many of these Leftist leaders are themselves Jews, they direct their attack against the "Jewish Establishment," "Jewish affluence," "Jewish middle-class mentality," etc.

Enjoying a recent revival is that obscene figment of imagination called "The Protocols of the Learned Elders of Zion," now being distributed as textbooks by advocates of anti-Semitism all over the world, including the Arab countries, most notably Saudi Arabia. The late King Faisal, termed "moderate" by the American media, enjoyed giving this publication as a gift. As in the edition first published in Russia in 1905, a plot is outlined by Jewish leaders to destroy Christianity and conquer the world. A map in the Protocols entitled "Dream of Zionism, a map of Greater Israel," shows "Greater Israel," including all or much of Egypt, Saudi Arabia, Iraq, Syria, Jordan, Lebanon, and parts of Turkey and Iran.

HA MATZAV (The Situation) - By Cherna Moskowitz

THE CANDIDATES

How simple it would be for us voters if we had a candidate for President such as Scoop Jackson, Daniel Moynihan, or Lowell Weiker. However, we must choose from what's available, a different task. The following analysis, based on the candidate's public records from the beginning of their political careers, may help.

I have not included information on President Carter as his policy vs. Israel is self-evident. The Carter Administration's vote on Mar. 1 against Israel in the U.N. is a clear indication of what could be expected, only intensified, of Carter if he were returned to office.

The analyses were taken from the Near East Report.

EDWARD M. KENNEDY

Few members of Congress have compiled as long and consistent a record of support for Israel as Kennedy. He was an early leader in the fight to provide more sophisticated arms to Israel and also in the effort on behalf of Soviet Jewry. In 18 years, Kennedy has never voted against an aid measure for Israel; he has voted against every measure proposed in the Senate to cut aid to the Jewish State.

In 1970, Kennedy was one of the initial signatories of a letter to Secretary of State William Rogers calling for the sale of Phantom jets to Israel. He was at the forefront of the effort to deny most-favored-nation trade status to countries that refuse its citizens the right to emigrate; he has personally intervened, successfully, with Soviet President Brezhnev in securing the emigration of numerous Soviet Jews.

In 1975, Kennedy introduced a bill calling for a moratorium on U.S. arms sales to Persian Gulf countries. In 1978 he opposed the "package deal" that tied approval of the sale of F-15s to Israel to congressional approval of a similar sale to Saudi Arabia.

Kennedy has consistently opposed U.S. dealings with the PLO, even on an indirect basis, until that organization renounces its pledge to destroy Israel. He has denounced the PLO as a "terrorist group" and pledge not to deal with it unless if he recognizes Israel's right to exist.

The senator has, since becoming a presidential candidate, stressed Israel's strategic as well as its moral importance to the U.S., citing the assistance Israel has provided for U.S. military and intelligence capabilities. This year he proposed an increase in U.S. aid to Israel at a time when the administration insisted the aid level must remain unchanged. He has identified "the real obstacle" to peace in the Middle East as the "refusal of the Arab world aside from Egypt to recognize Israel's rightful place in the Middle East."

Kennedy says that Israel's borders between 1948 and 1967 were "indefensible," and that "any final peace plan must provide Israel with secure, defensible and recognized borders." He says that recent events in Iran and Afghanistan "have only strengthened my appreciation of the geopolitical importance of the U.S. - Israel relationship." He rejects the connection between Israel and oil prices.

His supporters, who are also supporters of Israel, say Kennedy is a natural friend of the Jewish state who has worked closely with issues of concern to Jews throughout his political career. Others have misgivings and argue that despite his near-perfect voting record on Israel, he has not been "out front" on the issues and has missed several votes on foreign aid measures. They also argue that he has a weak record on U.S. defense, which is inconsistent with the support of a strong Israel.

RONALD REAGAN

Ronald Reagan has never held an elective office that involved voting on foreign policy. Consequently, his record on the Middle East is based entirely on public and private statements. The statements reflect the instinctive, strong, and consistent support of Israel.

While most of the presidential candidates have spoken of Israel's strategic importance to the U.S. as well as its moral significance, Reagan has drawn a particularly clear picture of Israel's strategic dimension that fits in with the rest of his foreign policy.

"I think, we have to recognize that, with the fall of the Shah, Israel remains the most stable ally we have in the Middle East," he said in an interview earlier this year, "with a combat-ready, experienced military that is a deterrent to further meddling in the area by the Soviet Union."

Reagan has stressed the benefits the U.S. derives from its relationship with Israel. "Israel's strength derives from the reality that her affinity with the West is not dependent on the survival of an autocratic or capricious ruler," he said last year in a nationally syndicated column. "Israel has the democratic will, national cohesion, technological capacity, and military fiber to stand forth as America's trusted ally."

Reagan is not, as some have charged, so "one-sided" on Israel as to be incapable of having any credibility as a mediator with the Arab world. In 1976 he told The Boston Globe that part of the reason the Arab-Israel dispute was so complex was that there is "so much right" on both sides.

When it comes to specific issues that reflect a willingness or unwillingness to safeguard Israel's security, however, Reagan has consistently come down on the side of defending the Jewish state. He has stressed Jordan's responsibility in solving the Palestinian problem, noting that Jordan is 80 percent of what was Britain's Palestine Mandate.

Reagan has been forceful in his opposition to U.S. dealings with the PLO until that organization "renounces terrorism, accepts U.S. Resolution 242, changes its charter, and recognizes Israel's right to exist." He asserts that OPEC pricing is "totally unrelated" to the Arab-Israel conflict. He advocates "defensible borders" for Israel.

He recently told a group of Jewish leaders that he believes in Israel's right to have settlements in the West Bank; he told the same group he

357

recognizes Israeli sovereignty over all of Jerusalem; although at times in the recent past he has been more cautious on the Jerusalem issue, declining to stake out a position.

Reagan's strong defense policy is consistent with a policy that advocates a strong Israel. He has expressed opposition to U.S. arms sales to Arab countries as opposed to the Israeli-Egyptian peace treaty and said that arms sales to Egypt should be linked to progress on the treaty.

Many people feel wary of candidates like Reagan, who has no voting record. More so than Carter in 1976, however, Reagan has a large stable of foreign and defense policy advisors with known histories of support for the Jewish state. Nevertheless, even with the best of intentions, some argue, Reagan's tack of experience in foreign policy could be as much of a handicap as it was for Carter

In Israel, voters select the party instead of the man. Thus, individual politicians do not need to review their past performance before the public. Long years of service to their party is more apt to get them on the list than the attributes of leadership. Only election reforms will give this small country the government it needs and deserves.

Chelm of the Day Award: Nepal, a country that recognizes the PLO, has a contingent of soldiers in Lebanon with the UN.

HA MATZAV (The Situation) - By Cherna Moskowitz

A recent renewed interest in Nazis living in the United States has brought to light some new information.

While we think in terms of justice, others with different priorities saw an opportunity to use select Gentians during the postwar period, irrespective of their pasts.

According to the U.S. Justice Departments and Congressional investigators, Operation Paperclip was responsible for bringing to the U.S. Germany's most valued doctors, scientists- and other experts, along with their dependents about 2,000 people. The CIA had their equivalent program, bringing over at least 100 Germans and their dependents.

Although Congressional sources suspected that source of the above had been Nazis, many today are working for U.S. military hospitals and installations, having been provided with top-secret security clearance by our government. A Congressional source claims to have seen evidence that some of the Paper clip doctors have conducted medical experiments on inmates at Dachau.

"But," The above-mentioned sources added, "we've received a major portion of the German patient office royalty-free which proved of considerable value to American corporations an industry." Expediency, as usual, takes precedence.

The FBI you suspected Nazi to inform on Emigres from Europe threats to deportation where enough to ensure cooperation.

The general accounting office, the independent investigation committee of Congress, notes in its 1979 report that the CIA contact at least 22 Nazis in the United States for information. Seven of them were paid. The FBI admitted to having a "confidential relationship" with' two alleged Nazis.

Our own government has helped many Nazis by less direct means: Vilis Hazners, the SS murderer in Latvia, was employed by Radio Liberty, which was founded by the CIA.

Three members of Congress introduced private bills on behalf of Andryia Artukovic, former Croatian Nazi.

The infamous Dr. Josef Mengele said to be securely living in South America was barred from receiving an American entry visa as recently as June 1979.

The investigation by GAO was hampered, and formerly Nazis were assisted, by possible undetected and deliberate obstruction of the investigation. Also, the GAO had only limited access to "sanitized" CIA, FBI, and other agencies' information.

Until two years ago, the State Department refused to cooperate with the U.S. Immigration and Naturalization Service's efforts to deport Nazi criminals because Communist countries would use its actions for anti-American propaganda.

For the same reasons, no requests for witnesses or documents from Communist countries were requested for nearly thirty years. There was also a widespread view that this was no longer pertinent information. One person observed, "It wasn't that the government was incompetent; it was just indifferent."

The victims of the Holocaust are with us today, as are many of their tormentors. There are many strange detours on the way to justice and many who stand in its path, but, fortunately, there are those who continue to seek out and find hidden Nazis. Some of those most actively urging action are Simon Weisenthal, Senator Max Baucus, Cong. (N.Y.) Elizabeth Holtzman, former Representative Joshua Eilberg, INS agent Tony Devito and others.

For the whole story, read Howard Blum's book, "Wanted: The Search for Nazis in America."

Note: In 1936, the Olympic Games were held in Berlin, lending prestige and political advantage to Hitler, while Jews were being persecuted, and anti-black sentiments were openly voiced.

In 1968 when Russia invaded Czechoslovakia, resistance posters were printed showing Russian tanks in Prague flying the Olympic flag. The driver of the tank is asking, "Which is the way to Mexico?"

In Munich 1972, Abraham Ordiah, the Nigerian President of the Supreme African Sports Council, was asked whether the Ugandan hockey team members would be sent to refugee camps after the games if they won a gold medal. Idi Amin had just announced that all Asians (all members of the team were Asians) would be deported, and their holdings expropriated. Ordiah replied, "I am a sportsman, not a politician."

In Munich 1972, the security of the Olympic compound was easily breached by Arab terrorists; eleven young Israelis were kidnapped and murdered," The Olympic games for 1980 in Moscow may be canceled under U.S. initiation because of Russia's involvement in Afghanistan.

In other international competition, so-called "sportsmen" have banned South African and Israeli athletes. The reality of sports being used politically is finally being recognized.

HA MATZAV (The Situation) - By Cherna Moskowitz

We are fast approaching that date, which brings songs of praise to Israel from politicians' lips. Between now and November 1980, you will hear more pro-Israel statements and read paeans of praise to Israel, the likes of which haven't been heard or seen for four years.

Yes, it's time to elect a president.

As you know, all contenders are, upon announcement of their candidacy, issued a waterproof bib (so they won't get spills from chicken soup dinners), a mimeographed copy of a pro-Israel party platform (good for millions of votes) and a list of the following statements to be read to Jewish audiences:

1) The U.S. embassy should be moved to Jerusalem.

2) Israel is the U.S.'s best friend in the Middle East.

3) The U.S. must be sure that Israel has secure and recognized borders?

4) Some of my best friends are Jewish, i.e., "The last time I spoke to Prime Minister Begin ...," etc.

5) Throw in a few Yiddish words like "L'chaim" and "shalom."

6) Big finish in a loud voice, "ISRAEL MUST LIVE!!"

It becomes confusing for the Jewish voters when all the candidates say the same things, go to the same number of kosher dinners, and have similar party platforms. Therefore, I suggest that the following kits should be distributed to Jewish voters:

1) Copies of the front runners' voting records vis a vis Israel.

2) Record of statements of politicians on Israel dated before November 1979. (For instance, Senator Kennedy's statements and votes show his position to be almost exactly like that of Carter's.)

362

3) Earplugs so as not to be swayed by political propaganda between now and election time.

4) A pledge card reading: "I swear I will vote for the candidate and party which will best understand and support the needs, politically and materially, of Israel, knowing full well that America's interests are best served by having a strong democratic country in the Middle East regardless of my party affiliation."

5) A copy of each candidate's position on the Jackson-Vanek Bill.

6) Family pictures showing candidates' brothers, with an attached list of their employers.

7) Statement from Andy Young as to his political preference for the presidency. (We vote for the other man).

Friends and fellow voters, step right up and get your "Presidential Election Kit." We can't guarantee satisfaction with your candidate but, if you use this kit properly, you will get the best results possible from your vote.

Footnote: Do not allow the audience to tie you down to admitting you think those borders should be the same as those of 1967.

HA MATZAV (The Situation) - By Cherna Moskowitz

For years, the paramount goal of American foreign policy in the Middle East was to prevent that strategic oil-rich area from falling under the domination of Russia.

Such domination would ruin the economics of the major industrial countries, undermine the support of America's allies, eventually isolate us, and effectively erode America's position of leadership in the free world.

The objectives of our foreign policies are obvious and understandable, But, as we used to say in what my children call the "olden days," something went wrong with the plan. Blunder upon blunder has done seemingly nothing towards changing the policies of our government. While Russian influence became compounded in land and naval bases in Iraq, Syria, South Yemen, Ethiopia, and Libya, the U.S. lost billions in aid and sophisticated weapons in Vietnam and Iran.

The U.S. is destined to play the same futile role in Saudi Arabia, a country that cannot secure even the holy shrine it guards for the Moslem world, let alone the Middle East. (The attack on the Grand Mosque was not the work of religious fanatics, but a planned general uprising by hundreds of Yemeni and Palestinian trained troops using Russian AK-47 rifles).

As far as Egypt is concerned, is there anyone willing to place bets on the preference of its next regime? The Egyptian people could swing from waving the American flag to tearing it up within days. Although that has happened in the past, the U.S. State Department seems bent on building Egypt up as our great deterrent against Russian influence in the Middle East...

How do you make the blind see? **Israel is the most important strategic dependable ally of the United States in the Middle East**. There is no reasonable substitute. America may have other friends and allies, but none can replace Israel.

How much stronger Israel would be today if the additional aid and war machinery so wasted in Vietnam, Iran, and Saudi Arabia had been given to Israel. Instead, U.S. policies have deprived Israel of its capacity to be oil independent, and Israel's best and most important training bases will be in the hands of Egypt.

Israel's citizens are encumbered with an unbelievable economic burden to help support Israel's defense needs which are identical to and should be subsidized by the U.S. Anything that weakens Israel will, in the final analysis, weaken the U.S. and make our country more dependent on the whims of fickle despots and kings.

U.S. political judgment and dependability are being seriously questioned by other nations. Pakistani President Muhammed ul-Haq described our foreign policy exactly as "big void." On the other hand, Russia's intentions and goals never change. It moves slowly over the globe with implacable single-mindedness. There is obviously nothing going wrong with Russia's plan.

One cannot help but be reminded of the story of the tortoise and the hare. Some look at accumulated results of U.S. cutbacks in defense, poor intelligence, and worse judgment in foreign policy and think the victor of the race is a foregone conclusion.

I think the trend can be reversed if the State Department can recognize Israel's potential at last. The first step should be U.S. support of Israel's presence in, and eventual annexation of the West Bank to effectively block the Russian supported Arab Palestinians from establishing a stronghold there.

Note: "Zins," a ZOA weekly bulletin, has recently published a comprehensive six-page study of prices in Israel, ranging from housing to insurance and food items. I think it would be most helpful to a family planning to make aliyah or live temporarily in Israel. A copy can be had by calling 426-7471.

HA MATZAV (The Situation) - By Cherna Moskowitz

Under the protection of the Shah, the ancient Jewish community of Iran prospered, becoming secure and affluent.

Since August 1978, when the stability of the Shah of Iran became questionable, the Israeli government has made special efforts to contact Iranian Jewish leaders and facilitate the aliyah of Jews to Israel from Iran.

Although approximately 18,000 Jews have left Iran in the past six months, about 50,000 remains, as with the German Jews, it was their position and affluence which trapped many of them. In turmoil resulting from political upheaval, business and property have been impossible to dispose of. Even 10% of poorer Jews in the outlying cities often own small shops.

Some have sent their children abroad to study, perhaps hoping to join them later. Six hundred such students have been accepted in Israel, but so far, only 100 have arrived.

In Iran, young men not studying (many schools have remained closed) are eligible for induction into the army, but parents also worry about their children being drafted into Israel's army.

Of the 9,000 Iranian Jews that have come to Israel, 1,000 have become olim; the others are registered as tourists. Many of these have visited Israel in the past; some have relatives and investments in Israel as well.

Israel, in an attempt to make the transition less difficult for Iranian olim, has waived the usual pre-aliya medical examination, offered special customs privileges, and additional loans of $2500 above the usual amounts. Apartments are made available immediately for them.

The large Jewish community remaining in Iran faces an uncertain future. Iranian Jewish leaders have felt the need to express their anti-Zionism and opposition to "Israeli propaganda publicly."

On February 13, thousands of Jews marched from the Saudi Synagogue to Ayatollah Khomeini's headquarters to pledge their support to him. The Ayatollah's son, Haj Ahmed, told them his father was ill but, "We love you. We are against the Zionists, but you are our brothers." I cannot help but feel fears for these captives.

In Syria and Russia, the words "Zionist" 'and "Jew" have become synonymous. And what will happen to those accused of Zionism by disgruntled business acquaintances and neighbors?

There is also fear of the leftists, the communists, the PLO (welcomed to Iran by the Ayatollah), and street mobs.

The Ayatollah has promised Jews the protection of Islam. Those who know of the Koran's special laws for Jews will find that statement more ominous than reassuring.

HA MATZAV (The Situation) - By Cherna Moskowitz

The political position of Jordan in the Middle East is intriguing. The tightrope walking act of the "little king" would turn a Wallenda green with envy.

Hussein has sometimes made astute moves, sometimes incredible blunders, but, like a bad penny, has always bounced back. Not only has he survived the assassination so often predicted for him, but he has parlayed a small country into a position where the U.S. provides all its requirements without relinquishing any control or giving any commitments.

Abduliah, the grandfather of Hussein and king of Transjordan, a small country east of the Jordan River, was recognized and supported by the British. His army of mostly Bedouins was turned into crack fighting units with English supplies and training.

In 1948, Transjordan troops, along with the armies of other surrounding countries, attacked the just reborn state of Israel, capturing the West Bank and East Jerusalem. At that time, Trygve Lie, UN Secretary-General, said, "The invasion was the first armed aggression which the world had seen since the end of the war."

Jordan became the country on both sides of the Jordan River for the following 19 years. Under King Hussein's rule, from 1952 on, the West Bank suffered desecration of religious Holy places, population transfers, and land appropriations. Many Palestinians who lived there were kept in camps subsidized by the UN and provided, not with Jordanian citizenship, but rather identity cards, requiring them to have special permission to travel or get work in Amman.

While Hussein's annexation of the West Bank was never recognized by the UN or indeed his Arab neighbors, neither were objections ever heard about his violation of the Geneva Convention rules as they applied to land conquered by aggression.

368

Enticed by visions of additional spoils, he joined with the Egyptians and Syrians in their attack of Israel in 1967. When the smoke cleared, East Jerusalem and the West Bank, 1/20th of the Jordan then existing, had been retrieved by Israel. (Time magazine, Feb. 14, 19977 reported it as half of Jordan).

In 1972, the Palestinian element led by PLO members became almost a government within a government in Jordan. Hussein acted decisively to secure his position by shelling the camps and finally driving them into Lebanon.

Jordan's role in the West Bank since 1967 is unique and difficult to define. West Bank Arabs allowed a free vote since 1972 by the Israeli government, elect officials loyal to Hussein, the PLO, or Communism. Jordan sends money to the various municipalities for streetlights, waterworks, teachers, and other officials.

Movement across the Jordan River is monitored to avoid terrorists to enter, but there is a free flow of workers, officials, and visiting families. Since 1976, Hussein has appointed West Bank Palestinians to serve on Jordan's Cabinet. Jordanian law still applies in local West Bank courts, and death sentences have been passed on West Bank Arabs who sold the land to Jews.

(Interestingly, West Bank law does provide for the death penalty in specific cases, whereas Israel's Administration (often called "inhumane") of the West Bank does not provide for the death penalty. The most severe penalties imposed by Israeli authorities to date are the destruction of the criminal's home and/or imprisonment.

In 1975, Jordan made a pact with Syria to train troops under a united command with Syria, thereby encouraging Syria to adopt a hardline vis a vis Israel and Lebanon.

Since 1975, Hussein has been cautiously renewing his friendship with the PLO, pledging to advance their cause and support them. (One can only ask why he didn't turn the West Bank over to them when it was under his control.)

This new alliance, now quite strong, has resulted in recent incursions by terrorists into Israel from the Jordanian border.

Hussein leaps nimbly from camp to camp when it suits his purposes. When the U.S. hesitated to sell 200 Hawk missiles to Jordan, Hussein threatened to go to Russia. When the U.S. capitulated, the price didn't suit him, and he again turned to Russia until a satisfactory deal was struck with the U.S.

Hussein has declared that he will participate in any future wars with Israel and has had planes and a tank assembly plant lavished upon him by the U.S. as well as a huge aid package because, as Henry Kissinger has declared, otherwise he will turn to the U.S.S.R.

The U.S. wooed Jordan in an attempt to keep Russia out of the area, but Hussein was quoted recently by Beirut newspaper Al-Hawadess as saying, "There must be a new international activity in which the Soviet Union and other parties concerned in the region could participate."

Although Jordan has taken part in every war against Israel, including the October War, (in October 1973) War he hedged his bets by sending troops to Syria instead of attacking directly and involving his own vulnerable border) our State Department insists on referring to Hussein as a "moderate" and stabilizing force.

In 1977, reports were confirmed by the Washington Post that Hussein had received over $15 million, often in cash, from the CIA. Most of it went to subordinates and tribesmen to ensure their loyalty and supply him with intelligence. The CIA also provided Hussein with other services, such as guarding his children.

It is evidently surprising to our government that Hussein has not applauded and joined the peace talks. On the contrary, special emissaries from the U.D. and all their assurances have not budged. Hussein from joining the rejectionist states. He demands that both the issue of Gaza and the West Bank be settled he will negotiate. Not only has he aligned himself with the Bagdad rejectionists, but he has pledged to help undermine the peace treaty. One official quoted by Newsweek said, "He was the first to go to Baghdad and the first to come out and cut relations with Egypt."

Some of our legislatures have asked for renewed consideration of Jordan's position. An authorization bill for 1980 economic aid to Israel. Egypt and Jordan ($220 million to Jordan) have been designed to assure that recipients are showing good faith to promote peace before being rewarded.

HA MATZAV (The Situation) - By Cherna Moskowitz

MEANWHILE, BACK IN LEBANON

While the process of turning Iran into another Lebanon continues, it might be interesting to evaluate the situation in Lebanon today. Last March; 1978, at great expense and the loss of 35 soldiers, Israel drove to the Litani River to stop constant terrorist incursions, put a halt to the shelling of Israel's villages, and relieve the beleaguered Lebanese Christians in the south.

Three months later, they withdrew at the insistence of the U.S. and the United Nations. Andrew Young (May 25, 1978) was quoted, "Well, I am sure the Lebanese Christians don't want the Israelis to withdraw now. One has to remember, in all fairness to everybody concerned, that there was a lot of turmoil in Lebanon before the Israelis got there."

Since then, news from Lebanon continues to be of death and destruction. Syria's "peacekeeping" forces remain, and that political comic opera called the United Nations still is maintaining a military presence (Unifil) to withdraw Israeli forces thereby "restoring international peace and security; and assisting the government of Lebanon in insuring the return of its effective authority in the area" (Resolution 425, 1978)

Israel Ambassador Yehuda Blum, in an address to the Security Council, charged that the only part of the Unifil mandate that has been unconditionally fulfilled was "Israel's withdrawal from Lebanon." He said that the other parts of the mandate restoring international peace and security and ensuring the return of the government of Lebanon's effective authority in the area had not been realized. The ineffectuality of Unifil is surprised only by the organization which spawned it. It has been unable to protect either Lebanese citizens or the border.

After Israel pulled its forces out of Southern Lebanon, and Unifil took control, Moshe Dayan wrote Dr. Kurt Waldeim that hundreds of PLO men had re-infiltrated into the areas." Dayan noted that certain Unifil units even had PLO liaison officers attached to them (June 14, 1978). To date, 20,000 PLO terrorists have crossed Unifil's lines south of the Litani River.

Interestingly, Unifil's French and Irish battalions known for their military expertise were stationed around Christian enclaves. In contrast, key areas such as the Litani River and opposite Tyre, a major terrorist stronghold, had Unifil troops with no battle experience such as those from Senegal and Fiji. Norwegian troops abandoned at least one village to the PLO after being fired on. Recently, Israel temporarily closed the "Good Febce" to Unifil personnel after a Senegalese soldier was arrested for smuggling explosives to terrorists in Israel.

Over forty Iranian soldiers stationed in south Lebanon have defected to the PLO. Terrorists entering Israel invariably come through Unifil lines. Some units, such as the French and Iranian, will be withdrawn from the 6,000-man U.N. force by their respective countries soon. The Mandate, renewed until June 1979, will be bolstered by Dutch troops, among others.

The situation today in Beirut is somewhat calmer. Although murder and kidnapping take place daily, there is no major fighting between various factions. The last heavy battles in October were directed against Christian forces by Syrians who hold the western suburbs. While massive Syrian bombardment went on against civilians desperately in need of food, water, and medical supplies, the U.N. passed a resolution asking for a cease-fire without once remotely referring to Syria.

In the South, there are many elements of Christian and Moslem. Today, there are about 60,000 people in the area, 90% Moslem, 7% Christian, and 3% Druse. Many of the Moslems cooperate with Major Saad Haddad, who is head of the Christian militiamen controlling a 10-kilometer-deep strip from the Mediterranean through the Golan foothills along the border. There have been assassinations of these Moslems by PLO men.

Major Haddad and his Christian militiamen have been reluctant to turn their arms and protected enclaves over to either the Unifil or Lebanese forces, understandably. However, the government will no longer pay the militiamen. A spokesman for Haddad indicated that Israel would be asked to pay his men.

The Arab Palestinians already have their own law and well supplied armed forces in the south and are paying high prices for houses and property there. (The PLO budget is almost equivalent to that of the Lebanese state.)

If Lebanese or Unifil forces were to replace Christian forces, it would lead to more attacks, more terrorism, the closing of the "Good Fence," (today six stations are serving South Lebanon, each with a clinic and post office) and the creation of a "Palestinian State" in South Lebanon.

Impotent Lebanese or Unifil forces in the South would fall into Syria's strategy and allow them with the PLO, to destroy the remaining pockets of Christians in Lebanon handily.

Northern Israeli towns such as Kriyat Shemona are again being rocketed from Lebanon, and terrorists come through Unifil lines at will, causing seemingly endless rounds of attack, retaliation, and death.

Will there be a free Lebanon when the smoke finally clears? I don't know. Syria shows no signs of leaving, and the Arab Palestinians get stronger thanks in part to the U.S. bundling of foreign affairs. As far as the Lebanese are concerned, in general, world response has run the gamut from disinterest to indifference.

HA MATZAV (The Situation) - By Cherna Moskowitz

NUCLEAR POWER

Three of the world's most prestigious sources of Military information, the International Institute for Strategic Studies, the Stockholm International Peace Research Institute, and Jane's All the World's Aircraft claim that Israel has nuclear weapons.

The CIA has estimated that Israel has 10-20 nuclear weapons; Time Magazine is more precise with a guess of 13. These reports are all based on assumptions rather than concrete evidence.

There seems to be no disagreement among its friends that Israel, in its unique position, should have such weapons. First, the Yom Kippur War showed that the Arabs, supplied and trained by their mentors (Russia and the U.S.), can be a formidable challenge to the Israel Defense Forces. Reliance on conventional arms becomes riskier as the quality and quantity of sophisticated weapons accelerate.

Secondly, Israel has the choice of being politically subservient (a situation repugnant arid dangerous. to any sovereign state) to the U.S. as its only weapon supplier or somewhat more independent by building nuclear weapons.

Thirdly, nuclear weapons held by the superpowers are considered a deterrent, How much more necessary it is for a small country surrounded by enemies to develop this "deterrent."

Fourth, no one doubts Israel's ability to develop or deliver such weapons. Israel possesses two nuclear reactors, one supplied for research by the United States; the other, near Dimona, was built with help from Prance. The Dimona reactor, guarded closely, is capable of producing enough plutonium for one or more nuclear weapons yearly and has been in operation since 1964.

The crux of the nuclear option lies in the next step: a chemical separation plant. At this time, such a plant either is well concealed or has-yet to be constructed in Israel. The building of a plant to separate plutonium and produce an atomic weapon would take approximately two years.

Israel's position regarding its nuclear · capability has been ambiguous. Shimon Peres said in 1966, "I know that this suspicion is a deterrent force. Why, then, should we allay these suspicions?"

Israeli leaders have often pledged that Israel has not and will not initiate the introduction of such weapons in the Middle East.

And so the guessing game continues. Hopefully, Israel will grow so strong and secure that the Arabs will consider the war option to be futile, and we will never know whether or not Israel possesses atomic weapons.

HA MATZAV (The Situation) - By Cherna Moskowitz

Secretary of State Cyrus Vance said, "This is a very serious matter that affects U.S. Soviet Relations." Admiral Moorer, after reading a letter, expressing the concerns of 1.678 retired U.S. Generals and Admirals before the Senate Foreign Relations Committee, added that the events revealed a "Soviet grand design which had already been demonstrated in Africa and Elsewhere."

Senator Frank Church said that this "particular action comes so close to home that unless the matter is corrected in a manner acceptable to the United States, I would think it would prove impossible to prevent it being linked to SALT as the Senate takes up the treaty."

The cause of these strong words and ongoing debate as to how best to alleviate the crises was a disclosure by Senator Church on August 30 of 2,000 to 3,000 Russian troops, which have been in Cuba since the mid-1970s. The Soviet force consists of motorized rifle battalions, tanks and artillery, and combat service elements. Also, there are 1,500 to 2,000 Russian military advisers and technical military personnel in Cuba. By no stretch of the imagination could one call this force a threat to the U.S.

However, a Soviet military presence of any tiny size and capacity in Cuba 85 miles away from U.S. shores is considered a "grave matter," a threat to U.S. Soviet peace treaties and relationships, and the cause for grim comments from the U.S. President and security advisors.

How then can one explain the reaction of the U.S. government to Israel's security situation, which is so much graver?

Israel, one-fourth the size of Cuba, has no sea or distance between it and the countries which have attacked it in the past and are preparing today for the annihilation of Israel. Israel's major cities are within easy striking distance of Jordan and Syria.

Moreover, if Israel would allow the West Bank to come under Arab control, a plan which is now being diligently pursued by the U.S.

Administration, the border would almost touch the Israel population centers. The border would be five miles Netanya and Hadera and would almost surround Jerusalem.

Instead of facing Russian combat brigade with the rifles and tanks, Israel shares mutual borders with enemies heavily armed with the world's most sophisticated planes and weapons mostly supplied by Russia and Israel's "best friend," the U.S.

In Syria, there are many thousands of Soviet military advisors and technical military personnel. If that were not enough, the Arab armies of Syria and Jordan have pledges from numerous Arab countries for men and equipment to fight against Israel.

Also, the peacemaker President Sadat of Egypt has stated very implicitly, that in the event of a war between Israel and its Arab neighbors, his pledge to fight on the side of his Arab brothers and open another front against Israel takes precedence over any peace agreement signed between Egypt and Israel.

When you are asked why Israel refuses to give up the West Bank, answer with a question an old Jewish custom. If U.S. leaders react so strongly to the Cuban situation, what would their reaction be in a situation such as the one Israel faces? Would they allow Washington to be surrounded by foreign forces?

If Mexico declared war on the U.S., would we be interested in negotiation with them to give them land along the Rio Grande?

Or perhaps show good faith by returning California to them? Why does the U.S. need a huge stockpile of nuclear armaments when it has never been invaded and is now at peace, but objects strenuously to the possibility of Israel's having nuclear power?

These ideas would still allow the U.S. to defend itself successfully with its great military capacity but would never be considered as anything but absurd. However, the U.S. government takes very seriously its demands upon Israel, which without doubt, jeopardizes Israel's very existence.

The double standard adopted for Jews through the ages is alive and well and is now being translated into a double standard for Israel compared to other nations of the world. The Near East Report lists a few relevant examples (Oct. 10, 1979):

For six years after 1776, the British pressed Americans to permit the United Empire Loyalists, the colonists who had remained loyal to the Crown to return from Canada and reclaim their property. The Congress adamantly refused. But Israel has often been called upon to repatriate a host of potential enemies within her borders.

In 1963, President Kennedy risked global conflict when he forced the Soviets to withdraw their missiles from Cuba. But Israel is urged to accept the massing of enemies on her old border who could be in a position to push her people into the Mediterranean Sea, only eight miles away.

The United States dropped atomic bombs on Hiroshima and Nagasaki to force Japan's unconditional surrender. But Israel's military triumphs have always been frustrated by diplomacy. Israel could win wars but never win the peace: in 1948, in 1957, in 1967, and again in 1973.

Our government has retained a base at Guantanamo, a strategic trusteeship over Okinawa for a quarter of a century, was long reluctant to withdraw from Panama, and still holds a trusteeship over Micronesia remote outposts which Washington deems essential to security. At the same time, Israelis are diagnosed as "paranoid" about security.

Try as we might, we cannot seem to convince the world that Jewish blood and the security of a Jewish homeland are equal to the value and need of others. We have to be sure that we do not become brainwashed into accepting that which is unacceptable to others, what the great U.S. need for defense purposes while at peace with the nations of the world is the very minimum that tiny Israel must-have.

HA MATZAV (The Situation) - By Cherna Moskowitz

On June 3, 1978, there was an ad on the first page of the Jerusalem Post that read "The First Anniversary, Thank You Mr. Begin and the People of Israel. We all love you for· saving our lives and allowing us to live in a free democratic country like yours. From all of us, the refugees from Vietnam."

Since then, as before, hundreds of refugees have been turned away from southeast Asian ports to face hunger, thirst, and ultimate drowning.

Thousands of more fortunate refugees from Vietnam have found homes in a variety of countries, including the U.S. The Knesset of Israel just voted to absorb another 100 of these refugees. A boatload of refugees who were given a choice of destination in January were somewhat less than anxious to throw in their lot with the hard-pressed Israelis.

There is, however, another group of people, threatened with extinction, who dream of becoming Israelis. You won't read about their fate on the front pages, nor will the U.N. lend its auspices to the rescue of the Falashas, the Black Jews of Ethiopia.

There has been a trickle of Falashas to Israel to date, despite the opposition of Haile Selassie and the lack of interest on the part of the Israeli government. Abba Eban called their plight "a very marginal problem," while debates raged over their Jewishness. Rabbi Yosef ruled that the Beta-Israel (Falashas) were the lost tribe of Dan, but Rabbi Goren expressed "dissatisfaction" with the 1975 ruling that recognized them as Jews under the Law of Return.

The Falashas have shrunk from an estimated one million (400 years ago) to approximately 28,000 due to war, conversion, and poverty. Living mostly in 490 isolated villages, they are at the mercy of bandits and feudal landlords.

Although pressured to convert to Christianity, the Falashas remained Jews with the belief that they were only Jews left in the world. Every village has a Kohan (priest) and synagogue, but they lack scrolls, prayer books, and ritual objects. They are too poor to buy rifles (at $250 each or three year's wages on the local market) to protect themselves and suffer terror and rape by various rebel groups. At least 7000 have been forced to flee their homes and are facing starvation on the outskirts of Gondar. Many have been captured by rebels and sold into slavery.

The Beta-Israel community · in Israel has fared well. All adult members are working ten are university students, one is an Orthodox rabbi, seventy-five are in the army (two were killed in the Six-Day War). Perhaps they call themselves Beta-Israel because Falasha means stranger, and they are no longer strangers.

The Ethiopian government will not let its citizens leave the country, but the Israeli community of 300 Beta-Israel are desperately trying to bring the attention of the world to the plight of their brothers - our brothers. They charge the white Jewish world with complacency. They tell us that Ethiopian Jews, now suffering murder and slavery, face extinction unless they can be rescued.

Note: Your concern can be expressed to:

Charlotte
World Zionist Organization
515 Park Avenue
New York, N.Y. 10022

Irwin Field
UJA General Chairman
P.O. Box L
Norwalk, Ca. 90650
For more information, call the American Association for
Ethiopian Jews (714) 642-8613.

HA MATZAV (The Situation) - By Cherna Moskowitz

For centuries Jerusalem has been known as the crossroads of the world. While someone stationed in the lobby of the King David Hotel can no longer watch camel caravans go by, they will certainly see every Jew they know who is traveling in Israel. During a month-long visit in June, we were delighted to bump into many old friends from the States as well as renew acquaintances with Israeli friends.

Among the "bumpees" was Eli Weisel, who has promised the proceeds of his next book to the Anti-Defamation League to combat the Arab boycott. This book will be based on information from the Polish government, never before released, about the Jews of Poland during World War II.

We heard from a reliable source that when Eli Weisel was in Washington talking to Kissinger, Kissinger pointed to a picture of Secretary of State Dulles and said, "Aren't you glad that a Jew is now Secretary of State instead of him?" Weisel replied, "If the secretary of State is a Jew like me, I would rather have the Jew, but if he is a Jew like Dulles, I would rather have Dulles."

Mrs. Joe Hirsch, the wife of Undersecretary of the American embassy, told us that, since working by the officials' wives is crowned upon, she is keeping busy by scheduling programs and meetings with Israelis for the other Embassy wives. Her purpose is to introduce them to Israelis and educate them.

Until now, there has been little socializing between Israelis and foreign embassies on an informal level. Most Embassy children do not go to school with Israeli children. Consequently, embassy families can spend a tour in Israel and leave without ever raving close contact without ever having close contact with the people of that country, their problems, and their feelings.

Hirsch said that she and wives from other Embassies have found the program rewarding and discovered it gave them some insight into the problems and pressures that beset Israelis.

We visited the graves of boys who died in defense of Israel since 1947: young boys, without having tasted the joys of adulthood, never knowing what it means to live in security. From the time they were old enough to understand, they knew at 18 that they would have to face death in the service of their country. We watched their parents watering plants around the graves. What a waste. What a terrible waste. And for what? The dates on the tombstones told us that each war had only been a preliminary to the next.

We joined 20 thousand people at a rally in Tel Aviv to protest ·possible retreat from the Gidi and Mitla passes. Even then, the feeling was that it was a futile exercise - that Israel had no choice in the matter. Would the Israeli Government dare send Kissinger home empty-handed again?

The best joke we heard while in Israel was about an Israeli helicopter pilot who ran out of gas while over the ocean and landed on an American destroyer. When the Americans rushed up and demanded an explanation, the pilot said, "Sorry, I thought it was one of ours."

We spent an evening with a couple who had met in prison during the British Mandate in Palestine. He was caught while robbing a British bank for funds to buy arms for the underground. She, still strikingly beautiful, was imprisoned for killing a man. You would be hard-pressed to find two more charming people, and I couldn't help think of the desperate deeds done by Jews, not by choice, but for survival. Do you ever wonder what choice you would make under like circumstances?

We shopped at Zion Square when there was still broken glass from the terrorist born b that took 1 7 Jives. The business was going on as usual. I found myself looking under the seats when I boarded buses. However, never did I feel uncomfortable in Israel as I did in London on our return home. Our hotel was host to many Arabs, and I realized my reply to "Your: name, please?" was much more subdued than usual because I was standing in a group of Arabs who were also checking in. A common sight in London is veiled women in passing Rolls Royces.

Rental agencies in London have reported demand by Arab visitors for expensive flats in London during the summer months that surpassed the supply. They spoke of Arabs paying six months' rent in advance with cash carried in suitcases.

We had the pleasure of having dinner with Arnold and May Forrester of the Anti-Defamation League and other friends at the "Versailles" in Tel Aviv. Mr. Forester was in Israel to film and tape some TV and radio shows.

The new "Civil Guard" can be seen patrolling the streets. Except for their guns, you would say that they were grandfathers, aged 60-75, out for an evening stroll. Somehow, I didn't doubt that these kindly grandfathers could and would use their guns if necessary.

Security measures at the Knesset are stricter than ever before and now include a body search. We were luncheon guests thereof Menachem Begin, Knesset Member, and leader of the Likud Party. As we entered, the sounds of a furious debate from the Knesset could be heard from the hallway.

We felt certain that the discussion was about the impending agreement in the Sinai. What else could bring forth such impassioned oratory? No, we were told that the Knesset was discussing the Port of Ashdod, which had been closed by Yehoshoa Peretz, Workers' Representative of the Port, in a fit of anger over not being recognized by the gate guard.

Every evening we were treated to a beautiful sunset on the Mediterranean. Later, we sat on the balcony and watched the moon on the water. We have been to some of the most famous beaches in the world, but nowhere have I seen more beautiful beaches and sunsets than from my balcony in Netanya. Some day when there is peace in the Middle East, Israel will become the New "Riviera," and pleasure craft from all over the world will dock at Cesarea.

HA MATZAV (The Situation) - By Cherna Moskowitz

I rarely have ambiguous feelings over an important issue; I am equally positive, regardless of whether I am right or wrong. However, the question of whether the UJA should support Soviet "dropouts" leaves me perplexed and undecided. On one hand, nothing is more important than Jewish survival. The State of Israel is our best guarantee for that survival, and Israel itself is weakened without an influx of Jews from other parts of the world. Therefore, the settlement of Russian Jewish in Israel is critical.

On the other hand, surely, Russian Jews who choose America have a right to our aid and encouragement. It is "Jewish" to refuse them necessary financial help? Besides, what right do I have to insist on Israel for them while I enjoy the luxuries and comforts of Long Beach?

Here are the arguments pro and con. The case for supporting Russian noshrim (Russian Jews who opt for the U.S.) with community funds is as follows:

1.   35% of UJA funds are spent in the U.S. for noshrim. It costs $25,000 per family to settle a Russian family here. The same family resettled in Israel costs $100,000.

2.   The Soviets can cut off Jewish immigration at any time. Considering the growth of anti-Semitism in Russia and the cooling-off of detente, the most important objective is to save as many Jews as quickly as possible - their destination should not be a factor.

3.   Because of housing shortages, economic difficulties, fears of war and being drafted into the army, etc. most Russian Jews who prefer to live in the west will eventually leave Israel anyway. Only the dedicated who would opt for Israel are apt to remain.

4.   It is discriminatory to provide aid to Russian Jews who have relatives in the U.S. and not do so for others who are not as fortunate.

The argument against are:

1. Only Russian Jews holding Israeli visas are allowed to leave except for rare exceptions. In 1979, 25,000 noshrim were resettled in the U.S. In January of 1980, 2,900 Jews left Russia, 900 fewer than January 1979. According to Leon Dulzin, chair of WZO, the dropouts are jeopardizing the emigration of remaining Russian Jews.

2. An informal survey showed that if there were no funds to settle in the west, most noshrim would emigrate to Israel rather than remain in Russia. Later they would, of course, be free to resettle in the west, but U.S. refugees benefits would not be available to them. Hopefully, a large percentage would remain.

3. Each year additional Soviet Jews in the west draw even more noshrim as families encourage other family members to join them.

4. Israel is besieged by problems: defense, public relations with the outside world, economic difficulties, demography, yoridah. An influx of thousands of Jews from outside is essential for each of these problems.

In the early 1970s, over 95% of emigrating Jews from Russia went to Israel. Today less than 30% settle there. A compromise program has been developed by a committee appointed by Prime Minister Begin.

1) No Jew will be denied a letter of invitation by Israel.

2) Financial aid will go to:

(a) Jews settling in Israel

(b) Jews settling in the U.S. who have immediate family living here.

Under these guidelines, all Soviet Jews can freely choose their destination, but if they do not fall within the above two categories, communal funds will not be made available to them.

In 16 cities such as Miami, Cleveland, and Los Angeles, this plan has already been put into effect. More communities are struggling to decide on this difficult issue.

HA MATZAV (The Situation) - By Cherna Moskowitz

Imagine a beautiful sandy beach; Bedouins on camel's ride by. Offshore is an island crowned by the ruins of a crusader castle. The sea is warm and filled with multi-colored corals and fish of every color and description.

This isn't the setting for an exotic movie; it's the southern coast of Sinai.

On our first visit to Eilat and southern Sinai this summer, we were overwhelmed by the underwater beauty in the Red Sea and the unique vistas everywhere. The Red Sea is a paradise for snorkelers. Only the distant hills of Saudi Arabia and the bright lights of nearby Aquaba at night remind you that all is not tranquil.

As Israel is a land of extremes, it seems appropriate to discuss the disaster of the economy after the beauties of the Red Sea. Here are some of the forecasts for the 1979/80 IL 304 billion budget; bread ·products· will go up 150%, eggs 80%, milk 75% chicken 68%, (you will note that these are all necessities) cost of living increments to salaried persons will increase 18% in April, another 15% in October.

Obviously, managing to feed a family and afford housing - which are critical problems in Israel now - will become even greater; the number of families that need help to exist will increase.

Israelis also have to cope with strikes that paralyze some of their most needed services: post office, nursing, water, electricity, buses, etc. We got a small taste of Histadrut strikes when the water and electricity in Netanya were cut off all day. Tourists carried buckets of water to wash it up the stairs of a 16-floor building. Take a large purse with you on your visit to Israel next summer - the Israeli pound will be worth less than 4c.

We had the pleasure of meeting the internationally respected physicist, Professor Yuval Ne'eman. He is heading up a new political party that sees itself as carrying out the policies of Herut.

Members of the party feel that the Begin administration has fallen far short of the economic reforms promised and are afraid that the West Bank, as well as Sinai, will be sacrificed to the Arabs. Their support comes mainly from Herut, the Land of Israel movement, the N.R.P. and Gush Emunim,

Many Israelis we spoke to expressed· fears about Israeli security and American pressure. Such well known political figures as Moshe Arens, Geul Cohen, Shmuel Katz are also part of this opposition party, which became active this month.

Their performance at the polls depends upon the situation at the time of the election and, as I expect Begin to retire in the next few months, his predecessor. The new party called is expected to pick up 5-20 seats in the Knesset.

Geula will be visiting California soon. Prof. Ne'eman will be here at a later time. His work with American physicists on a yet to be announced, but vital, project brings him to the U.S. often.

In two months from now, groundbreaking will take place simultaneously in Germany and Israel for factories to produce a device which will extract shale oil. Using a patented Israeli invention and German financing, this project could put unlimited oil on the market for between $4 to 11 per barrel, of which $1 of every barrel will go to Israel.

Let's hope that some other comparable products won't be marketed first. At any rate, someday, in the future, we will have the pleasure of telling the Saudi Arabians to drink their oil.

There was broad news coverage when El Arish in the Saudi was turned over to Egypt. I wonder if the following facts were in the local news: Egyptian authorities have taken reprisals against at least a dozen residents of El Arish on the ground they "collaborated" with Israel. (This appeared in pages of the Federation News-Ed.)

Approximately 1,000 El Arishis, mostly Arab Palestinians, left at Egypt's request and are now the new "refugees" in the Gaza strip. Israel is rehabilitating them. Many will be provided with housing near Rafah.

The government of Israel just made it legal for Jews to buy land on the West Bank, a long-overdue action, I believe. Hopefully, many will take advantage of this and buy property such as the Jewish National Fund did before Israel was proclaimed as a state, thereby paving the way for a large Jewish presence. This is an opportunity that could have far-reaching consequences.

Our five weeks in Israel were packed with excitement, sandwiched between lovely days at the Netanya and Cesaerea beaches.

I hope G-d will grant you all health and happiness and the opportunity to be in Israel in the coming year.

HA MATSAV (The Situation) - By Cherna Moskowitz

United Nations Resolution 242, confirmed by Resolution 338, has been accepted as a framework for peace in the Middle East by Israel, Egypt, Jordan, and Syria. Despite occasional threats to repudiate or alter them, their acceptances have never been withdrawn. Although China condemns both resolutions, the United States and Russia, have given full support to them.

In May 1975, I heard former United States Ambassador to the United Nations, Arthur Goldberg, who was the moving spirit behind the drafting of resolution 242 and one of its authors, clarify some of the most critical aspects of the Resolution.

Both expressly and by implication, it repudiates the concept of an imposed peace and calls for "agreement" an "accepted settlement" by and between the parties.

Regarding borders, the proposal by Russia calling for Israel's withdrawal to the lines of June 5, 1967 - did not receive strong enough support to pass. Instead, 242 endorses "withdrawal of Israel's armed forces from territories occupied in the recent conflict" and interrelates this to the principle that all states have the right to "secure and recognized boundaries."

Goldberg states that in his and other legal experts' interpretation, there are no specific borders or territories involved. The meaning is that Israel will move, the extent relies upon negotiation and security. The crucial omissions of the words "the," "all," and " June 5, 1967, lines" make this clear. French and Russian texts differ, but it is the English version that was voted upon.

The Arab nations call for Israel's complete withdrawal to 1967 borders based on the Resolution and the United Nations Charter's language regarding "The Inadmissibility of The Acquisition of Territory By War." This is a weird statement since the Arabs acquired and retained territory (some of the same territory in question) in the 1948 war, contrary to the United Nations Partition Resolution. Russia supports this Arab claim, although Russia still holds territories from Finland, Poland, Rumania, Japan, and other 'states taken in World War II.

Summing up this issue, Arthur Goldberg states that 242 "neither commands nor prohibits, territorial, adjustments in the peace agreements. It does call for adjustments to ensure secure boundaries for Israel; whose, borders were so often the victim of the violation."

Resolution 242 calls for free passage in International Waterways. It refers to the usefulness of demilitarized zones but mentions no specifics. A notable and intentional omission is the status of Jerusalem. There is no mention of the PLO, Palestinian state, or West Bank. It speaks simply of "a just settlement of the refugee problem... " This has become the issue over which the Arab states and their many committed supporters now call for a revision or reinterpretation.

The United States cannot agree to any changes in Resolutions 242 and 338 without breaking a major written commitment to Israel. Article 4 of the United States-Israel Memorandum of Agreement on the United States political, economic and military assurances to Israel, for which Israel gifted Egypt with the Abu Rodeis oilfields and strategic passes in the Sinai reads:

"The United States will oppose and, if necessary, vote against any initiative in the security council to alter the terms of reference of the Geneva Peace Conference adversely or to change Resolutions 242 and 338 in ways which are incompatible with their original purpose."

This memorandum also constrains the United States from dealing with the PLO unless the PLO accepts Resolutions 242,338 and Israel's right to exist. It further states:

"Similarly, the United States will consult fully and seek to concert its position and strategy with Israel with regard to the participation of and other additional states. It is understood that the participation at a subsequent, phase of the conference of any possible, additional state, group, or organization will require the agreement of all the initial participants."

In effect, pressure on Israel to accept PLO, participation at the Geneva Conference would be contrary to such written agreements, without Israel's express acceptance, even if the PLO were to accept 242, 338, and Israel's right to exist.

The PLO, despite all the debate and gentle prodding by the West, continues to reject 242 and 338, mainly because they refer to "refugees," which would include Jewish refugees as well, and make no mention of Palestinian rights such as a Palestinian Arab state.

Although President Carter has indicated that unprecedented talks between the PLO and the United States would be possible if the PLO accepted Resolution 242, the PLO had refused and turned down these overtures; calling them United States cooperation with Zionism and imperialism When asked, if the PLO decision was an "obstacle to peace,." Administration officials answered. "No comment." It is believed that there will be no United States reaction to the PLO's rejection, in order not to anger the Arab states.

The Damascus newspaper "Al-Ahram" reported recently that a "silent dialogue" between the PLO and the United States is already underway.

As if to underscore the United States Administration's overtures to the PLO, President Carter has signed legislation, which eliminates the requirement that the PLO obtain a special waiver from the Justice Department to enter the United States. Senator George McGovern introduced the bill removing the PLO and other groups from the designation "terrorist."

This erosion of support for Resolution 242 and 338 as originally interpreted by the United States and Israel, as well as the behind the scenes maneuvering by the U.S. to "legalize" the PLO is causing concern among Israel's friends. It is hoped that a rift will not be caused between Washington and Jerusalem because of Israel's insistence on exercising rights agreed upon by international legal means and already bought and paid for with far-reaching and valuable concessions.

HA MATZAV (The Situation) - By Cherna Moskowitz

On May 3, I heard one of the most inspiring speeches I have ever heard from a young man who became the seventh man in history to resign from an important position at the White House. Mark Allen Siegel, President Carter's aide arid chief liaison with American Jews, was the man who drafted the Democratic party platform on the Middle East, which was the most pro-Israel platform ever and was unanimously adopted at the convention.

According to the President's pollsters, the votes in the states which won for him and made the difference were states where the Jewish vote was most critical, such as New York. A total of between 70 and 75% of American Jews in the last election voted for Jimmy Carter. A good deal of that support was based on the pro-Israel Democratic party platform.

For Mark Siegel, - who served Hubert Humphrey for two years, the Democratic party for four years, and President Jimmy Carter, - his resignation was traumatic but unavoidable.

When Jimmy Carter went into the White House, he firmly believed that all parties in the Middle East desired peace, including Fassad of Syria and Yasir Arafat of the PLO. Zbigniew Brzezinski also concurred in that. In February of 1977, the issues were broken down by Cyrus Vance as falling into three categories: the nature of peace, withdrawal from occupied territories, and the Palestinian problem.

In March of 1977, for the first time, President Carter used the words "Palestinian homeland." An uproar was heard throughout the land because of his usage of these words, which were clearly read to mean a state for the Palestinians on the West Bank.

Hamilton Jordan and Mark Siegel were called in to try to understand the nature of the reaction and possibly eliminate it. From that point on, Mark Siegel was a part of the negotiations going on in the White House involving the Middle East, sat in on all conferences relating to these issues, and was able to observe very closely at hand what was happening.

In June of 1977, there was an official change from the usage of the word "homeland" to the Palestinian "entity." There was no change of purpose; however, there was a change in semantics, which was thought to be more acceptable.

On July 6, 1977, President Carter met with the Conference of Presidents of Major Jewish Organizations at the White House and came out strongly against a Palestinian state. He reiterated that all arms promised to Israel would be given to Israel and was very, very reassuring.

In July of 1977, there was a cordial meeting between Prime Minister Menachem Begin and Jimmy Carter. On October 1, the United States and the Soviet Joint Declaration of Principles were released. It angered Israel as well as the Arab states because it had been prepared in secret negotiations unknown to both the Arabs and Jews. Hamilton Jordan and Mark Siegel were not aware of this Declaration of Principles before it was announced. In it was the usage of the words "legitimate rights of the Palestinian people," which is known as code words for a Palestinian state. Four thousand telegrams a day came across Mark Siegel's desk in protest to that Joint Declaration, (Yes, someone does read and count those telegrams and letters.)

On October 3, Moshe Dayan came to Washington to meet with Carter, and between them, they worked out a joint working paper. However, immediately after that, Sad at, acting without the knowledge or the encouragement of Washington, made his statement announcing his desire to go to Jerusalem and seek peace.

There was no reaction from Washington. Brzezinski had put all his efforts towards going to Geneva for peace talks, and he was J caught totally unaware of his plan awry. He could not cope with the idea of a bilateral peace between Israel and Egypt.

A word from Washington had a very ambivalent tone about the peace initiative between Sadat and." Begin. In a meeting, it was decided that it would be best for Carter to ignore the issue unless he was asked about it by reporters.

Mark Siegel argued for a clear statement - of support, and ultimately he prevailed. However, after that, he was relegated to the role of representing the White House to Jewish Americans and was no longer invited to take part in policy decisions.

In December, Carter again met with Begin. Soon after, Carter took off for parts around the world. One of the places Carter visited was Saudi Arabia, where he met with King Khalid, who told him very bluntly that he demanded the F-15 bombers for proof from Carter that he was as good a friend as was the Shah of Iran. In Aswan, Anwar Sadat spoke to Carter and made him promise to put pressure on Begin.

In January, the one-sided criticism of Israel began. Hostility was shown not only to Begin and Israel, but also there was a distinct cooling toward the feelings of America's six million Jews.

Mark Siegel feels that it was the dual-threat and pressure from Egypt and Saudi Arabia, which caused Carter to link the arms sales of Egypt, Saudi Arabia, and Israel - a package for which there is no precedent.

This is particularly difficult for Israel to accept, because Israel released parts of the Sinai, including the Mitla and Gidi Passes and the Abu Rodais oil fields (Sinai Accord # II) specifically because of the promises made by the United States for these very warplanes.

Mark Siegel argued with the Administration, putting forth this argument as well as others. He asked how, if Israel cannot trust the United States, its best friend, to hold to an agreement that it, made two years ago, could it possibly trust Egypt, a country with which it has been at war for thirty years, and go into negotiations and pacts with them?

At that time, President Sadat broke off negotiations with Israel; I understandably, because after all, he felt that President Carter could get for him a much better deal than he could get with direct negotiations. At that time, there was no criticism of Sadat at all from Jimmy Carter, although we can all imagine what the circumstances would have been, had Begin broken off the peace talks.

In February of 1978, Brzezinski and the White House staff met with the Conference of Presidents. He very clearly told them that he no longer had to listen to their views. He told them that Israel and the United States had different national goals and that there is a special relationship between the United States and Saudi Arabia.

On February 28, 1978, Mark Siegel made his last speech for the White House to the Young Leadership Council. The State Department read over his speech and changed it. Although he had reservations, he delivered it as they wished, but it was met with booing and hissing. Although he was dismayed at that reaction, Mark Siegel couldn't help feel that had he been sitting in the audience listening, he probably would have reacted the same way. Later that day, he checked with the Defense Department and found that indeed the Young Leadership Council had been correct - his speech had been full of inaccuracies and lies. There was no longer doubt in his mind that despite what perhaps were good motivations of the government, its policies and attitudes were negative and were serving as an obstacle to peace.

In March of 1978, Mark Siegel spoke at length with President Carter and gave him the reasons why he felt he had to resign. The last paragraph of his letter of resignation read, "If I am nothing to myself, who will be for me? And if I am for myself only, what am I? And if not now, when?"

Tom Braden, a columnist, wrote after his resignation, "This guy better decide, is he an American or is he an American Jew?"

The answer of Mark Allen Siegel to Tom Braden was, "Mr. Braden; I am a Jew."